A NEW PUBLIC MANAGEMENT IN MEXICO

Other Titles in the Political Economy of Latin America series

The Policy Process in a Petro-State
César E. Baena
ISBN 0 7546 1070 5

Bureaucracy and Politics in Mexico
Eduardo Torres Espinosa
ISBN 0 7546 1104 3

Dollar Diplomacy
Francis Adams
ISBN 1 84014 741 5

South American Free Trade Area of Free Trade Area of the Americas?
Mario Esteban Carranza
ISBN 1 84014 795 4

The Failure of Political Reform in Venezuela
Julia Buxton
ISBN 0 7546 1346 1

The Political Economy of Mexico's Financial Reform
Osvaldo Santín Quiroz
ISBN 0 7546 1447 6

Structure and Structural Change in the Brazilian Economy
Joaquin J.M. Guihoto and Geoffrey J.D. Hewings
ISBN 0 7546 2000 X

Urban Environmental Governance
César Nava Escudero
ISBN 0 7546 1564 2

The Reconquest of the New World
Pablo Toral
ISBN 0 7546 1669 X

State-Society Relations in Mexico
Kenneth Edward Mitchell
ISBN 0 7546 1718 1

A New Public Management in Mexico

Towards a government that produces results

ESTEBAN MOCTEZUMA BARRAGÁN

ANDRÉS ROEMER

LONDON AND NEW YORK

First published 2001 by Ashgate Publishing

Reissued 2018 by Routledge
2 Park Square, Milton Park, Abingdon, Oxon OX14 4RN
711 Third Avenue, New York, NY 10017, USA

Routledge is an imprint of the Taylor & Francis Group, an informa business

Publisher's Note
The publisher has gone to great lengths to ensure the quality of this reprint but points out that some imperfections in the original copies may be apparent.

Disclaimer
The publisher has made every effort to trace copyright holders and welcomes correspondence from those they have been unable to contact.

A Library of Congress record exists under LC control number: 2001094261

ISBN 13: 978-1-138-70121-2 (hbk)
ISBN 13: 978-0-415-79292-9 (pbk)
ISBN 13: 978-1-315-21008-7 (ebk)

Contents

List of Figures

List of Tables

Acknowledgments

This book has a history forged of convictions about what a good government should be and, together with this, an efficient public administration. It began with my interest, as a senator, in contemplating, and working hard, in order to propose a bill for professionalizing and evaluating the performance of public servants in Mexico – a law that would strengthen the development of human "assets", that would generate institutional arrangements that were efficient with respect to objectives, indicators of performance, legal certainty, administrative transparency and, of course, of a responsible way of serving. Andrés Roemer joined this cause in order to fit the civil service into a model of result-oriented public administration. We worked together for nearly 21 months on theoretical and practical aspects, and evaluated evidence from national and international cases. Of course, the history and background of the topic played a relevant part in the study: political, institutional, situational, normative, demographic, territorial, sociological and cultural variables. However, fundamentally, what made this book possible was the invaluable, unconditional support from friends, colleagues, and national and foreign institutions concerned with a common cause: Mexico.

In spite of the impossibility of naming here all those who cooperated during this long process in investigating the problems of administrative efficiency, and in particular in regard to the aspect of institutions and their human resources, we are deeply grateful to all of them.

We especially owe our gratitude for their work, collaboration, reading, editing, comments and co-responsibility (sometimes co-authorship), to the following personalities in the field (in alphabetical order): Jorge Asali (legal analysis), Juan Manuel Calderón (theoretical introduction), Ana Leticia Cuéllar (institutional analysis), Enrique de la Madrid (administrative-institutional analysis), José Rafael García Córdova (appendices), David García Junco (national cases), Sergio García-Bullé (institutional-administrative analysis), Hugo Alejandro Garduño Arredondo (translation and edition), María Eugenia Gómez Guerrero (editing), Fernando Gracia (international cases), José Octavio López Presa (institutional-administrative analysis), José Luis Méndez (theory and national and international cases), Pablo Ojeda Cárdenas (legal analysis), Gary Reid (institutional analysis), Everardo Rojas (edition), Aleida Ruiz (institutional analysis), Gabriela Saldate (appendices), Federico Seyde (theoretical analysis), Fanny Slomianski (final revision), Paul Slomianski (international cases), Edwin Villarreal (international cases), Carmen Zárate (writing, style and edition).

We are also grateful to our distinguished colleagues and friends: Luis Fernando Aguilar Villanueva, Manuel Arango, Eugene Bardach, José Luis Barros Horcasitas, Michael Barzelay, Javier Beristain, Federico Berrueto, Edgardo Buscaglia, Felipe Calderón, Bonnie Cohen, Robert Cooter, Miguel de la Madrid Hurtado, Manuel Herrera Rabago, Roberto Ducoing, John Ellwood, Carlos Elizondo, Arsenio Farell Cubillas, Arturo Fernández, Bruno Ferrari, Jorge Ferrari, Roberto García Requena, Hugo Alejandro Garduño Arredondo, José Alberto Garibaldi Fernández, Daphne González, Claudio X. González Guajardo, Natividad González Parás, Guillermo Güemez García, Rony Heifetz, Luis Alberto Ibarra, Enrique V. Iglesias, Carlos Jarque, Kate Jenkins, Santiago Levy, Florencio López de Silanes, Luis Maldonado Venegas, Luis Antonio Márquez, Raúl Méndez, Edgard Mercado, Adela Micha, Michael O'Hare, Pedro Ojeda Paullada, Adolfo Orive, Oscar Roemer, Jesús Rojas, Alfonso Romo, Guillermo Ruiz de Teresa, Moisés Saba Masri, Liébano Sáenz Ortiz, Octavio Salazar, Alejandro Saltiel, Jairo Sánchez, Lucía Segovia, Boris Shwartzman, Fernando Solís Cámara, Francisco Suárez Dávila, Javier Treviño Cantú, Ernesto Zedillo Ponce de León and, especially, Mónica Hurtado Padilla.

We also owe our appreciation to various academic and government institutions, as well as to international organizations that contributed in a vital way to the preparation of this work, in alphabetical order: the Bank of Mexico, Booz Allen and Hamilton of Mexico, the Center for Strategy and Development (CED, initials in Spanish), el Centro de Investigación y Docencia Económica (CIDE), the Department of Social Development of Mexico, the Department of the Comptrollership and Administrative Development of Mexico, the Department of External Affairs of Mexico, the embassies of Mexico to the following countries: Argentina, Bolivia, Chile, Colombia, Ecuador, Peru, Venezuela, France, New Zealand and the United Kingdom; the Graduate of Public Policy of the University of California at Berkeley, Grupo Pulsar Internacional, the Inter-American Development Bank, the John Fitzgerald Kennedy School of Government of Harvard University, the Latin American and Caribbean Law and Economics Association, the Mexican Senate of the Republic, the Mexican Academy of Law and Economy, the Mexican Society for Geography and Statistics and, especially, the National Water Commission; the National Geography and Statistics Institute, the Organization for Economic

Cooperation and Development, the Office of the President of the Mexican Republic, the World Bank,

We would especially like to express our appreciation to our friend George Philip for his help, support and intelligence as well as to our publisher of this book for their invaluable work and generosity: Ashgate Publishing Ltd.

All the errors in data and interpretation are, naturally, our own responsibility.

To Cecilia, for her daily love and her enjoyment of life.
To my children, Ana Cecilia and Juan Esteban,
for their interest in getting to know our country
and be better Mexicans

ESTEBAN MOCTEZUMA BARRAGÁN

For Alejandro, David and Valeria: my reason for being and
for existing. To Fanny Slomianski, for her
vitality and unconditional love.

ANDRÉS ROEMER

Introduction

Let us imagine the following scenario: you, dear reader, are designated the new head of an important department in the public sector of your country of residence. You are warned that in order to work here, you must observe all existing restrictions. You cannot acquire work implements (e.g. paper, ink, pens, tables and computers) without going through the required channels (which are complex and strictly controlled by one or two central units). You have no flexibility or autonomy (or, if you do, it is in a very restricted sense) in handling human, material, financial and administrative resources. For various reasons, part of your personnel is non-removable, and cannot be discharged from their posts no matter what their performance is like. On top of this, you face serious problems of institutional culture (the personnel is unmotivated: their confidence is at a critical low, they have no expectations for betterment and receive a very poor salary). In fact, nearly 70 % of the good elements of the previous administration, will probably be leaving their positions during the next two weeks, in order to join the person you are replacing, in her new job. For these and other reasons of a cultural nature, you will have difficulty finding documents and information on projects already carried out (diluted institutional memory). As a result, the mission of your department is not very clear. On the other hand, you must carry out 57 programs, 850 activities and approximately 2,500 procedures whose real costs and benefits are unknown to you. And, as if this were not enough, you are advised to bear in mind that one of your incentives is to perform tasks which will please your boss, because he is the main judge of your services (don't worry about the citizens). As for your salary, do not compare it with other equivalent positions in similar sectors, since they operate under different market systems.

Situations such as the one described occur frequently in the Public Administration System that today holds sway in Mexico and in many other parts of the world. As a result (of this lack of institutional arrangements and efficient incentives), governments have been helpless to obtain the results expected, which has dramatically undermined their credibility in the eyes of society. We are experiencing a loss of the social assets of our institutions, our public servants, our political parties and our authorities.

Credibility reflects society's confidence in the capability and efficiency of institutions and persons in leading a country toward objectives that are beneficial to the majority. Credibility is built by fulfilling expectations. It is based on the past through reputation (earned by achieving results), it is materialized in the present with deeds, and is projected toward the future with vision and hope.

But Mexico and Latin America have suffered, and continue to suffer, from this problem to a great extent. In the United States, by the mid-sixties, three quarters of the voters had absolute confidence in the federal government's ability to lead the country successfully; however, by 1995 surveys revealed that this confidence had plummeted to only 15 percent, and among the causes were inefficiency, wasting of resources and the corruption of the machinery of government.[1] A very similar tendency has been observed in countries such as Canada, Great Britain, Italy, Spain, Belgium, Holland, Norway, Sweden, Ireland and Japan.[2]

The World Bank has estimated that the levels of government credibility, registered by the Latin American nations, taking credibility to be reflected in the confidence shown by businessmen and investors in the institutional structure and in the government's capacity and efficiency, are much lower than those observed in member countries of the Organization for Economic Cooperation and Development (OECD), as well as the countries of southern and southeastern Asia, the Middle East and northern Africa, and central and eastern Europe. The only levels of credibility lower than those found in Latin America are to be observed in the countries in the southern Sahara region in Africa and in the Community of Independent States.[3] The World Bank concludes that the levels of administrative efficiency, economic growth and investment flows show a high degree of correlation with the credibility level of the different countries.[4]

As we have already pointed out, among the main causes for credibility loss in many of the countries of the world are inefficiency, wasting of resources and unnecessary expenditure on the part of the governments. On one hand, it has been quite clearly argued that the government has extended its participation to a great number of activities that go beyond the fundamental functions of the State[5] and that, in many cases, could be carried out more efficiently by the private sector. On the other hand the citizens observe very poor performance on the part of the government and its institutions in regard to results obtained by the implementation of policies, plans and programs.[6]

Due to flaws in institutional arrangements and in the system of incentives, many governments, far from participating in the solutions demanded by society, become part of the problem. To correct this tendency is, and will be, one of the greatest challenges of the turn of the century, as regards public policy. The present situation of highly competitive, global markets requires of the governments, not so much the role of protagonist as that of prompting, promoting and facilitating, at the same time as it involves a redefinition of its mechanisms for protecting the less advantaged sectors of the population in order to lead society as a whole toward goals of solidarity. Therefore, it is necessary to offer results and recover society's belief and confidence in its government in order to establish conditions that would promote sustainable development.[7]

The need to create efficient and effective governments, close to the citizenry, based on visible, long-term results and improvements, has led academics, leaders and social groups to institute administrative reforms known as the "new public administration", "administrative reform" or "administrative modernization".[8]

Administrative modernization consists of envisioning an administrative-institutional policy of the State, based on a re-engineering of procedures in government institutions, motivated by the aim of achieving efficiency and effectiveness in its management by transforming departments into independent units, oriented toward achieving results by means of a clear definition of the goals to be reached over the middle and long terms.

Our fundamental purpose in this book consists of identifying the factors that determine the process of public sector modernization, in order to analyze the predominant tendencies in this area, as well as to examine and compare the experience observed in the processes of implementing reforms in different countries and in various departments of the Mexican government itself. This will allow us to identify "better practices", which constitute a frame of reference for facilitating the reform process in the case of Mexico.

Our reform proposal for the Mexican public administration is based on a philosophy of granting freedom and autonomy to public servants in order for them to make better decisions. We propose a philosophy of *entrepreneurial* public servants with greater responsibility, one in which the centralized, highly controlled management would be replaced by flexible, efficient processes. In other words, our proposal involves a process of transforming the power, so that it moves from the centralized organisms and departments toward the operative bureaucracy, and within the bureaucracy itself, from the highest echelons to the middle and lower ones. At the same time, in order to ensure a mechanism that would guarantee a democratic allocation of the responsibility and commitments that the bureaucrats must undertake toward the citizens and toward the elected officials, our proposal emphasizes the need to orient efforts toward the professionalization of the public servants' performance.

The heart of the institutions consists of people who, under correct (namely, good and efficient) institutional rules, norms and arrangements, are able to offer the citizenry more and better products and services, using fewer resources and avoiding waste. By virtue of the fact that organizations do not function adequately if the personnel that form them lack the required aptitudes, a rigorous process of professionalization of the civil service is proposed in which efficient mechanisms of selection, training and evaluation of the personnel's performance are to be included, as well as an appropriate system of remuneration and incentives. These should be designed and instituted completely consistently with the objectives and vision of the modernization of the public administration as a whole.

The main hypothesis presented in this work is that the institutional arrangements in Mexico and Latin America have become less efficient in executing their objectives. The results obtained by public sector policies and programs fail to meet society's expectations and, consequently, its institutions and rulers are losing credibility. We believe that foremost among the causes for this phenomenon is the lack of an established, regulated and efficient career civil service. There is no adequate structure of incentives for public servants to carry out their duties correctly, and the result is a greater deterioration in the functioning of the machinery of government. In other words, we need to make our public administration more efficient, reforming the institutions and bureaucracy in a context in which results constitute the most important element of management.

Based on this, our book is composed of five chapters. The first one offers an exhaustive look at the origins, objectives and characteristics of the reforms that lead to administrative modernization. For this purpose, its theoretical underpinnings are analyzed, placing special emphasis on the theories of the new institutionalism and of public choice, as well as on the way in which these are linked to the process of modernization. Also studied are some fundamental elements that should be considered in any process of administrative modernization, such as incentives, accountability, culture and some strategic principles.

Chapter 2 introduces the concept of career civil service, its origins, advantages and disadvantages. In chapter 3, an analysis of the Latin American experience is presented with regard to administrative reforms. In particular, background, characteristics and results of the reforms adopted in Chile, Argentina, Colombia, Bolivia, Ecuador, Venezuela and Peru, are examined. Based on these experiences, recommendations are made for the case of Mexico.

Chapter 4 reflects on the experience observed in different OECD member countries, placing special stress on the study and evaluation of three particular cases: the United Kingdom, New Zealand and France, countries where the magnitude of the reform and its characteristics, as well as the impact of the results obtained, are of vital importance for our present study. This chapter also reviews those policies that were applied by the countries studied and that were appropriate and productive in carrying out their objectives, as well as those that proved not to be successful. Based on this, at the end of the evaluation of each of the countries mentioned, a list of recommendations for the case of Mexico is also included.

Chapter 5 deals with the experiences in civil service reform of different departments and organisms of the Mexican government itself. The cases of the National Institute of Statistics, Geography and Computing (INEGI, initials in Spanish), the External Affairs Department (SRE), the National Water Commission and the Teaching Profession are specifically examined. An analysis is also made of the way in which the public sector in Mexico now generally administers its human resources.

Finally, the general conclusions of our study are presented and a synthesis offered of the main lessons and implications for public policy that we have obtained from this work. We consider that it constitutes a valuable aid for one of the great challenges of the next millennium: how to execute government functions efficiently, incurring fewer costs and achieving better results.

Notes

[1] For a more extensive explanation of these figures see Joseph Jr. Nye, Phillip Zelikow and David King, *Why People don't Trust Government,* Harvard University Press, 1997. See also "Washington Post/Kaiser Family Foundation/Harvard University Survey Project", 1996; "Harris Poll", 1996; and "Hart-Teeter Poll for the Council for Excellence in Government", presented in the *Washington Post*, March 24, 1997.

[2] Joseph S. Jr. Nye, "The Decline of Confidence in Government", in Joseph S. Jr. Nye *et al., Why People...*, *op. cit.*

[3] For further detail see the World Bank, *World Development Report 1997: The State in a Changing World,* Oxford University Press, 1997.

[4] In relative terms and according to the most recent *Global Competitiveness Report*, out of a total of 53 countries analyzed, Mexico occupies 32nd place in general classification. However, if the strength and efficiency of the institutions are considered exclusively, the country falls to 43rd position. Indicators such as fulfilling commitments undertaken by previous administrations; stability and continuity of the institutions; competence of the public servants; obstacles to opening new businesses; independence of the judiciary; impartiality of the courts; efficiency of the police forces; as well as incidence of organized crime, place Mexico among the lowest positions of the countries studied. There is also evidence that the people's confidence in a great number of Mexican states (governed by different political parties), as well as in institutions such as the Bank of Mexico, the General Attorney's office of the Republic and the federal, state and local governments, is generally declining. (See World Economic Forum, *The Global Competitiveness Report 1998,* in collaboration with the Harvard Institute for

International Development, 1998, as well as the Banamex/Accival survey, "Qué tanta confianza tiene usted en..." ["How much confidence do you have in..."], published in the magazine *Este País*, no. 55, February, 1999.)

5 According to the World Bank, the fundamental functions of the State should be limited to the following: a) administering justice, b) maintaining macroeconomic stability, c) providing basic social services and infrastructure, d) protecting vulnerable groups, and e) protecting the environment. See World Bank, *World Development Report 1997, op. cit.*

6 Regarding this last point, there is the complex problem of determining parameters that would allow us to evaluate the government's performance. That is, what criterion can we use to measure the performance of our public administration? There are several possible parameters: the citizens' expectations, previous experience, experiences in other countries, the performance of the private sector and civil organizations in activities similar to those carried out by the government, to mention only the most relevant.

7 It is important to mention that society's dissatisfaction with and lack of confidence in the government and public policies are, to a certain extent, necessary for the proper development of the democratic life of a nation. However, when the limits of that phenomenon are crossed, extremely negative and even irreversible consequences can result, such as the reduction in tax revenues because of the citizens' refusal to pay taxes; disobeying laws on the part of society; as well as deterioration in the bureaucracy due to the loss of interest of qualified and specialized personnel in joining or remaining in the public sector. Without these valuable resources, the government would show worse and worse performance, and the country would enter a dangerous, negative spiral.

8 Great Britain was the precursor in this revolution when, in the eighties, during Margaret Thatcher's administration, it implemented a rigorous institutional reform to endow the different departments and organizations in the public sector with new mechanisms that would allow them to reach the levels of efficiency required by the country and expected by society. Reform was necessary, because the institutions had been penetrated by important interest groups who obtained benefits for themselves at the expense of the rest of the taxpayers; the government's expenditure had grown at a rate that was unsustainable over the long term and, at the same time, public services were very poor, and insufficient to satisfy the demands placed on them by society.

1. Administrative Modernization

The object of this chapter is to introduce what is known today as *administrative modernization*. For this purpose, reference is made first to its origin, strategic objectives pursued, and institutional characteristics. The theoretical underpinnings are then analyzed, emphasizing their scope and implications. Finally, practical lessons are presented that were obtained from countries where this model has served as a basis for making governments more efficient.

It is important to point out that an exhaustive analysis of administrative modernization as a theoretical model is not claimed to be carried out, but rather the development of a general diagnosis of the practical virtues contained in this model is proposed, presenting guidelines that can be useful to those governments interested in modernizing their administrative structures and taking as a basis the fact that any modernization strategy should have as its starting point a continuous, permanent, contextual and historical analysis of the structural particularities of the country in question.

Origin, objectives and characteristics of administrative modernization

In the last few decades, the world has experienced a dizzying transformation. Today economies are more integrated into the context of the world market, and their internal processes depend inevitably on the complex dynamic of globalization. Unlike what used to happen a few years ago, it is now practically impossible for a society to set in motion successful strategies in economic development based on protectionist policies that isolate it from the world economic dynamic. The challenge lies in designing development strategies capable of giving national economies viability in a global market that is increasingly specialized and competitive.

In the framework of the previously valid model, encouraging development, the governments tended to confront upsets of an economic type by adopting survival strategies focused on attaining achievements over the short term. This myopic vision of economic problems generates enormous costs for the developing economies by encouraging governments

1

to concentrate their efforts on attacking the superficial expressions of the crisis, ignoring structural causes. At present, the fundamental concern lies in undertaking institutional and legal reforms which actually make it possible to transform structures and undertake development strategies with possibilities of success over the long term. The project of this book is located precisely in the framework of this logic of radical modernization.

As was mentioned, the complexity of the problems that afflict contemporary societies and the increasingly generalized perception on the part of society that the government has ceased to "participate in the solution which favors development" and has become "part of the problem and an obstacle to development", has generated a serious crisis of confidence. Far from being the result of a single line of causal determination, this crisis seems to be the synthesis of a complex set of processes. Foremost among these is the growing incapacity of the government to attend to society's basic demands, a situation that arises out of the conjunction of two fundamental problems: the lack of clarity in the objectives and functions of government, and its lack of efficiency and efficacy in carrying them out. With respect to the first point, governments have obviously lost their sense of *mission*, so that at the present time there exists no consensus as to what they should and should not do nor, of course, as to how to do it efficiently. With respect to the second point, governments, in their keenness to eliminate corruption and wasting of resources, have introduced a profusion of controls and regulations that have ended up creating considerable costs in terms of effectiveness and efficiency as well as in terms of equity. This has meant that the government has had to spend more in order to accomplish the same, which leads to an increase in public expenditure above its fiscal capacity, and to a systematic decline in the quantity and quality of the goods and services it offers to society.

This situation has made the successful operation of the government, as based on traditional practices and structures, unsustainable, demonstrating the urgency for introducing substantial changes both in the way it administers social resources and in the way it implements and evaluates public policy. This idea is reinforced by a report by the OECD, the conclusion of which is that political leaders do not seriously deal with the roots of the problems of their nations until the situation nears critical proportions. And it is at this point, close to the disruption of the social and political order, that the need for a deep structural reform becomes evident and is finally accepted by a great number of relevant social actors.[1]

In this context, many governments have undertaken to review their organizational basis thoroughly. In many countries, there has been a political will to create a new legal and institutional structure to make it possible to correct the rigidities and inadequacies of the prevailing administrative models. Rather than bringing about superficial modifications, they recognize the need to have a new model for public administration that would serve as a theoretical and methodological basis for undertaking radical reforms both in the way the government administers society's resources and in the way it executes the decisions of public policy. The challenge lies in designing and applying formulas that, based on obtaining *results*, permit the effectiveness of the institutions to be increased in order to make the management of resources more efficient and make the decisions and actions of civil servants fundamentally more professional and accountable.

Based on the theoretical model that proposes administrative modernization, several countries[2] have set reforms in motion whose purpose is to replace the traditional rigid, centralist structures with a system of institutional organization and bureaucratic behavior, in which the public administration operates in a similar way to the best practices in environments of competitiveness and accountability.[3] One of the important points of departure of this new model considers that the origin of the government's problems lies in the prevailing organizational-administrative culture and not in the persons who make up the public sector. The basic idea is that it is not possible to attribute responsibility for the government's failure to people who are constrained by obsolete regulations and excessive controls. On the contrary, administrative modernization seeks to vindicate public servants, granting them greater confidence, stability and better work conditions, in order to increase their productivity so as to be in a position to attend to society's demands more effectively, efficiently and equitably.[4]

In short, the point is to strive to turn the government into an organization that works better and costs less,[5] with the understanding that present-day societies require public administrations that are changing, sensitive to their surroundings, provided with units which, in spite of their technical complexity, are effective in terms of producing results based on previously established indicators of performance, thereby achieving an optimal combination of quality and sustainable productivity.[6]

The model of public administration proposed encourages governments to establish clear, result-oriented missions and to endorse performance agreements committing the administrative units to responding to citizens, thus obtaining concrete, quantifiable results in terms of management and provision of public goods and services. Institutional commitments that form part of performance agreements involve granting civil servants greater levels of freedom in administering and organizing their funds as well as in operating their different programs. The point is to grant directors, or those in charge of administrative units, the elbow room necessary for producing the results expected of them, precisely defining their levels of responsibility and the volume of resources they can use in order to attain a certain goal.

This allows for an increase in productivity and the level of accountability of public servants, who must then find a balance between greater margins for operational capacity and greater levels of responsibility. This logic of government functioning involves a powerful decentralizing inertia that guides the redesigning of the functions and powers of the central departments and agencies. This redesigning implies leaving the task of strategic planning based on the formulation and evaluation of middle- and long-term public policy in the hands of the central government, in order to concentrate the execution of the short-term actions contemplated in the program goals, in the local administrative units.[7]

In conclusion, and in order to increase the government's efficiency in the production and provision of public goods and services, the new model recognizes the need to promote the use of marketing techniques.[8] In these it is considered particularly important to create an environment of competitiveness between public agencies and companies in the private sector. It is necessary to get over the idea that a public sector company is, by definition, unable to compete successfully with private units. *The challenge lies in generating sufficient incentives and precisely defining the rules of the game.* In order to achieve this, it is essential for public institutions to adopt ideal systems for the administration of human and administrative resources, which ought to be complemented by the development of areas of planning, evaluation and marketing that would let them study the demands and preferences of the users of their products and services thoroughly.

To summarize, the government reforms undertaken by various countries on the basis of the model of administrative modernization have had three characteristic elements: the introduction of greater levels of flexibility and autonomy in the management of public servants and administrative units based on clear, specific missions; the endorsement of agreements that would enable the performance of bureaucrats to be evaluated, based on the obtaining of *results* and not only in terms of carrying out *formal procedures*; and finally, the use of marketing strategies aimed at improving the productivity of government agencies and companies in order to enhance the quality of the goods produced and services provided.

The fundamental objective of these efforts is to restore citizens' belief in their governments by making their administrative structures more efficient and, above all, more involved in the true demands, expectations and needs of society.

Theoretical underpinnings of administrative modernization

The central aim of administrative modernization is to improve efficiency and effectiveness in order to strengthen the processes of equity in the institutions that comprise the government, as well as increasing the professional quality, accountability and sense of commitment toward the community on the part of public servants. This means a project aimed at raising society's confidence in its leaders through structural changes in the administrative machinery that would provide an effective solution to problems, an economical use of political resources and the growing provision of high-quality goods and services.

As a theoretical point of view, administrative modernization is situated in the field of economic analysis of the law, of the theory of the new economic institutionalism and of the theory of public choice.[9]

New economic institutionalism and the economic analysis of the law

One of the main characteristics of administrative modernization is the use of a neo-institutional focus on the analysis of the impact of public policy on the behavior of individuals.[10]

The economics of property rights and transaction costs, also known as the new institutional or neo-institutional economics, had its modest origins in the late 1950s in the work of Armen A. Alchian.[11] With the support of seminal articles about transaction and information costs, written by Ronald H. Coase and George J. Stigler,[12] this area of research attracted other authors and, by the mid 1970s, had generated a considerably increasing body of theoretical and empirical research.[13]

The work of this school is sensitive to organizational subject matter and analyzes how the structure of property laws and transaction costs affect incentives and economic behavior.

The new institutional perspective tries to show that institutions count. Every different organizational structure affects incentives and behavior; however, institutions themselves are considered legitimate objects for economic analysis. Coase indicates that it is possible to use theory to analyze institutions in such a way that their operation is explained and forms an integral part of the economic model. Most authors have accepted this point of view and, consequently, recent efforts to broaden the applicability of traditional institutionalism have led to new methods on how to interpret economic doctrine as applied to public administration.[14]

The new institutionalism considers how the distribution of property rights and transaction costs affect incentives for public servants and consequently their behavior.

This perspective underlies three elements inherent in the model of public administration: methodological individualism, which considers bureaucracy as maximizing its utility function; and which implies that the rationality of individuals is limited; and that there are individuals who behave opportunistically. These postulates translate into four axioms in administrative modernization:

First: administrative modernization reinterprets the role of the public servants' interests within the government, starting from the assumption that an analysis of the functioning of the government should be based on a *methodological individualism*; that is, in an evaluation of the situation and of the incentives that affect the persons that make up the government.

Second, instead of considering that civil servants have the priority of maximizing the objective function of the government, it considers that bureaucrats are rational actors who seek to maximize their personal benefits.[15]

This situation often leads civil servants to make decisions that turn out to be inadequate and inefficient for the general interests of society. The logic of personal benefit is imposed, from this theoretical point of view, on the logic of the public service, causing the policy implemented by the governments to tend to deviate from the objectives that originally shaped it.

We can find one clear example of this in the public servants in charge of deregulating administrative procedure in order to give the citizen faster, more efficient service. Even though the objective of the public policy is clear, it often happens that the bureaucrats in charge of applying it see the opportunity for improving their income precisely by not carrying out this deregulation, or by not carrying it out completely. The logic of personal benefit indicates to them that the slower and more complicated the procedure, the greater the possibility of demanding more money from those citizens interested in having fast service. In other words, the bureaucrat finds greater incentive in terms of personal benefit in the act of corruption than in that derived from the adequate performance of his deregulating efforts.[16]

Third, in order to find a more faithful model of the conditions of the real world of institutions, administrative modernization replaces the assumption of "complete rationality" with one that states that individuals have a limited capacity to gather and analyze information, as David Kreps indicates:[17]

> A *completely rational* individual has the ability to foresee everything that might happen and to evaluate and optimally choose among available courses of actions, all in the blink of an eye and at no cost. A boundedly rational individual attempts to maximize but it is costly to do so and, unable to anticipate all contingencies and aware of this inability, provides ex ante for (the almost inevitable) time ex post when an unforeseen contingency will arise.

Finally, administrative modernization considers that, besides incorporating the concept of bounded rationality, it is necessary to foresee the possibility that some incomplete contracts will not be carried out due to fraud committed by one of the parties, since it is possible that some public servants may not be honest and may deliberately attempt to distort or hide information relevant for decision-making in order to maximize their own interest, in bad faith.

Based on the perspective of the new economic institutionalism, the public administration can form organizations that can correctly define property rights, reduce transaction costs, and establish incentives for public employees to provide goods and services efficiently and promptly to society, thereby avoiding the opportunistic conduct which is undesirable for the "public good".

Public choice

The theory of public choice, according to Dennis C. Mueller, is the economic study of taking decisions that pertain to non-market activities or, simply, the application of economics to political science.[18] Administrative modernization uses public choice to evaluate bureaucratic behavior, based on the postulate that individuals are selfish, rational beings, maximizing their own utility. This would then purport to explain the way the problems faced by public officials affect the government's strategic conduct, as well as its performance.

Generally, models of public choice assume that the process of design, definition and implementation of public policy is determined according to the efforts of interest groups and individuals to promote their own interests, which is usually known as "income hunting".[19]

However, the problem of income hunting is assuaged because of what Mancur Olson calls, in his theory of collective action, the problem of the *free rider* (opportunist).[20] Olson mentions that if the number of persons in a group is sufficiently small, or if there is coercion or some other special mechanism for individuals to act in favor of the common interest, rational beings guided by their own interest will not act to achieve the common or group interest.[21] This is due to the fact that each individual will contribute only in a small measure to the collective action; the withdrawal of this contribution is not considered sufficient to affect the expected success or failure of the collective goals. Consequently, due to this problem of the opportunist, interest groups are obstructed in their attempt to commit themselves to an action that is to their collective advantage.[22]

In this way, just as in the case of the New Institutionalism, the theory of public choice is based on the assumption that, in order to understand the government's behavior, it is essential to understand first the behavior of the persons who comprise it. In this respect, the theory of public choice is a basic tool in administrative modernization, due to the methodological emphasis on incentives on which it is based, and to the fact that it has its axiological origin in the principal that no discernible social value exists independently of individual values, so that individual actions offer elements that are significant for public policy to evaluate collective action.

As Mercuro and Ryan mention:

> ...rational, utility-maximizing individuals act not only in the marketplace, but also participate in the political decision making process to enhance their utility. Consequently resources may be allocated, either via the marketplace or via the political process by the same individuals acting in several different capacities.[23]

Finally, the normative focus of public choice is on the process of exchange and not so much on that of choice, which usually constitutes the center of attention in the traditional, neo-classic economic analysis. Buchanan describes it in the following way:[24]

> I have maintained that the contractual or Paretian norm is relevant, based on the simple principle that "we start from here". But here, the status quo is the set of institutions and legal regulations [...] I have tried to argue that, insofar as property rights are specified in advance, authentic exchanges are reproduced, with reciprocal profits for all parties. However, insofar as rights are subjected to a constant redefinition by the State, nobody has incentives to organize and initiate business dealings or contracts. This is equivalent to saying that when the political body begins to be openly concerned about sharing the cake, under the designations of property rights and legal dispositions; when we begin to think about personal gains derived from not complying with the law, in private or in public, or in the disparities between real allegations and those that it is estimated will be found under any idealized anarchy, we are preventing and impeding, by force, the execution of structural changes potentially capable of increasing the size of the cake for everybody.

Therefore, the theory of public choice stresses the exchange based on the rule of consensus and compensation. Thus, both the new economic institutionalism and the theory of public choice offer a recent theoretical model for public administration that will enable it to be more efficient because it is based on axioms with greater predictability on the behavior and essence of individuals, groups of individuals, and institutions.

Definition of goals

Starting from theoretical assumptions on institutional and human conduct, the first thing to be done to define the mission or goals is to establish "where we're coming from" and "where we should be heading" (later we will discuss "how" to go from one to the other).

Having clear, worthwhile goals gives meaning to the existence of institutions. Government organizations need a mission to accomplish which must be assessed by the actors and, besides, must be able to spread itself over concrete goals whose accomplishment presupposes complying with certain determined results. As Peter Senge clearly establishes: a shared vision is vital for every organization, since it provides it with the focus and energy to learn. Although it is possible to have adaptive learning without a clear vision, creative learning only happens when people try to achieve something that is important to them.[25]

A government that lacks clearly defined goals and functions will have problems motivating its members and generating in them the sense of commitment necessary for serving society effectively, efficiently, honestly and innovatively. In general, the lack of vision will prevent the creation of the inter-institutional synergy necessary for innovating the machinery of government. In the absence of clear government objectives, that permit the different institutional actors to recognize compromises and priorities, the granting of greater levels of autonomy will become a formula for chaos.[26]

Administrative modernization has as its governing principle the improvement of the way in which the government operates, granting maximum priority to the satisfaction of the citizens' demands, delegating authority to the administrators, replacing excessive rules and regulations with adequate incentives for increasingly highly qualified civil servants, calculating budgetary allocations based on the results attained by the institutions and, as far as possible, introducing market mechanisms to raise the productivity of government agencies and to enable them to offer the community an ever-increasing volume of high-quality goods and services.[27]

One of the greatest challenges facing the contemporary State consists, precisely, in defining the optimum terms for the structural relationship between the government and the market. Determining the extent and characteristics that the regulations for the economic activities of private individuals should have, constitutes a problem of a political nature, rather than of a technical or administrative one. This is particularly clear if we consider that the government is not an abstract entity but a complex, inter-institutional network, historically constituted, made up of persons and groups of persons who have their own interests and expectations.

The problem gets more complicated when the government's general objectives depart from or fail to coincide with the individual and group goals of the people who make up the bureaucratic structure. This conflict presents the challenge of designing a public administration made up of institutions with the autonomy necessary for operating effectively and efficiently that, at the same time, have incentives and are subject to controls that are able to prevent the personnel in charge of using its resources and operating its programs from putting the satisfaction of private or labor union interests ahead of the achievement of the government's objectives. The challenge of constructing institutions that would truly enable the government to promote the interests of society, constitutes one of the main concerns of administrative modernization.[28]

As the theory of public choice points out, every constitutional democracy faces problems of this type because society forms a government to promote its interests, and then returns to its private activities.[29] For administrative modernization to achieve its objective of creating institutions that are able to respond effectively and efficiently to the demands of society, besides a precise definition of the government's objectives and functions, it is necessary to solve the problem of the conflict of interests between a bureaucracy that resists change (agent) and the person or group of people in charge of designing and implementing the processes of public administration reform (principal). This conflict, which has been called "agent-principal" in the theoretical literature, arises from the presence of asymmetric information in the government environment. Asymmetric information implies that certain persons or groups of people within the bureaucracy are in a position to obtain incomes ("extranormal" benefits) as a result of their privileged access to useful and reliable data which would be extremely expensive to obtain for other actors.

The presence of asymmetric information in the government, and the monetary interests that this creates, transforms the bureaucracy into a factor of resistance to the reformist strategies proposed by administrative modernization. In order to solve or minimize the "agent-principal" problem, this theoretical model recommends implementing two major strategies. The first has to do with public servants and involves establishing objectives, incentives and comprehensive systems of human resources for those people who perform their tasks adequately, and the establishment of effective sanctions for who those who do not. This apparently simple idea becomes complex by virtue of the complications involved in defining what is truly functional for government agencies, in terms of both incentives and sanctions for bureaucrats.

The second strategy refers to government institutions and consists of introducing market practices which, through competitiveness, could reduce the levels of asymmetric information that make it possible to obtain monopolistic income and for corporate interests to develop within the bureaucracy.[30] Both strategies will be developed extensively in the following chapters by means of a comprehensive, efficient system for the professionalization and performance evaluation of public servants.

Incentives: service ethic

A fundamental challenge of the project of government transformation presented by the model of administrative modernization consists in inculcating an entrepreneurial mentality in public officials. This should be imposed on the traditional, "clientelistic" culture [Tr. note: "clientelism" is the practice of obtaining support with promises of government posts, financial help, favors etc.] that is characteristic of the bureaucracy in many societies. The new public servants must be professionals imbued with a vocation for service to the community and truly concerned about achieving results, solving concrete problems and systematically improving their professional capacities and aptitudes. The challenge lies in replacing an idle, unimaginative bureaucracy, with a professional one that is fully convinced that it is consolidating a service ethic based on the importance of maximizing the government's positive effect on society.

In the framework of the model of traditional public administration, the "agent-principal" problem has generally been faced by introducing tighter regulations and controls. This type of vertical, centralist strategy has failed to give satisfactory results in most countries. By limiting the freedom of public administrators and forcing them to follow rules and procedures, there is an increase in formal control, but almost always at the cost of reducing the levels of effectiveness and efficiency of government agencies. On the other hand, the dishonest behavior of public servants and the obtaining of incomes by using asymmetric information, usually continues because of the fact that the benefits implicit in these actions remain, in spite of the introduction of greater formal obstacles that, far from solving the basic problem, only cause a rise in transaction costs to the detriment of the citizens and private economic units.

Due to the evident failure of this type of strategy, some countries that we will study here, inspired by the principles of administrative modernization, have found an alternative way to modify incentives for the public servants in order to convince them of the service ethic proposed. The transformation of the system of incentives within which the bureaucracy operates, represents a pragmatic solution by minimizing the "agent-principal" problem and by reducing the conflicts of interests that necessarily arise when the bureaucracy becomes a power structure with its own ends, often contrary to the government's explicit ends as an institutional network, and to the general interests of society. This modification of institutional incentives, as a reform project, is based on the introduction of economic market principles into the government's functioning, foremost of which are the realization that competitiveness is essential for encouraging innovation and improving the quality of goods and services offered by government agencies, and the fact that the bureaucracy should be made up of highly qualified career professionals, with an ever-increasing level of specialization in the tasks that they carry out, and imbued with a deep desire to serve the citizenry.

A large number of the government agencies work as monopolies. These are static structures whose existence is established by law, and is rarely questioned. These bureaucratic domains lack the incentives to innovate practices and procedures to eliminate inefficiencies and to operate more effectively. One possible solution to this dilemma consists in introducing the principle of competitiveness. By subjecting them to the pressures of a competitive market, and confronting them with the possibility of being displaced by other structures, these agencies will be aroused from their lethargy and busy themselves designing and adopting better practices that will permit them to do more, and better, work, using their resources and experience more economically.[31]

As we shall see in chapter 4, one example of the successful introduction of the principle of competitiveness into public administration is the case of New Zealand, where a recent reform process separated the two functions of acquisition and sales from the government agencies.[32]

At the present time, agencies that are buying must invite tenders in order to acquire goods and services. Private companies and public agencies participate in the bidding. Thus the government agencies involved in producing goods and providing services, are forced to compete with their counterparts in the private sector. By separating the government's interests as producer from its interests as consumer, the monopolistic power of the institutions has been reduced, which has facilitated the adoption of measures aimed at improving their effectiveness and efficiency.

Those agencies that do not compete with the private sector, will end up losing their formerly captive clientele and running the risk of being privatized if their function is not high-priority or strategic to the government. In addition, the obligation to invite tenders for acquiring goods and services on the part of government agencies, has made it more difficult for the civil servants to conceal information and has thereby reduced the deviation of revenues toward the bureaucracy.

Accountability

From the point of view of administrative modernization, the lack of accountability, a characteristic of traditional bureaucracy, is related to the presence of asymmetric information and, in this respect, fits into the framework of the theoretical problem previously described, the "agent-principal" problem. The expensive, difficult access to reliable information in the government environment represents a source of power for sectors of the bureaucracy interested in obtaining a percentage of the social income by promoting its own interests at the expense of the public interest. The asymmetric information and lack of accountability allow domains to be formed inside the bureaucratic machinery that, by means of different strategies, are able to manipulate the institutions' operations, distorting the government's ends. The final result of this process is a political one: a government controlled by corporate and union interests will be unable to define, and successfully implement, development policies oriented toward the benefit of society as a whole. In addition, a government lacking accountability, where the administrative machinery is unable to give a clear account of itself and where the bureaucracy does not assume responsibility for its actions, is one that will gradually find the basis of its legitimacy undermined in the eyes of society.

In answer to these complex problems, administrative modernization proposes increasing the accountability of the administrators, and of the institutions they belong to, creating a direct link between the objectives of the agencies and people responsible for attaining them. In order to establish a greater level of accountability, it is necessary to distinguish among the resources that agencies receive (inputs), the goods and services produced (outputs), and the results produced (outcomes). By way of illustration, let us think of the different stages involved in the work process of a government agency in charge of providing health services. As a first phase, the agency will receive the resources that allow it to operate, from the Secretary or Ministry in charge of allocating public budgets. The second phase will develop as a result of the implementation of health campaigns (public health education, vaccination, direct medical attention, preventive medicine, etc.), in which the government agency will produce goods and services earmarked for different sectors of the population. Finally, in a third phase, the results of health campaigns will be evaluated according to different indicators of effectiveness and efficiency (for example, reducing the incidence of some type of epidemic at the least possible cost for the government). As figure 1.1 shows, it is possible to represent this process graphically.

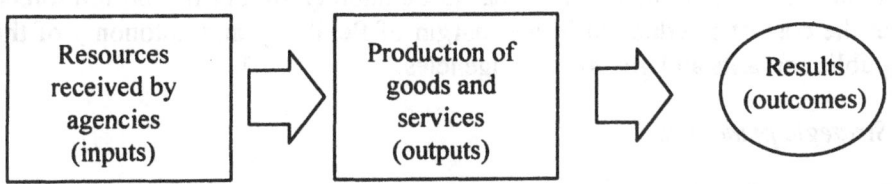

Figure 1.1 Stages involved in the work process of a government agency

One problem of the traditional public administration is that it does not consider mechanisms that are effective in evaluating the government's productivity and results. Usually the programs are evaluated in terms of the tax revenues used (first phase in the process), and not as a function of the goods and services produced nor, even more importantly, as a function of the objectives of public policy reached through their implementation (second and third phases). The overseeing concentrates on the procedure of exercise of expenditure and on applying accounting methods, leaving aside the obtaining of results and the accountability of government actions. By not concentrating on the productivity of the work and the obtaining of results, this model for evaluating public management does not create the appropriate incentives for public servants to make an effort to improve the competitiveness and response capacity of the agencies, which produces a bureaucracy that is more concerned with the level of expenses incurred and the activities or programs carried out, than with its capacity to produce results efficiently.

Administrative modernization proposes raising the level of public servants' accountability, having the evaluation mechanisms concentrate on the second and third phases.[33] Countries that have adopted a strategy that concentrates on the second argue that, without denying the importance of the evaluation of results over the middle and long terms, over shorter periods it is more practical to assure the fulfillment of objectives based on the production of a certain number of goods and services.[34] On the other hand, countries that have increased their level of accountability, concentrating their evaluations on the third phase, base their arguments on the fact that the most effective thing for managing to increase effectiveness and efficiency in public administration is to create a direct bond between civil servants and the results of the programs that they are to operate. Essentially, these are complementary strategies that, ideally, should occur simultaneously, remembering that accountability should not be reinforced at the cost of a reduction in the margin of flexibility and autonomy of the public servants and government agencies.

Strategic principles

In order for the reforms presented by the model of administrative modernization to have permanent positive effects and not only short-term impacts, it is essential to apply two guidelines for action. In the first place, an authentic strategy should be defined, a plan of action, provided with clear, realistic objectives, that would seek to modify the processes by means of which public policy is planned and executed, that would make it possible to redefine criteria for evaluating their effectiveness, that would grant institutions greater functional autonomy and that would increase the accountability of public servants. The successful implementation of the reforms presented by administrative modernization presupposes a proactive attitude on the part of the government and, in this respect, implies producing the necessary political consensus. In the second place, it is essential to understand that the introduction of functional market criteria, such as the systematic increase in productivity and the creation of an environment of competition among government agencies, should not occur partially and in isolation but, on the contrary, should form part of a joint, encompassing strategy of inter-institutional efforts. In order for these regulating mechanisms to provide the desired effects, the functioning of the government should be generalized as a whole, thus producing the necessary synergy to actually transform institutional practices and cultural patterns.

Culture

Clarifying the objectives of the government and of its institutions, establishing adequate incentives and raising the level of accountability of the public servants, are necessary, but not sufficient, conditions, for operating an overall transformation of the public administration. In addition, it is essential to generate a new culture among public servants based on an ethic of professional responsibility and deep commitment to public service.

All governments possess specific cultural models that are the product of their formative process. In these historical processes, the interests and power strategies of the groups, and the people that make them up, play a central part. Most governments reflect the superimposing of different cultural forms, some of them inclined toward tradition and others committed to reform strategies. This reality was expressed by analyzing the "agent-principal" problem, in which the values, norms, attitudes and expectations of "conservative" sectors of the bureaucracy reflect interests created inside the machinery of government. These cultural forms related to obtaining incomes and thus protecting particular interests, are present in many governments and constitute serious obstacles to the introduction of the reforms proposed by administrative modernization.

In this regard, the project of administrative modernization implicitly includes the cultural transformation of the bureaucracy. In order for the government to work according to the principles of effectiveness, efficiency, productivity, quality and honesty, it will be necessary to overcome behavior patterns inherited from the past that, to a considerable degree, explain the growing discredit that at this moment affects the bureaucracy of most countries. In spite of its evident complexity, changing attitudes and ways of thinking do not constitute an unattainable goal. The introduction of principles of productivity and competitiveness from within the institutions, the modification of legal and institutional frameworks according to clear objectives of public policy, the introduction of adequate incentives for the work of public servants, the carrying out of periodic, objective evaluations of their performance and, basically, the professionalization of the public service, constitute strategies whose adequate implementation will surely create the context necessary for changing the government's image in the minds of the bureaucrats and, even more importantly, in the minds of the citizens.

Administering the cultural change requires involving and listening to citizens, those who benefit from the services, taxpayers and public servants themselves, and getting them to participate in the change. This cultural change cannot be established "by decree" nor can it be brought about "overnight". In addition, the administration of the cultural change requires a serious communication strategy based on immediate, visible and significant results.

It is important to plan timetables and methods cautiously. Administration strategies for culturally changing the organizations, if they are not carried out completely and fundamentally, become "vaccines against believing in change". On the other hand, non-inclusive reforms imposed "from above" are translated into uncertainty, fear and, of course, enormous probabilities of failure.

Conclusions of the chapter

In order to actually transform the administrative machinery of government, it is pertinent to begin by systematically diagnosing the problems and trying to specify their nature. Thus it is also necessary to acknowledge that many governments lack the institutional mechanisms capable of requiring public servants of all levels to carry out their responsibilities towards society; and finally, we cannot ignore the fact that homogeneous administrative plans and procedures are frequently imposed on all government units, even when their strategic objectives and nature are completely different.

The creation of administrative regulations, generalized from particular experiences and situations, has meant that the controlling departments exercise an excessive, and frequently unnecessary, rule over the rest of the departments and government agencies. Since these regulations often do not take into account the operability and nature of the regulated agencies, there has been excessive, dysfunctional interference by the controlling authorities in the process of decision-making. Among other problems, this situation reduces the accountability of government agencies, as well as their capacity to successfully implement policies and programs.

In addition, the centralization of the process of decision-making and excessive regulations hamper the execution of actions aimed at making the exercise of public expenditure more and more efficient. It often happens that, when a public institution wants to modify its way of operating in order to streamline its expenditure and produce budgetary savings, the central, controlling authority imposes a long, winding path of negotiations and normative interpretations that end up wearing it down and inhibiting its will to bring about improvements.

When these structural problems of public administration are increased and surpass the limit of what is strictly bureaucratic, they become problems of a political nature. The incapacity of institutions and officials to attend effectively and efficiently to society's complaints, which are becoming more and more plural, informed and participative, undermine the legitimacy of the State. In this respect, one of the most characteristic features of contemporary political crises is their close connection to administrative processes with no economizing, where the basic aims of the government appear to be subordinate to the reproductive imperatives of an inflexible, costly, deprofessionalized and often corrupt bureaucracy. This results in a crisis of credibility that weakens the tax-collecting power of the machinery and inhibits the legal framework.

The historically dominant model of public administration has favored formal issues and neglected the basic ones. The obtaining of *results*, in terms of satisfying social needs, has been subordinated to the priorities implicit in determining an optimum volume of public expenditure and in establishing efficient control mechanisms over its exercise. According to this logic, it is more important to regulate the amount spent than to determine whether public funds are actually being channeled toward solving real problems and generating the goods and services demanded by society. In addition, the verticality and centralism inherent in the model create perverse incentives among bureaucrats by inhibiting their creative capacities and by making institutional processes inflexible, costly and slow. This leads us to conclude that not only do the present structural profiles of the public administration prevent it from becoming an effective instrument for the government's attending to and solving social problems, but that the persistence of corrupt practices and ineffective, inefficient institutions constitute a real threat to the preservation and strengthening of democratic systems.

The model of administrative modernization is not concerned with how many programs have been carried out nor is it based on how many activities have been performed. It does not matter if more beds were placed in a hospital or more vaccines given; what does matter is knowing for example how much the sick rate and incidence of tuberculosis has been reduced, and how much the programs and activities carried out contributed to reducing those rates. Here it is unimportant to know whether more patrol cars were bought or more policemen hired; what counts is reducing the crime rate. This is a view according to which results are more important that programs.

From a theoretical standpoint of the economic analysis of the law, in its aspects of the New Institutionalism and Public Choice, it can be seen that one of the most important causal explanations for the present crisis being experienced by the State, is an ineffective, inefficient definition of responsibilities, and institutional incentives deficiently established by the government, which are found at the root of many economic, social and political problems. A government that does not orient its resources in order to offer *results* to society, is a government that finds its legitimacy undermined and sees its capacities for political leadership and social regulation systematically reduced. Because of this, it is essential to review and fundamentally change the process of definition, implementation and evaluation of political policy, in order to generate new mechanisms and institutions that actually motivate the actors and enable the government to respond successfully to the mission of the institutions based on social demands.

Transcending the old model of public administration with its profiles of bureaucratic inflexibility, incapacity for innovation and costly, over-regulated and inefficient institutions, means undertaking a task that goes beyond the scope of what is strictly administrative. Successfully redesigning the public administration requires renovating the mechanisms, incentives and processes of governing. Having administrative modernization not only requires the creation of institutions that promote a better performance of the civil servants, and enable the expenditure to be streamlined, but also the creation of institutions that make the relation between government and citizens more flexible and legitimate. There must be some progress made in the area of effectiveness and efficiency in managing public matters, as well as in the area of legality and accountability of policy decisions made by public servants.

As we have already explained, and are borne out by the "best practices" in the citizens' opinion (see figure 1.2), renovating the government and its administrative structures requires a political effort to build flexible, autonomous institutions, and at the same time create a legal framework that promotes the transparency of a meritocratic system in the administration of human resources. Also, the legal framework should encourage the economical allocation and exercise of public resources, the efficient management of limited resources, the precise definition of the scope of powers and responsibilities of the public servants, the definition of clear rules that minimize friction among diverse organizations, and precise attention to citizens' real demands and expectations.

The challenge lies in reaching a balance between flexibility and control or, in other words, between the capacity to imagine solutions and to design processes that would allow services to be improved, and the need to count on responsible public policy whose process of formulation, implementation and evaluation would actually make it possible to produce results within the framework of budgetary restrictions. Lastly, the new institutional design must be sufficiently solid as to establish precisely the spaces of relative autonomy between the heads of the administration, and society. This relative autonomy should be expressed in terms of capacity for execution on the part of the administrative machinery, and capacity for influence on the part of the social authorities. Autonomy demands a clear, conclusive accountability on the part of the public policy-makers and the respective institutions. *Autonomy through results*, is the combination that is required and that has been shown to work.

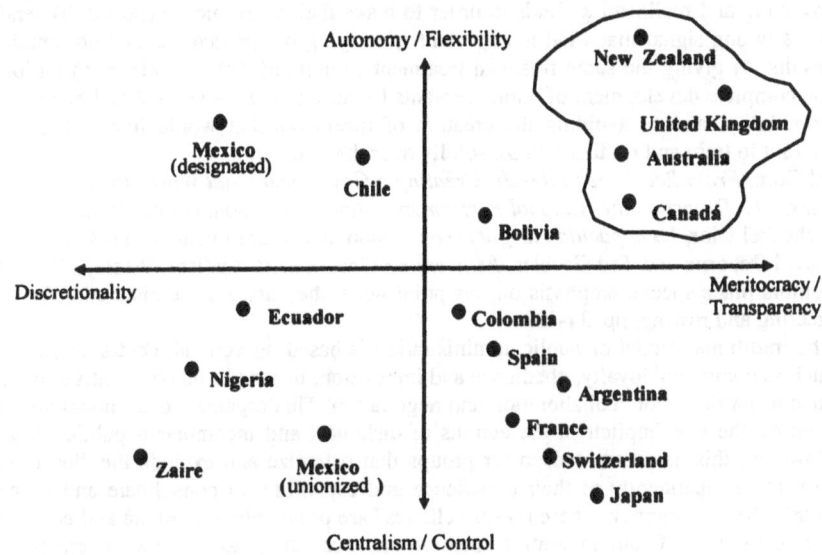

Figure 1.2 Mapping that identified the best services with pertinent administrative models

Notes

[1]   OECD Why Economic Policies Change Course, Paris, 1988.

2   Among those countries that have taken specific measures to adopt a system of this type are the United Kingdom, New Zealand, Australia, Canada, the United States, Ecuador and Bolivia, among others.

3   Colin Campbell, "Does Reinvention Need Reinvention? Lessons from Truncated Managerialism in Britain", *Governance: An International Journal of Policy Administration*, no. 4, October, 1995, p.480; Les Metcalfe, "Public Management: From Imitation to Innovation", *Australian Journal of Public Administration*, no. 3, September, 1993, p. 293.

4   The traditional (or old) model of Public Administration suffers from deficiencies that do not allow for an administration that offers better services at the lowest possible costs; this model implicitly involves: 1) an increase in operational costs of the public machinery, 2) increase in transaction and delay costs in the administration of the government due to the process of authorization that the departments must carry out in investing and reallocating funds in order to make their work more efficient, 3) sending out a wrong signal that what is important is carrying out procedures and not obtaining results, 4) giving the same financial treatment to units of different kinds, 5) inhibiting the complete development of public servants because of their – vertical and horizontal – immobility, and 6) avoiding the creation of incentives that would induce the public servant to train and professionlaize solidly over the long term.

5   Al Gore, *From Red Tape to Result: Creating a Government that Works Better and Costs Less: The Report on the National Performance Review*, Random House, 1993.

6   Yehezkel Dior, *La capacidad de gobernar*, Fondo de Cultura Económica (FCE), 1996.

7   David Osborne and Ted Gaebler, *Reinventing Government*, Addison-Wesley, 1992. The authors place special emphasis on this point when they discuss the distinction between steering and rowing, pp. 34-42.

8   The traditional model of public administration is based on vertical, centralist concepts, such as command, loyalty, obedience and imposition, instead of on cooperative concepts such as participation, collaboration and negotiation. This organizational model aimed at limiting the risk implicit in the actions of dishonest and incompetent public servants. However, this has permitted power groups that ostracize and exclude the "loser" civil servant, independently of their experience and capability, to consolidate and multiply within the bureaucracy. These power "cliques" are often able to regulate and coordinate the activities of administrative institutions according to outside interests and, occasionally, in a way that is openly contrary to the aims of public policy.

9   For an exhaustive study of the economic analysis of the law and its perspectives on government, see Andrés Roemer, *Introducción al análisis económico del derecho*, 1st reprint, Instituto Tecnológico Autónomo de México, Sociedad Mexicana de Geografía y Estadística, Fondo de Cultura Económica, 1998.

10 The following analysis is based on the book by Andrés Roemer, *op.cit.*

11 Armen A. Alchien, "Private Property and Relative Cost of Tenure", in Phillip Bradley (ed.), *The Public State in Union Power*, University of Virginia Press, 1959, pp. 350-371; as well as Arnem A. Alchien, *Some Economics of Property*, Rand Corporation, 1961.

12 Ronald H. Coase, "The Problem of Social Cost", *Journal of Law and Economics, vol.* 1, 1961; and George J. Stigler, "The Economics of Information", *Journal of Political Economy*, vol. 69, no. 3, June, 1961, pp. 213-225.

13 Louise de Alessi and Robert J. Staaf: a) "Property Rights and Choice", *Law and Economics: An Introduction,* 2nd. ed., Academic Press, 1988, pp. 175-200; and Louise

de Alessi: *b)* "The Economics of Property Rights: A Review of the Evidence", *Research in Law and Economics, vol.* 2, 1980, pp. 1-47.

[14] Unlike the new institutionalism, traditional or historical-descriptive institutionalism has its origins in the work of John R. Commons, Thorstein Veblen, Henry Carter Adams, Jerome Frank, Walton Hamilton and Roscoe Pound. These authors represent a tradition that, above all, concentrates on the inter-relationship between the processes of the State and the economy, and involves more than an application of economics to public administration. The historical-descriptive institutionalistic point of view has never been completely articulated, and for this reason it is difficult to elucidate precisely what the concerns and achievements of this point of view are. However Thomas Ulen's work distinguishes a common theme in this model that results in dissatisfaction regarding the formalism of modern microeconomic theory, especially when applied to matters of public policy. Ulen also distinguishes two groups separated by this dissatisfaction: one, discontented with the extremely formal, mathematical character of microeconomics and that sees in this formalism the reason why the traditional neoclassical economist does not pay enough attention to the influence of a specific time and place and to the institutional context in which the economic decisions are adopted; and the other, which does not object to the formalism of modern microeconomics, but rather to the fact that institutions are typically considered exogenous variables when, in fact, they are endogenous. On this point see Robert Cooter and Thomas Ulen, *Law and Economics,* Harper Collins, 1984.

[15] For a more detailed analysis of the maximizing bureaucracy, see William Niskanen, "The peculiar economics of bureaucracy", *American Economic Review,* Papers and Proceedings, no. 58, 1968, pp. 293-305; William Niskanen, *Bureaucracy and Public Economics,* Edward Elgar, 1994.

[16] See Mancur Olson, The Logic of Collective Action: Public Goods and the Theory of Groups, Harvard University Press, 1965; and The Rise and Decline of Nations, Yale University Press, 1982.

[17] David M. Kreps, *A Course in Microeconomic Theory,* Princeton University Press, 1990, p.745.

[18] Dennis C. Mueller, "Constitutional Public Choice", in Dennis C. Mueller (ed.) *Perspectives on Public Choice: A Handbook,* Cambridge University Press, 1997, p.1.

[19] Income hunting should be understood as the attempt to obtain economic earnings through the intervention of the government in the marketplace. A classic example is the attempt by a company to obtain monopolies granted by the government, since they enable the company to raise their prices above competitive levels, so that their income increases. See Mercuro and Timothy P. Ryan, *Law, Economics and Public Policy,* JAI Press, 1984.

[20] Mancur Olson, *op. cit.*

[21] Mancur Olson, *op. cit.*

[22] Gary Becker points out that most groups involved in politics will encounter the problem of the opportunist. However, the important thing is the relative rather than the absolute degree of the figure of the opportunist, given that this is what determines the relative power of the group. See Gary Becker, "A Theory of Competition among Pressure Groups for Political Influence", *Quarterly Journal of Economics,* vol. 98, 1993.

[23] Mercuro and Ryan, *op. cit.,* p. 141.

24 James M. Buchanan, "Politics, Property and the Law: An Alternative Interpretation of Miller et al. v. Schoene", *Journal of Law and Economics*, vol. 15, no. 2, October, 1972, pp. 439-452.

25 Cf. Peter Senge, *The Fifth Discipline: The Art and Practice of the Learning Organization*, Doubleday, New York, 1990.

26 Peter Senge, *op. cit.*, p. 235.

27 Al Gore, *From Red Tape to Result: Creating a Government that Works Better and Costs Less: Report on the National Performance Review*, Random House, 1993.

28 For a better understanding of the important effects of institutions and constitutional provisions on the way governments function, see Werner W. Pommerehane, "Institutional Approaches to Public Expenditures: Empirical Evidence from Swiss Municipalities", *Journal* of *Public Economics*, vol. 9, 1978. pp. 163-201; Rexford E. Santerre, "Representative versus Direct Democracy: A Tiebout Test of Relative Performance", *Public* Choice, vol. 48, 1986, pp. 58-63; Rexford E. Santerre, "Representative versus Direct Democracy: Are there any Expenditure Differences?", *Public Choice*, vol. 60, 1989, pp. 145-154.

29 Dennis C. Mueller, *op. cit.*, p. 140.

30 Dennis C. Mueller, *Public Choice II*, Cambridge University Press, 1989, p. 245.

31 The subject of competitiveness in the government as a measure for stimulating the implementation of better practices is developed succinctly by Graham Scott, Ian Ball and Tony Dale, "New Zealand's Management Reform", *Journal of Policy Analysis and Management*, vol. 16, 1997, pp. 357-381.

32 Herman M. Schwartz, "Reinvention and Retrenchment: Lessons from the Application of the New Zealand Model to Alberta, Canada", *Journal of Policy Analysis and Management*, vol. 16, 1997, pp. 405-422.

33 The decision to center on the second or third stage is a matter for discussion. In administrative modernization a dominant strategy does not exist, as is shown in the case of New Zealand, which fixes the accountability at the second stage, while Australia fixes it at the third. A detailed explanation of the differences and coincidences between the models of New Zealand and Australia is given in José Edgardo Campos and Sanjay Pradhan, "Evaluating Public Expenditure Management Systems: An Experimental Methodology with an Application to the Australia and New Zealand Reforms", *Journal of Policy Analysis and Management*, vol. 16, pp. 423-445.

34 Not all the results can be measured, although indices are generated that can approximate it. Similarly, an agency is not the only one that affects a result; rather, it is the effort of several agencies, and the problem is to measure the impact that each one has. Finally, the problem of temporariness refers to what measures taken today can only have an impact over the long term, so that if they are measured over the short term one might think, mistakenly, that they have been inadequate.

2. The Career Civil Service: A Comprehensive System of Professionalization, Evaluation and Performance of Public Servants

Origins and definition of the career civil service

The reform of the career civil service constitutes one of the fundamental principles of administrative modernization. Career civil service claims to create clear incentives for improving the development of public services, reduce discretion in the organization of positions, and corruption; but in order to carry it out, it is necessary to establish control mechanisms which are difficult to monitor, such as performance evaluation and accountability. Career civil service guarantees continuity and *institutional memory*, but, on the other hand, generates power domains, so that it is necessary to consider an optimum scheme combining flexibility and good management of human resources.

As we will see in the next chapters, in the governments that have implemented reforms in the management of human resources, three guiding principles can be identified: 1) the preparation of professional and labor contracts for definite periods, 2) the inclusion in these contracts of clear objectives and commitments that enable the performance of the civil servants to be measured objectively, and 3) the granting of greater levels of freedom to the administrators and heads of government agencies in order for them to achieve the goals and tasks that are entrusted to them.

The fact that contracts are signed for a definite period, but based on principles of job certainty in exchange for praiseworthy performance, allows administrators to make adjustments in their payroll lists in order to increase the efficiency and effectiveness of the institution, within short periods of time. In addition, by defining a work period in the contracts,

25

time limits for obtaining results from the public employees are more effectively established. Also, by including in the contractual instruments a list of the commitments undertaken and the goals pursued, a greater level of accountability is created in the public servant and objective parameters are established in order to use the comparison of goals and results as a basis, and decide legitimately about renewing the contract and granting benefits. Lastly, a fundamental aspect of this reform strategy lies in the responsibility granted to institutions to hire and fire the personnel under their jurisdiction – justifiably, not discretionally –, and to modify the operative procedures of the agencies. The main limitation imposed is that the agency's affairs must be handled transparently in order to facilitate accountability.[1]

As shown in figure 2.1, it is evident that those countries that have a system of human resources administration based on merit, are significantly related to a more efficient bureaucratic performance, less corruption and, generally, better government.

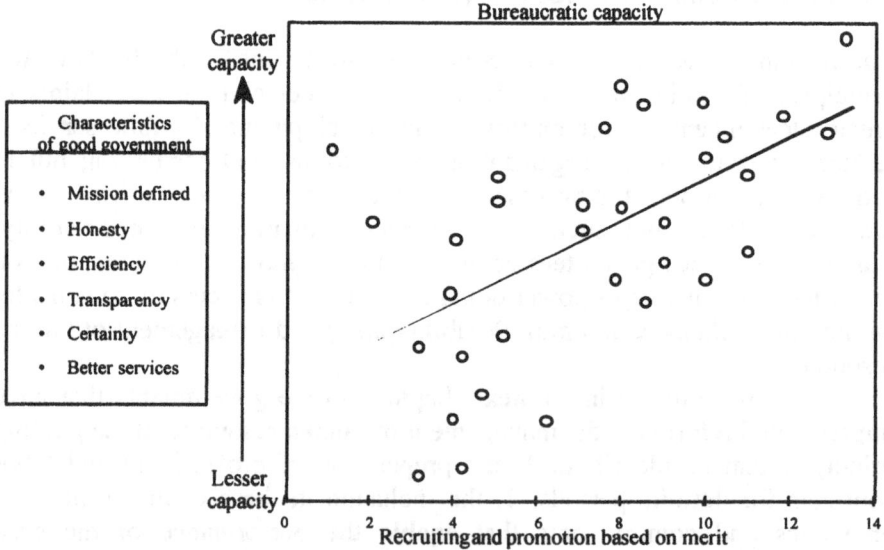

Source: World Development Report, World Bank

Figure 2.1   Merit vs. better government

The desire to have a professional public service is not a new one.[2] For quite a while, the career civil service has emerged as a reaction of governments to the crisis in the public administration caused by political immobility, corruption and lack of professionalism of public servants.[3] That is to say, the career civil service arises as an answer to three administrative challenges: 1) the demand for personnel highly qualified to confront the new challenges taken on by the public function; 2) the new, prevailing conditions in the world environment, and 3) the deep discredit of public officials due to cases of corruption, abuse of functions and impunity in the exercise of their functions.[4]

To solve these problems, the career civil service proposed creating an efficient public administration that is based on merit, defends the public interest, is service-oriented and has institutional memory. This is achieved by means of a system that regulates the entry by means of a rigorous selection, one that encourages prior training and satisfactory performance evaluations, and that dismisses an employee from his position for unsatisfactory performance evaluations. In addition, the system demands neutrality from the civil service in partisan questions.

To reach these objectives is a complex, hazardous task that involves costs and benefits. The main advantages and disadvantages that the career civil service presents are examined below in order to evaluate later the dilemma facing the governments that consider establishing a system of this type in administering public servants.

Advantages and disadvantages of the career civil service[5]

The career civil service, of course, is not the solution to all the problems of government. On the contrary, it is a system that presents diverse advantages, and disadvantages, that should be evaluated in the particular context of each case before any government decides to adopt it.

Advantages

1. *Eliminating the culture of individual loyalties*. This culture, which still explains the way many government teams are made up, cannot be replaced in a short time by a culture of responsibility and impartiality, given that a far-reaching, constant process of changes in the values of the public officials, and a system of incentives and penalties, are required. Under these circumstances, a well established civil service will greatly contribute to the change.

2. *Creating job security based on merit*. Another situation that is appreciated in the public service in general, as evaluated by the citizenship, is that officials of the middle and upper ranks giving excellent performance often do not have security in their job. This uncertainty partially explains corruption in the public administration. There should be mechanisms for separating functions for irresponsible servants (who do not "respond"

efficiently to their obligations) and security in their employment for those evaluated as excellent in performance. Also, the absence of, or inadequate, legislation in this area leads to arbitrariness in selecting personnel with criteria other than merit. These problems will be decreased if there is an efficient, professional, career service.

3. *Maintaining institutional memory.* Instability in the jobs of good civil servants, besides creating incentives for developing corrupt behavior, also leads to the elimination of their accrued experience. This loss not only results in costs in time and information, but is also an obstacle to the constant flow of administrative services. In this regard, an efficient career civil service is not limited to a simple regulation of the formal relations between the government and its agents, but also establishes the basis for reaching objectives and creating future structures and techniques that will make up the administration of human resources within the framework of modernizing the public administration.

4. *Training.* Training public officials permanently and continuously for a better performance of their functions, besides generating an increase in productivity, provides quasi-economic incentives that allow them to know that the task they carry out is appreciated, respected and valued.

5. *Results.* Because systems of personnel administration, such as those described in this work, create incentives for public servants to carry out their work efficiently, there is a smaller demand for resources on the part of each agency, which allows the results achieved to translate into gains in productivity.

6. *Feasibility of implementation.* Professionalizing the public administration in countries where there is widespread mistrust of the government, seems an extremely difficult task. However, this is precisely where it is possible to obtain substantial results over a relatively short period of time.

Disadvantages

1. *Decrease in opportunities.* The professional career systems have come to be associated very frequently with important problems; for example, they have generated an oversupply of government employees, at the same time as they reduce the opportunities for professionals not inside the systems, to accede to public employment. Job security has often tended, unfortunately, to accentuate rather than solve the problem of inefficiency, due to difficulties in installing the processes for evaluating public servants. Also,

the principles and advantages of the merit systems are not easy to achieve, since these systems are difficult to define and administer.

2. *Inefficiency.* Although a career civil service would foster a culture of efficiency in those employees worried about promotion, these systems would sometimes be displaced by appointments of a political type that lead to traditional problems, such as rigidity, slowness, bureaucratization and excessive autonomy, among others, that involve inefficiency.

3. *Bias in the selection and evaluation systems.* Although the members of the civil service ought to have enough possibilities to accede to the higher positions as opportunities arise, access to them should be granted to the most qualified after an impartial, fair evaluation, which in some cases would imply that the best candidate, whether from inside or outside the civil service, would receive the appointment. However, an excessively closed career system would be negative, just as an excessively open one would, because it lends itself to appointments that are too political and self-serving. Besides, the establishment of a meritocratic system calls to mind the need to have mechanisms for monitoring the public servants' performance, which turns out to be very costly.

4. *Institutional complexity.* Unfortunately, administrative reforms have often proven to be elusive and complex. To change formal structures, and especially real practices, is an extremely complex task. Even worse, there is not only one complex problem to be solved, but several at the same time, since administrative problems are interrelated; for example, developing an administrative career with clear, official paths should be accompanied by the development of efficient evaluation and training systems.

5. *Isolation, discretion and determining the government agenda.* The first consequence, once there was a system of career civil service, is that public officials would conceivably be encouraged to lock themselves up in a particular area of specialization, isolating themselves from the influence of the needs of the other areas of the government, with the result that public policy would be executed in a disjointed, incoherent way. Also, specialization would produce a broad, discretionary power on the part of the employee who, by becoming the possessor of knowledge, would create a sphere of influence and control within the department, a fact that would make it possible for public employees to develop their own programs in order to increase their influence on the government agenda.

6. *Immobility.* A civil service which ends up protecting the rights acquired by the public servants, and incapable of demanding co-responsibility and results, is the maximum obstacle to the efficient development of the public administration. The challenge is to break off the immobility of the "bad" civil servant and to guarantee certainty to the "good" one.

As can be observed, the system clearly involves costs and benefits, so that the point is not to define whether or not it is advisable to establish a system of human resources, but rather *what* type of system, according to *what* institutional arrangements, based on *what* principles and with *what* vision of the country and public administration.

Table 2.1 Advantages and challenges of the Career Civil Service

Advantages	Challenges
Creates clear incentives for improving performance of public servants	Creates the need to establish control processes, which are difficult to implement, for: • Performance evaluation • Accountability
Reduces discretion in the organization of posts	To prevent the loss of flexibility from becoming a factor in limiting performance
Reduces corruption	To prevent the creation of power domains
Guarantees continuity and institutional memory	To limit the increase in recruiting, selection and training of personnel

Challenges of the career civil service

The introduction of a career system implies several challenges. The first one is that, on one hand, bureaucracy should be subordinated to political authorities, as well as to national laws and institutions and, by the same token, to the society that chose those in charge of making decisions or passing laws. On the other hand, public servants should, to a certain extent, attend to the groups most involved in their work area.

A second challenge is that, somehow, employees should simultaneously have autonomy in management to attend to the particularities of their professional field and also a minimum of rights, such as the right to job security. But, at the same time they should be relieved of their posts if it is proven that they do not fulfill the established objectives. The development of a career system should, therefore, be accompanied by the development of effective and sufficiently clear evaluation systems.

The third challenge is that public servants will be obliged to provide services fairly and, to a certain point, uniformly, but at the same time efficiently and flexibly.

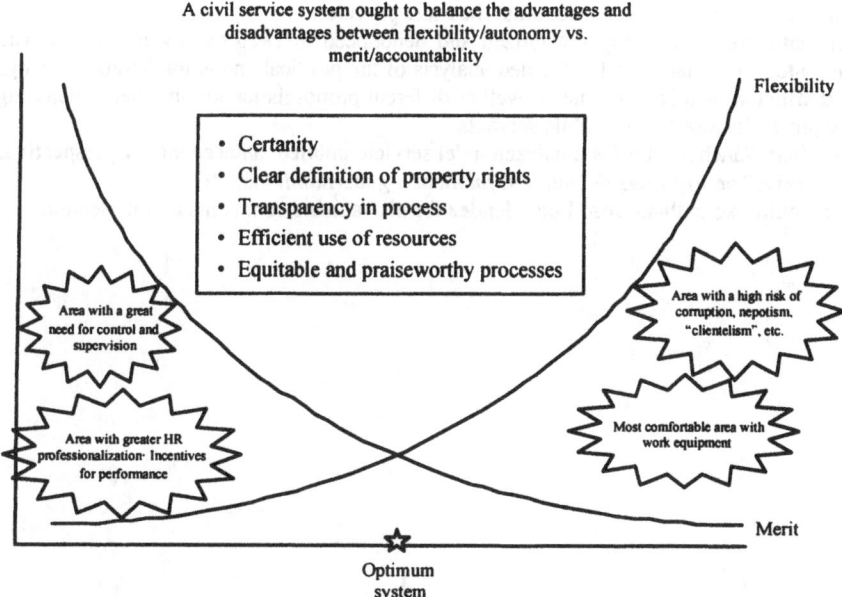

Figure 2.2 Balance flexibility vs. merit in the management of human resources

To meet the challenges in question successfully, and to mitigate the disadvantages of the system and to strengthen its advantages, is not an easy task, but neither is it impossible. For this reason, the systems of career civil service of different countries are evaluated in the following chapters, which will put us in a better position to propose mechanisms that would offer systems of human resources that work and that serve society.

Notes

[1] As Bardach points out, the prevailing high indices of discretion make public administration an unpredictable organization, with a high degree of power concentration among its most important members, which promotes the creation of agent-principal problems. For an analysis of this topic, see Eugene Bardach, *Getting Agencies to Work Together: The Practice and Theory of Managerial Craftsmanship*, Brookings Institution Press, 1998.

2   Due to the complexity of the public function, for more than one century the public services have been divided into two types of personnel administration systems: the military service, whose object is to regulate the personnel responsible for defending national sovereignty; and the civil service, which is in charge of providing and administering the public services that the State provides.

3   This situation was clearly recognized and denounced in 1826 by Javier Burgos, who presented to Fernando VII a detailed analysis of the political and administrative wrongs that afflicted Spain at the time, as well as different proposals for solving them, including the professionalization of public servants.

4   José Juan Sánchez, "Profesionalización del servicio público: antecedentes y perspectivas en México" en *Enfoques de políticas públicas y gobernabilidad,* 1999.

5   We would like to thank José Luis Méndez for his valuable comments on this section.

3. The Latin American Experience

Introduction

The objective of this section is to describe the laws and preliminary results of the career civil service in Latin American countries in order to identify and propose recommendations for Mexico. To carry out this analysis and focus the research effort, critical points were identified for establishing the career civil service in our country. These points center on the high-level structure of the organism that regulates the civil service and the criteria for the public servants' performance evaluation, selection, recruitment, training, promotion and separation. The differences in contexts, organizational cultures and demographic and social structures are also considered, in order to recognize the benefits and limitations of other practices in our national context.

The analysis of the critical points centered mainly on four countries: Chile, Argentina, Colombia and Bolivia, which are representative of innovative and divergent practices that have been established for a significant period of time. Each of the cases has strong and weak areas. At the end of the chapter, the strengths of each country that are applicable to the case of Mexico, and their weaknesses, have been selected in order to avoid repeating errors from other practices in our national context. Experiences of countries such as Venezuela, Ecuador and Peru are also included.

The Latin American countries began reforms of their public administrations because of fiscal restrictions that necessitated a reduction in their work force, at the same time as better-quality, more efficient programs and services were needed. In addition, the national debt crisis, experienced in almost all the countries in the region, greatly weakened the administration, making it difficult for it to meet the challenges imposed by the new environment, created by the structural reforms. The commonest practices in human resources management in the region are examined below.

Typical patterns of human resources management in Latin America

In several countries (particularly in Mexico, but also in Chile, Colombia and, to a lesser extent, Argentina), the effectiveness of the upper echelons allows the administrative inefficiency to be overcome to a certain point, in the management of human resources as a whole.

In this regard, Mexico has the most stable upper echelons in the region, with ministers remaining in their posts almost twice as long as their Chilean counterparts, and three times longer than the average in the zone.[1] Similarly, when contrasting compensations, Mexico is the exception, since it pays them salaries nearly four times greater than the average for the region, and two times more than in Colombia, its closest competitor.[2]

In fact, where the Mexican system resembles the behavior of the other Latin American countries, is in the operation of its lower levels.[3]

In general, in the whole region, it can be observed that the rigidity of the system is due to the poor functioning of the basic processes of the system of personnel management. Recruitment, evaluation, dismissal, promotion, compensation, and revision and adjustment of salaries, are the basic tools with which a civil service operates. In these areas, the Latin American systems rarely have systems that encourage a greater competitiveness in merit among the servants that work in the service.

Legislation and formal and informal institutions in Latin America tend to affect the stability of the public posts, without at the same time providing measures that would promote a performance of the employees oriented toward obtaining the results and goals sought by the department and desired by society.[4]

These restrictions accompany all the processes of the system, from recruitment to termination of employment. Thus it usually happens that, along with provisions that protect the job stability of the public servant, the legislation includes others that prevent the recruiting of civil servants that come from the private sector, or that stipulate that they can only be hired if there is no candidate among all the public servants. Similarly, the recruitment systems assure the virtually monopolistic control of an agency or department over the recruitment and selection of personnel. These practices are usual in the region, and are illustrated here with the Argentinean, Chilean and Venezuelan legislations.

In addition to the similarities, as we shall see next, there exist particularities in the handling of the professionalization, evaluation and performance of the public servants in the countries to be analyzed that, in many cases, can be complementary (and not exclusive) in order to strengthen a comprehensive system in the case of Mexico.

The case of Chile

Background

Chile made significant attempts between 1974 and 1990 to strengthen its economy, to privatize the services that it offered the public sector and to decentralize, at the lower levels, many of the functions of its government. In fact, the system dropped from approximately 350,000 people in 1971 to slightly under 140,000 in 1991. However, it still maintains practices in common with those of other Latin American public services with regard to the management of their central systems of the civil service, in particular in the ministries (secretaries of State in Mexico), "intendencias" or administrative divisions (states) and "gobernaciones" (local governments). These practices, regulated by the New Administrative Statute (Law 18.834 of Nov. 23, 1989) reduce the efficiency and effectiveness of the civil service, but are compensated to a certain degree by the functioning of the upper levels of their administration, which are not found inside the civil service.

At present, the Chilean public administration is made up of almost 150,000 people. Around 96% of the total unionized civil service (without including those hired or those in the health services) have their job stability guaranteed.[5] The remaining 4% are appointed personnel who serve at the discretion of the president, his ministers and the senior members of the administration. Within the system, pressures encouraging a better performance are very low, and most of the provisions relating to evaluation and training are either very sketchy or ineffective. Chile has a civil service system that grants great freedom to the ministries, state governments, local governments and to the organizations and centralized and decentralized public services in managing human resources. There exists a central law that establishes guidelines that control the entry, promotion and separation of the Chilean civil servant; however, the law grants freedoms to the departments so that they can make modifications they consider pertinent.

The controlling organism is the Treasury Ministry. The law does not specify what kind of accountability should be observed in the case of human resources, but it is known that a budgetary ceiling is set for funds allocated to the public servants' payroll. Each department is therefore free to establish the salary scales, catalog, hierarchies and number of people that it needs to carry out its functions. It also has the authority to decide on the number of people that enter as civil servants, hired by honorariums.

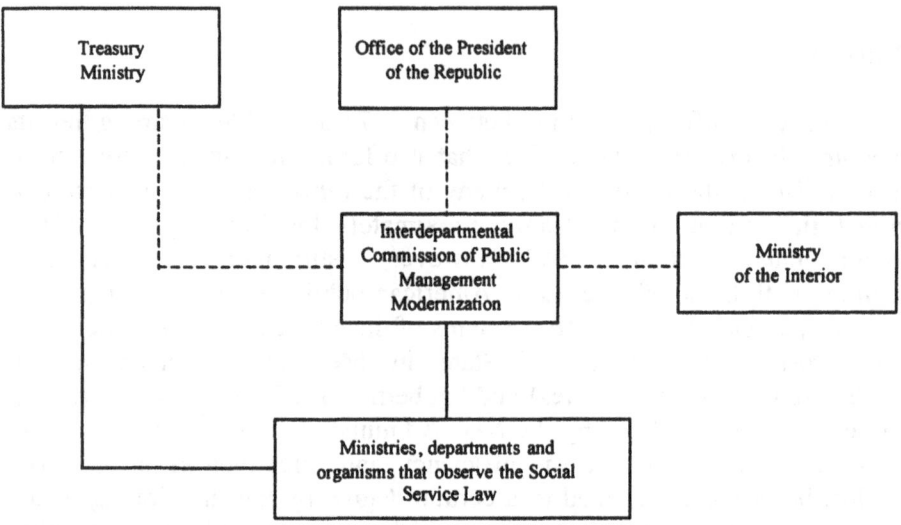

Figure 3.1   Organic structure (b)

One attempt at a mechanism for measuring the departments' performance is the Inter-ministerial Commission for Public Management Modernization, made up of representatives of the Ministries of the Interior, treasury and the President's Office, which aims at establishing management commitments between the ministries and the Ministry of the Interior, as well as at regulating and supervising compliance with the civil service laws.

The scope of Chilean law extends from the lowest positions to those of head of department. From head of department to minister the positions are called "confidence" (designated) posts and are handled similarly to their counterparts in Mexico. The lowest positions are equivalent to Mexican unionized workers and are affiliated to the National Association of Fiscal Employees, which does not enjoy the power boasted by a union. (In Chile it is illegal for a public servant to be affiliated to a union.)

Entry, recruitment and training

Entering career posts as head only happens by public competition in the lower-ranking posts or when it is not possible to promote a civil servant to the vacant position. The public competition consists of two sections, technical and objective. In each competition, factors must be considered such as studies, educational and training courses, job experience and specific aptitudes for performing the function in question. Each of the departments is entitled to define the weighting of each factor and the minimum points necessary to qualify as a suitable candidate.

There is a selection committee that prepares and directs the process, made up of the head of personnel and a committee of representatives of the department's central and regional offices, and that is responsible for submitting the names of the three best-qualified candidates to the authority that has the power to make the appointment for that position.

External recruitment is only possible at the initial levels of the administrative career. The entry of persons from the private sector at other levels is permitted only when it has not been possible to find other employees inside the administration who are able to occupy these positions.

The objective of training in Chile is to develop, complement, perfect or update the knowledge and skills necessary for the efficient performance of duties or abilities of public officials, and to prepare the public servant for positions of greater responsibility. There are three types of training: promotion, polishing skills, and voluntary. Each department establishes the prerequisites necessary to be a candidate for the training courses, depending on the course requirements. Each department is free to make arrangements with universities and other educational institutions according to its needs.

On the other hand, the system allocates very few resources to the training of its personnel. According to the Public Sector Budget Act of 1992, for example, less than 0.5% of the expenditure on personnel in four of the most important Chilean ministries (the President's office, Finance, Economy and Education) was allocated to training their personnel.

Evaluation and promotion system

The Chilean system of performance evaluation is based on merit and demerit points. The mark is given by the immediate head of the unit to which the official belongs. The points are based on the performance of the public servant during the twelve months corresponding to the evaluation. Three areas are evaluated specifically, based on the demands and characteristics of the post:

1. Behavior, which considers aspects such as morality, loyalty, obedience and discipline.
2. Judgment and discretion, which includes the capacity to discern accurately, tactfully and with reserve.
3. Productiveness and capacity, which include aspects related to accomplishing the functions inherent to his position with respect to time, manner and quantity.

Merit points will highlight those actions which involve personal behavior or performance as an outstanding official, while demerit will include those which record negative actions or omission of responsibilities. Based on the number of merits and demerits, performance is evaluated in each of the areas of evaluation, according to the following scale: excellent, very good, good, adequate, inadequate, deficient and poor.

Once the merit and demerit points have been counted in each area of evaluation, the officials are classified into one of four lists: distinction, normal, conditional and deficient. Like many systems used in similar administrations, the system of evaluation creates strong pressures on the immediate bosses not to give unfavorable marks to their subordinates. As a result, for lack of any other criterion, most of the promotions are granted mainly for seniority. This, in turn, generally causes salaries to be assigned for the same reason, rather than for better or worse performance.

Promotion is considered the right of an official to accede to a vacant post at a higher level in the hierarchical line of the department to which he belongs. If the employee does not have an evaluation included on the "distinction" or "normal" list in the previous period or has been sanctioned in the last twelve months, he will not be eligible for a promotion in the ladder.

Chilean law establishes that an official will be entitled to promotion to a position of an immediately higher staff level, enjoying preference over the employees of this staff level, when he is at the top of his category, has the necessary qualifications for the position and has a greater number of points in the evaluations than the officials of the level to which he is acceding.

Separation from the service

In the Chilean Civil Service Act, the grounds for termination of employment of a civil servant are specified:

1. Resignation accepted.
2. Retirement obtained.
3. Vacancy declared.
4. Dismissal.
5. Position eliminated.
6. Decease.

The declaration of vacancy will proceed for any of the following causes:

1. Health ruined or incompatible with duties of post.
2. Loss of any of the requirements for entering the position.
3. Official's evaluation on the "deficient" or "conditional" list.

The law stipulates that only in the cases of *job elimination* due to the processes of restructuring the department, will civil servants who are removed from their posts and who do not have the qualifications to occupy another, be entitled to severance pay as indicated by the corresponding law.

A designated civil servant and those hired by honorariums can be removed by means of a resignation petition to be formulated by the authority who granted the appointment. Under no circumstances will the designated public official be given severance pay or honorariums when he is removed from office.

Evaluation of the Chilean civil service and recommendations for Mexico

At the present time, the Chilean government is obtaining acceptable results in its administration without managing to eradicate completely the problems of a bureaucracy. The law now in force was introduced when Pinochet's dictatorship ended, placing as transitory articles the non-removability of public servants of that time and their not being subject to the new law. In this law a maximum term for transforming all government posts into civil service posts was not considered. This has caused a double organization in the machinery of the Chilean government composed of old, non-removable public servants and the new ones hired by honorariums.

This problem, besides not making completely clear who is responsible for which task, demands a greater investment of financial resources to carry out the same function, a situation that is also occurring in Colombia, and that Mexico ought to take into consideration.

The low level of competitiveness of the civil service is compensated for by the effectiveness of its upper echelons. Here the service restrictions related to salaries can be eliminated. In this way, the State offers more competitive salary packages with respect to those of the private sector, and attracts people with competitive qualifications for the internal market.

The system of performance evaluation, as in other Latin American countries, does not achieve its goals, mainly because of a lack of incentives for the middle and higher levels to evaluate their subordinates strictly. Nowadays, almost 90% of the evaluations carried out annually are "with distinction" in the evaluations given.

Mexico should take advantage of the Chilean experience to avoid the flaws in the system of performance evaluation, double organizational structure and limitations of career positions, since they directly threaten the efficiency and motivation of public servants.

In the same way, it should attempt a similar model with respect to the autonomy of the ministries for the development of their administration through performance agreements with the Chief Executive.

The case of Argentina

Background

In the contemporary history of Argentina there have been several attempts at administrative reform. For example, in 1955 the Institute of Higher Studies in Public Administration tried to promote a reform according to the report of Northcote and Treveylan of England, but without much success.[6] Later attempts had the same results. Critics say, generally, that there were two main obstacles. One, the lack of commitment on the part of political leaders who often only took it as a means of achieving their purposes and getting rid of those subordinates who did not share their view. And two, the high degree of organization and cohesion of the civil servants in the Association of Civil Personnel of the Nation. It was possible to persuade them to accept reforms that would improve their working conditions and their expectations of making a career for themselves as civil servants, but not to accept conditions for tenure in their post based on their performance.

In 1966 a stage of "administrative streamlining" began. One of the government's first goals at that time was to reduce the number of civil servants in order to increase efficiency and get rid of the "political protégés". The Argentinean government applied new methods and procedures to eliminate the work that was not strictly necessary (process re-engineering), announced that a redistribution of the responsibilities would be made and that any unnecessary personnel would be dismissed, the most capable officials would be kept on and each would be paid according to "his capacities". Although about 80,000 officials would thus be dismissed, which would involve a major unemployment problem, the first step was taken in 1967 with the passing of Law 17343, which would make it possible for civil servants to be relieved of their duties and which repealed Law 6666 of 1957.

This project, however, did not regulate the grounds for dismissal in detail, so that the ministers began to fire those officials whom they did not esteem for personal or political reasons, without taking into account the functioning of the Ministry in their charge. There was great resistance to all these proposals of administrative reformation, from the Association of Civil Servants, arguing that there was no way of knowing who or how many employees were "superfluous", since the administration departments did not have a homogeneous organization and, besides, lacked a definite study of their departments and their personnel. It was not until the 1980s, with the arrival of the democratic government, that important steps began to be taken to improve the public function.

In addition, the Secretariat of the Administrative Profession and the Government Administrators' Training Program (Profag, for its abbreviation in Spanish) under the National Institute of Public Administration (INAP, for its initials in Spanish).

In order to create that new system, the public function was first evaluated. The following diagnosis was the result:

1. There was a large turnover of personnel responsible for leading the government; between 1940 and 1980 the turnover rate for ministers was 13.7 months in their post; for secretaries of State, 12.2 months; and for governors, 14.1 months.
2. There was no continuity in the programs, mainly for two reasons: on the one hand, because the transitory leaderships managed only

incompletely to recognize the mission of their organization, the relative priority of the problems and the adaptation and suitability of the personnel in their charge; and on the other, because new governments tend to ignore the programs in effect and to develop a new plan of action that would bear the mark of their own government.

3. Discontinuity in leadership tends to dilute the responsibility even more and it serves as an argument to justify poor performance.

4. Due to the large volume of matters to be decided, the senior administrators often had to limit their efforts to ratifying the judgments of their subordinates, which affected the quality of the decisions when the subordinate personnel was not ideal.

5. As regards the selection and incorporation of personnel, there were few organizations that had procedures that incorporated criteria of merit, competitions or opposition. In other cases, in spite of having stipulated a recruitment mechanism, in practice this was ignored.

6. Regarding promotion, the official's advancement responded to "clientelistic" criteria, and merit, aptitude, capacity or calling played secondary parts.

7. Remuneration in the form of special compensations was very much gaining in importance compared to the basic salary. The problem worsened when its growing importance was reflected in an ever-increasing number of promotion ladders and a different ladder for each institution.

8. Lastly, it was found that there was a total lack of evaluation mechanisms for both the employees' performance and for the results in general.

Thus, in order to begin to tackle this situation, the Program of Administrative Modernization was developed in 1990. Its first concrete actions were:

1. It was decided to reduce drastically the government secretariats and undersecretariats of State, concentrating the units in only 36 undersecretariats dependent on 8 ministries. All hiring was also frozen starting from that moment (decree 435/90).

2. At the end of September, 1990, the Executive Comptroller Committee of Administrative Reform (CECRA, for its initials in Spanish) aimed at formulating and applying a major restructuring of the public administration (decree 1757/90).

3. This process culminated in the declaration of new, homogeneous, organic structures for all of the public administration. The administrative areas of each ministry were unified; each of the undersecretariats could have a maximum of three national directions; unnecessary functions were eliminated.

The reform of the public service was made in three big areas: 1) reduction of employment, 2) creation of a general system of human resources administration that would operate at the national level - called the National System of Administrative Profession (Sinapa, for its abbreviation in Spanish), and 3) development of a Training Program for public officials (Profag, for its abbreviation in Spanish).

Sinapa originated as a system whose aim was to unify several differing régimes. It sought to establish the elementary principles of the public function in order to achieve definite, uniform and flexible bases in their scope and area of application. Before this system originated, there were several statutes and promotion ladders for each activity, approved by the previous Law 6666/57, all of which disappeared when Sinapa established a single scale. At the present time, the system of remuneration is centralized; it includes supplements, bonuses and extras, which caused controversy due to their growing importance and because they distorted the salary system.

Profag took charge of training the human resources who aspired to be government administrators and belong to the career civil service.

As for the government administrators, once incorporated, their career is regulated by the Statute For the Body of Government Administrators and the Promotion Ladder For the Body of Government Administrators. According to the ladder, the career is made up of three classes (A, B and C, in order of decreasing rank), divided into grades, where grade 1 is a lower and grade 3 a higher level.

This structure is related, not so much to the type of duties or functions carried out by the officials, as to the hierarchy of these functions by virtue of the fact that, when entering, the officials are automatically incorporated into class C, grade 1, which is the lowest grade in the scale.

Selection, recruitment, and training in the system

In Argentina the process of selecting government administrators is closed, since only the first job competition is open (only professionals are invited for the group of administrators). In order to enter the applicant is required to pass a strict training process and, more significantly, regardless of the aptitude level with which he passes the training stage, all those who enter the public function do so at the lowest grade in the hierarchy.

The selection process consists of several exams. First there is an anonymous, written exam, with logical problem-solving, general culture, information about the real-world situation and reading comprehension; the "best" answer must be chosen, not the "correct" one. The second is for those who pass the first exam and consists in giving a solution to a "case", which is answered by giving an "advisory" report, with another report explaining the reasoning on which such and such a solution was based. In the third exam (when the process is no longer anonymous) a series of personalized interviews begins, with a psychologist who specializes in selection from outside the public function, using evaluations and workshops. Here the candidates' capacity for solving problems in a group is observed. Finally, there is a professional interview, given by a selection team.

Once the interview stage is over, a ranking is done and, based on this, the final selection. This process is anonymous and is done by mostly external, specialized personnel.

Once accepted, the applicants begin a period of study that will last two years. As it is necessary for them to devote themselves full time to it, from this moment on they are allocated a salary that is the responsibility of the National Public Administration Institute. Only those applicants that pass all the courses at the end enter the public function.

This process is made up of a System of Training that is established through a Permanent Career Commission that controls subdepartments in the different ministries and decentralized organisms, and that acts as an advisory organism in administering human resources, as well as in work and institutional relations. It is made up of representatives of the administration and of the unions.

There also exists the Technical Advisory Committee of Training Policies with representatives of the office of the President of the nation, of the SFP and of the INAP. A representative of this last organism presides over it and his responsibility is to advise regarding the best design and execution of training policies, to consolidate the needs to be covered every year, to coordinate the training offers and propose opportune measures that he considers advisable.

The concrete assignment of the new members is related to a previous study of profiles done by the Secretary of the Public Function (SFP, for its initials in Spanish), on the basis of the best alternative in order to take into consideration the most developed knowledge and capacities of the individual, as well as his interests and personal concerns (this is established in an interview whose aim is to complement the file in question).

Evaluation and promotion

The Secretary of the Public Function is the one in charge of coordinating, advising, monitoring and controlling the evaluation, as well as of improving the System of Performance Evaluation. This evaluation is done every year and follows the procedure below.

At the beginning of the year, the evaluator and the one evaluated agree on the objectives, activities and results to be reached during the period, which are set down in form "A" (management plan).

At the end of the first six months, the one being evaluated will fill out form "B" (progress report) and will send it to the evaluator in the first phase; he, in turn, will fill out form "C" (evaluation report) and in turn send it to the evaluator of the second phase as background for the final evaluation. When the procedural period is over, the previous step is repeated (now with forms "B" and "D", a procedural report and evaluation report by factor). The evaluator of the last phase (according to the case) will issue an Overall Procedural Evaluation, according to form "E".

The agent is entitled to obtain a copy of each of the forms at the end of the process and to know his overall mark, which is also to be sent to the department and added to the employee's file.

There are three central factors for promotion: performance evaluation, training and seniority. The requirements for promotion are the following:

The prerequisite for grade promotion are: to have the minimum seniority required for each grade and to have been marked satisfactorily on the annual performance evaluation. For class promotion it is necessary: to have fulfilled the conditions for grade promotion and, also, to pass (when this is indicated) the training activities established by the Secretary of the Public Function.

Separation from the service

Law 22.140 of 1980 established, in article 30, that personnel could be dismissed for abandoning the service, unjustified absences (more than 10 in one year), offenses to superiors, crimes that affect the decorum of the public function or for a deficient mark in two consecutive years or three alternate years during the last ten years of service.

The margin of time was later reduced, since decree 993/91 approving Sinapa, in section IV, article 42, establishes that: "stability will be acquired whenever the agent earns a *Good* mark in each of the periods evaluated". As the scale of marks of the evaluation system includes three levels -excellent, good and deficient -, this means that the first time the agent earns the mark of deficient, will be grounds for his leaving the civil service régime.

Evaluation of the Argentinean civil service system and recommendations for Mexico

In a study that was carried out shortly after implementing the new system, most (90%) of the officials stated that the most serious problem with the Sinapa is the low salary level at all levels of the ladder, although this does not apply to those who occupy positions of executive responsibility, since these employees are paid similarly to professionals of an equivalent category in the private sector.

By 1993 an opinion survey on Sinapa had been administered to a sample of officials attached to the program. The object of the study was to find out what idea the officials had of the structuring and functioning of the program. The most important discoveries included the following:

1. The officials continued to feel the presence of "the ghost" of the lack of transparency in the processes of assigning positions and in evaluating performance.
2. The officials, for the most part, were not motivated. They did not believe in the possibility of advancement in their career because all around them they saw political string-pulling instead of promotions for performance.
3. Although the training was appreciated, and they were willing to take it, there existed certain ignorance on the part of the employees as to the

profile of "desirable professionalism", which hampered a possibly greater incentive for them to achieve it.

4. Public servants maintained a positive image of themselves, but one that contrasted with the opinion that society had of them. At the same time, it was found that this could be attributable to a lack of efficient mechanisms of information and general communication about the Sinapa.

5. Some of the negative observations had to be interpreted with reservation, because they could be attributable to the short time the program had been in operation.

Several lessons can be learned from the Argentinean experience for the case of Mexico:

1. The procedures that are designed for selection, recruitment, evaluation, promotion and separation should be familiar to all public servants. In order for a system to work, it is necessary for all the officials of the department to be familiar with the work mechanisms. This is achieved through a strategic information campaign and a program made up of the officials and public servants themselves from different levels of the administration who are "believers" in the new system.

2. Remuneration in the form of compensations and bonuses should be transparent and integrated into the salary.

3. There is a need to create mechanisms for individual and group performance to assure that the public servant is focusing on the efficiency of the performance of his position without losing sight of the goals of the department in general.

4. The selection process, besides including exams to evaluate the applicant's theoretical and practical knowledge according to the function that he wants to fill, will contain a mechanism to evaluate his reasoning capacity when faced with situations or cases of the real-world situation, where the applicant will give the "best" answer, not a "correct" one. These evaluations should be established by each of the departments subject to guiding principles of merit and equal opportunities.

5. The evaluation process will begin at the beginning of the year, when the person being evaluated and his evaluators will agree on the goals, activities and results that the individual will attain during the following year of work based on their evaluations of previous performance. The

performance evaluation should be impartial and the results should be carried out conscientiously.

The case of Colombia

Background

Over four decades ago, Colombia began efforts at professionalizing its public servants. Just as in other countries of Latin America, the main reasons for introducing a civil service were based on professionalizing the public servant in order to guarantee the improvement of services, based on individual merit. From the beginning, they tried to follow a model similar to the French one: with centralized controls.[7] The Colombian pattern is made up of a National Civil Service Commission (CNSC, for its initials in Spanish) that is responsible for overseeing and enforcing the laws that derive from it in the area of human resources management, as well as the Treasury Ministry in charge of fixing budget and salary limits that other ministries should accept.

However, Colombia has not been successful in introducing its civil service, and this is clear from the number of variations and agreements undergone by the laws in the last five years, either from a lack of confidence of the employees in the system or the considerable corruption that exists, or from the amount of discretion that is allowed to the ministries (added to the poor mechanism for accountability at the central level). At the present time, the CNSC (initials in Spanish) is attempting to limit discretion in the selection and recruitment processes, as well as in the separation of public servants.

One of the advances that Colombia has made is an evaluation system of the ministries' performance on the part of the citizenry. The system, named *Trato hecho*, introduces a mechanism for passing or failing the performance of the ministries (and indirectly of the ministers and vice-ministers) similar to those existing in some of the OECD countries. However, the results of this system have been discouraging because little action is taken as a result of this performance assessment.

The scope of Colombian law includes all the employees of the State that serve in the agencies or organizations at the national, departmental (state), district (except for the Capital District), municipal levels and the decentralized organizations.

Organic structure

The levels of the government human resources in Colombia are divided into seven levels, in order of importance:

1. Directive: includes ministers and vice ministers.
2. Advisory: support personnel of ministers and vice ministers.
3. Executive: mainly directors general and heads of division.
4. Technical: head of section and group coordinators.
5. Professional: analysts.
6. Administrative: secretaries, etc.
7. Auxiliary: chauffeurs, gardeners, messengers, etc.

The levels included in the career civil service range from auxiliary to technical and, on occasions, executive (some heads of division). There is no definite criterion for establishing which heads of division should form part of the service and which should not.

The National Civil Service Commission is composed of:

1. The director of the Administrative Department of the Civil Service, who is to preside over the Commission. In his absence he will be replaced by the secretary general of the same department.
2. The director of the School of Higher Studies in Public Administration.
3. Two representatives of employees of the State.
4. A representative of the Federation of Municipalities.
5. A representative of the Confederation of Governors.
6. A member designated by the president of the Republic.

The Colombian president designates the members of the Commission for a two-year term to carry out their function, with the possibility of repeating the assignment for up to two more periods, if this is the decision of the head of state. This characteristic of uncertainty not based on merit in performance undoubtedly introduces a factor of instability in the policies regarding human resources, which seems to be reflected in the number of variations of the laws and agreements that have been made in the last five years (see figure 3.2).

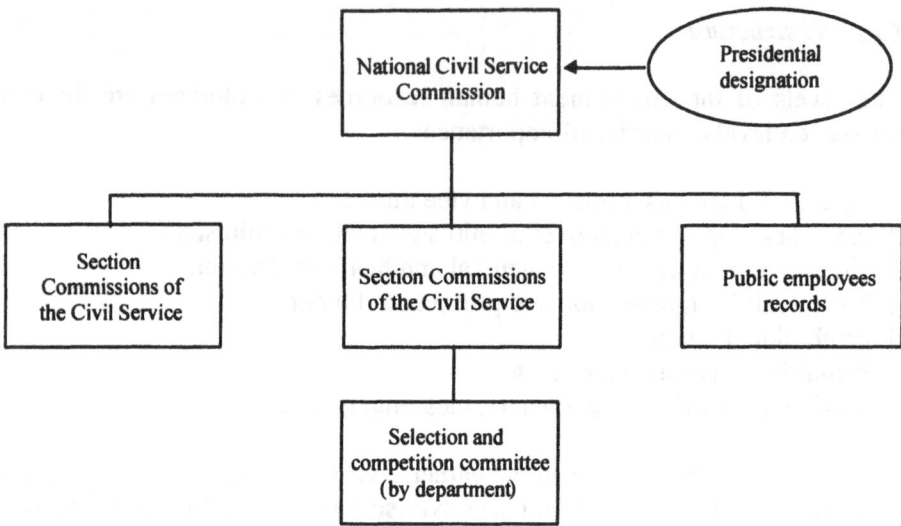

Figure 3.2 Organic structure (a)

In general terms, the key responsibilities of the CNSC are the following:

1. To oversee compliance with the career norms of the employees in the national and territorial environment. In the event of infraction not following the rules, to request the imposition of sanctions by the competent authority, in the form of a fine, suspension, or the dismissal of the offender.
2. To know, statutorily or by petition, of the irregularities occurring in carrying out the selection processes, being able to annul them, either totally or partially. To exclude people from the eligible lists who might have committed a violation of the internal laws or regulations of the administration of civil personnel serving the State and to order the revocation of appointments or other administrative acts.
3. To recommend to the Administrative Department of the Civil Service, initiatives, studies and investigations in areas related to personnel administration.
4. To make sure that the provisional appointments do not exceed the legal term. In the event of an infraction, to request from the competent authority the imposition of sanctions in the form of a fine, suspension or dismissal of the offenders.

5. To cooperate with the government and with the Administrative Department of the Civil Service.
6. To delegate functions onto the section commissions of the Civil Service.
7. To dictate their own regulations and those of the section commissions.
8. To know, in the second phase, the decisions adopted by the section commissions of the Civil Service.

The CNSC does not have political power comparable to that of a ministry; however, by presidential decree, compliance with all norms and regulations is obligatory.

The Commission delegates some of its functions onto section commissions that are located in some states of the country. These section commissions have the same functions as the CNSC, and their main objective is to delegate section work that is carried out in the central government. They are also made up of the counterparts of the members of the National Commission. When circumstances warrant it, the CNSC can temporarily resume the functions delegated while the causes that originated the decision are being resolved.

In addition, all agencies that have personnel registered in the civil service will have as part of their organizational structure, a Personnel Commission to oversee compliance with the norms issued by the CNSC. The Personnel Commission of each agency will be made up of two representatives of the head of the agency and a representative of the employees.

The CNSC will take the Public Record of Employees registered in the Promotion Ladder of the Administrative Career, that is to be made up of all registered employees or those who managed to apply for the promotion ladder of the administrative career. The main object of the record is to form a pool of personnel and to resort to it in case a vacancy occurs.

At the present time, the CNSC is saturated with work, does not receive enough resources and requires greater financial and technical support.

Selection, training and promotion in the system

One of the main concerns of the CNSC is to introduce clear procedures and norms for the selection and recruitment of personnel that will act as public servants. The selection process aims at guaranteeing the entry of ideal personnel into the public administration and to the promotion system for employees, based on merit, by means of mechanisms that will enable all Colombians who can show they have the qualifications to perform the jobs, to participate.

The selection of personnel for entering the administrative career or the promotion system inside it, falls within the jurisdiction of each agency or organization, under the direction (regulation) and monitoring of the National Civil Service Commission.

When a definitive vacancy occurs in a career job or there is an order to fill a new position, this is done according to an established order of priority:

1. With career personnel whose position has been eliminated and who have opted for the preferential right to be reallocated.
2. With the best employee in the agency at the level corresponding to the position to be filled, provided he has the qualifications for carrying out the duties.
3. With the person who occupies the first position on the list of those eligible for the promotion competition or open competition, at the moment in which the appointment is to take place.

When the selection is being made to fill an administrative career post, career employees have a preferential right to it. Otherwise, provisional appointments are made, lasting no longer than four months. If for some fully justifiable reason it is not possible to hold the competition to fill the vacant position, the term of service by provisional appointment will be extended by up to another period of four months. All cases in which there is free appointment, should be notified to the National or Section Civil Service Commission.

A substitute can be designated provisionally if an employee is on study assignment or filling a free appointment position in another department. This position will only be carried out as long as the assignment lasts.

Filling free appointment positions will be done by ordinary appointment by the head of the department; career positions will be filled by means of a competition. In both cases, the applicant for performing the functions of the vacant post should have the qualifications required for the job, according to the manual of functions and positions.

Also, the applicant who is to provide services in the position in question, in order to continue with his career, should fulfil the following requirements:

1. The last evaluation of services given to the applicant at the moment of the registration should be at least 70% on the scale.
2. Not to have been given disciplinary sanction during the previous year.
3. To have held his present position for a period of not less than one year, as career employee.

To create a closed or "promotion" competition, there should be at least two people interested in the vacant position that have the qualifications, and then the respective procedure will be followed. In the event this condition is not met, the competition must necessarily be declared void and an open competition announced as indicated by the norms.

Once an open competition has been announced, admission to it will be open to all those who can show they have the necessary qualifications for performing the duties and that can be legally appointed in the position.

The law establishes equal opportunities for all Colombians who can show they have the same qualifications for holding the position for which they are competing. This is "guaranteed" by means of the "eligible list", where the marks are published in descending order.

Each department and organization is to have a committee for carrying out the selection or competition processes. This committee is to be made up of the nominator (person with the authority to make the appointment) or his deputy, the head of personnel and the representative of the employees in the Personnel Commission of the agency. The committee will have the following functions:

1. To prepare the competition project for announcement, so that it meets the legal requirements and technical parameters, according to the type of post.
2. To make sure that the competition is carried out as established in the announcement and, in the event anomalies are found, to inform the nominator.
3. To designate suitable juries for each of the tests applied in the competition.

4. To sign the record of the applicants on the last day contemplated for applications.
5. To decide regarding complaints presented by contestants dissatisfied with the tests.
6. To prepare and sign the competition records.
7. To present the resolutions establishing the "eligible" lists or declaring the competitions void, as the case may be, to the head of department or organization for his signature.

Based on the result of the applications, the list of applicants admitted or rejected will be prepared and published, in the latter case indicating the reasons.

Once the competition is completed, the head of the department or organization will prepare the "eligible list" of candidates approved, given in strict order of merit. This list will be valid for up to one year as validation of the exams presented and in order not to ask the applicant to present the same exams within a short period of time.

The person selected by open competition is appointed for a trial period of four months, at the end of which his performance will be evaluated to decide whether he is to remain in the position or it is to be declared vacant. If he is given the position, the National Civil Service Commission will have to go through the procedure to include him in the career civil service, and he will then begin to obtain the corresponding benefits.

Evaluation and separation

Colombian law establishes criteria and ranks for marking the aspects to be evaluated for each applicant for a vacant position, in order to avoid as much as possible any discretion that might exist in the process. The results in this area have made it possible to reduce the weight of highly discretionary processes, such as interviews, and increase the weight of objective variables, such as exams of knowledge (while granting freedom to the departments to adapt procedures to their particular necessities). At the present time an effort is being made on the part of the CNSC to reduce the weight of the interview even more, because many complaints are still being received that are related to the subjectivity that exists in this process.

If the nominating authority makes appointments without complying with the norms established in the law and its regulations, and the members of the Section Civil Service Commission permit this either out of action or omission, this will constitute grounds of improper behavior and will bring about a concrete response, in the terms contemplated in the law. The National Civil Service Commission, ex oficio or at the petition of any citizen, will take the pertinent measures to verify the fact and to request that the corresponding sanction be applied.

The Colombian Civil Service Act clearly explains the grounds for employees' removal from the system:

1. Due to a declaration of his appointment being null and void, when he has obtained an unsatisfactory evaluation of his services.
2. Due to his resignation being accepted.
3. Due to the elimination of his job.
4. Due to his leaving, and being entitled to retirement.
5. Due to absolute disability.
6. Due to being of age for mandatory retirement.
7. Due to dismissal.
8. Due to a declaration of job vacancy in the case of job abandonment.
9. Due to expiry of the period for which he was appointed or elected.
10. The declaration of his appointment being null and void, mentioned in point one, refers to an unsatisfactory performance in the evaluations carried out annually. Once a public servant has obtained this mark, an "objective" (outside) opinion should be heard by the Personnel Committee of the department. If it is decided that the evaluation was "objective", the public official must be discharged. This system is considered very aggressive because it forces the evaluator to decide if the public servant cannot mend his errors and improve in a short interval. Consequently, most of the evaluations give the public servant a favorable result, which creates the perverse defect of tending to evaluate "kindly" within the organizations.

The law contemplates the possibility of declaring the change from a civil service position to one of free appointment, in which case the civil servant will be entitled to be placed in a position of similar characteristics with equal pay, provided a vacancy exists. In the event that a position is not opened with these characteristics, the employee will be entitled to continue carrying out his function and to maintain the career benefits as long as he remains there. The implications of following this procedure are quite harmful for the professionalization and efficiency of the public administration, since it leaves the door open for a double structure to be created with equal functions, maintaining one that is potentially expensive and another that is unprofessional and inefficient.

Every employee registered in the civil service system that is removed from his position will have a right to severance pay or to preferential treatment for placement in another similar post. In the event that it were impossible to reallocate the official to another department of the agency within a period of six months, he would be entitled to the severance pay established by law. In the event that a civil servant has lost his position as the consequence of a restructuring of the department, he will not be entitled to receive severance pay, but will receive preferential treatment in placement in a position of a similar nature.

An "Evaluation of Services" of each public servant is carried out annually. The employee's productiveness, quality of work and work behavior are marked. The Evaluation of Services is taken into account in order to:

1. Determine his continuance or removal from the service.
2. Incorporate his career into the promotion ladder.
3. Participate in promotion competitions.
4. Grant scholarships and study assignments.
5. Grant incentives to the employees.
6. Evaluate the selection processes.
7. Formulate training programs.

The marking procedures are established by the National Civil Service Commission and are to be accepted by all government organizations (except for the Capital District and municipal governments). Each of the organizations has the capacity to adapt the procedure, but any changes must be approved by the Administrative Department of the Public Function (central).

Performance evaluations should satisfy the basic principles dictated by the CNSC, namely, they should be:

1. Objective, impartial and based on principles of equity.
2. Fair, so that both positive and negative actions should be kept in mind.
3. Based on concrete facts and conditions demonstrated by the employee during the period of time included in the marking or evaluation, assessed under the circumstances in which he performs his duties.

The head of personnel of the department or organization should ensure the timely and appropriate application of the system of performance evaluation. To this end it should:

1. Inform the evaluators as to the norms and procedures that govern this area.
2. Promptly give out the application forms and other necessary material necessary for proceeding to the marking and evaluation.
3. Ensure that the marking and evaluations are properly carried out.
4. Prepare the averages necessary for obtaining the definitive mark and inform the interested party.
5. Present reports on the results obtained in the evaluation of services to the head of the department or organization.

The head of the organization assigns the duty of marking an employee to the employee's immediate superior for evaluation. An extension of 2 weeks will be given after the date set for handing in the marks. The employee evaluated will be entitled to request his mark two days after the period agreed on has expired. In spite of this being an annual process, the head of the organization may order an unscheduled evaluation if he receives information that some civil servant is not performing his duties efficiently. The result of the evaluation will be given to the employee directly.

Partial evaluations may be held of the officials who occupy temporary positions on assignment, substituting another official, in the event of changing posts outside of the dates of the normal evaluation, or if they become eligible to occupy another post inside the civil service, outside of the evaluation period.

In the event the employee does not agree with the result of his evaluation due to suspicions that one or more basic principles were not respected, he will be entitled to make a complaint, supported according to the law, for verification. In the event that the evaluation is unsatisfactory, the position will be declared null and void. Freely appointed employees are not subject to evaluation.

Evaluation of the Colombian Civil Service System and recommendations for Mexico

Colombia imposed a system lacking progression and systematization in implementing the act. Organizations were given six months to introduce the systems, organization, procedures, description of duties and everything related to the Civil Service Act. Such an ambitious plan meant that the organizations were not ready to introduce the whole process and this caused logistical, organizational and service problems. The introduction of the civil service system in Mexico should be gradual, controlled and focused so as not to negatively affect the service that the department offers to the community.

The CNSC has done positive work by carrying out changes in the civil service norms; one example of this is reducing the importance granted to discretionary tools in selection and recruitment.

It is highly advisable that in Mexico an efficiency unit, endowed with presidential authority, be created in order to oversee compliance with the norms established in the law for issuing resolutions regarding any irregularities found. However, the unit will keep these functions from interfering with the normative and study functions, instituting clear laws and rules, besides dividing its organizational structure into departments with specific functions and having sufficient resources to carry them out. This unit should be minimal in bureaucratic terms, and oriented toward a comprehensive, forward-looking vision in order to bring about an administrative modernization that is flexible, synergetic, effective and efficient; and, among other powers, responsible for the area of the civil service.

The performance evaluations play an important part again in this area: bosses are not motivated to mark their civil servants as "deficient" for fear of becoming unpopular or having problems with their subordinates. The system of performance evaluation in Mexico should, necessarily, be effective. The pragmatism of the law depends to a great extent on this.

Mexico should create a database similar to the Public Record of Employees Registered in the Promotion Ladder of the Administrative Career, where information is kept regarding current employees and those recently removed. The objective of this database would be to identify candidates with the appropriate profile to fill vacant positions.

In each department there should be a committee that would be responsible for executing the competition and selection processes, in order to guarantee their transparency and legality. This committee would have the same structure as its Colombian counterpart.

Mexico should adopt the mechanism of the Colombian system to guarantee the assigning of posts based on merit: to declare a closed competition valid, it will be necessary for there to be *at least* two qualified applicants to fill the empty position; if not, the competition will be declared void.

Colombian law limits the time for assigning posts by provisional appointments. Mexico could diminish the risk of the increase in freely assigned posts in the same way, that is to say limiting the time in which a freely designated civil servant can remain in the organization before an open competition to occupy this post is announced.

The case of Bolivia

Background

Bolivia attempted a reform of its civil service in the context of a set of structural reforms of its economy. In the early 1980s, Bolivia faced an acute process of inflation and recession that almost reached hyperinflation in 1985. The process of macroeconomic adjustment following this crisis prompted a process of state restructuring that included, among other things, a major privatization of services of the government sector and changes in the state financial system and in the provision of public services.

This process revealed the weakness of the traditional upper echelons of the Bolivian public administration, with the result that there began a process to bolster the civil service, particularly its upper echelons, which had been seriously weakened since the early 1980s.

Thus, by mid 1988, a strategy was designed that aimed at recruiting a considerable number of civil servants in middle and upper levels to distribute them through different agencies. Although initially the project only covered 653 positions, by the middle of 1992 this strategy was abandoned in favor of a second, more ambitious phase, which consisted of creating a new Civil Service Program (PSC, initials in Spanish) that would aim at reinforcing only the upper echelons of the administration, some 12,200 people, a little less than 6.7% of the existent civil service, whose payrolls of just over $128 million annual dollars constituted about 8.7% of the total salaries of the service.

The process sought to strengthen the central administration and to eliminate, besides, the irregular patterns of financing into which the administration had fallen, since a considerable number of these were financed with funds coming from multilateral assistance, and not clearly defined.

The government in turn proposed a period of 10 years of reform in order to make the transition from the old system to the new PSC. In this period, the State of Bolivia was to: 1) reduce the number of employees existing at the beginning of the reform; 2) incorporate personnel into the new system, and 3) obtain additional funds to finance this. In order to make the plan fiscally viable, it would be necessary to reduce this group of personnel by a little over 40% and obtain financing, both in domestic funds and in external credits. This presupposed an additional financing that would increase from $33 million a year for year one, to $78 million for year ten, as well as an external debt of a little more than $57 million to be distributed throughout this period.

By mid 1992, however, first the Bolivian government, and later the financial community, reached the conclusion that the continuous financing of this small group (little more than 6,500 people) would be fiscally impracticable, with the result that they changed their strategy again and decreased the object group: first to around 2,800 and then to 2,500 people. In spite of this, unlike the initial approach, this group would not be distributed equally throughout the whole public administration, but rather would be concentrated in a few departments to ensure the generation of "critical masses" that were favorable to the process of government modernization, in the rest of the departments.

To prevent a disorderly process, a legal framework was created that regulated:

1. Which agencies could receive selected public servants with high evaluations, who were well paid.
2. Which commitments the agencies should fulfil in order to receive these civil servants.
3. What objectives the departments as well as the new civil servants should achieve, once the latter took up their posts.

These reforms were regulated by law by means of a radical change in the system of public administration management (law 1168, in 1990), which included a set of "basic norms" for all departments (that functioned as a set of "minimum standards"), and then more detailed provisions for each of the systems of administrative support. To date, the program is still being introduced into different departments, beginning with a functional analysis of the National Secretariat of Industry and Trade. The process has been linked to the establishment of performance objectives, explicitly connected to the fulfillment, on the part of the Ministry of Finances, of a financial flow allocated to this process, in order to ensure that the changes are effective and visible. The process of incorporating other departments into this system has advanced at a relatively slow pace due to the need to have sufficient financing for each case.

To accomplish this, the Bolivian system is based on the following organizational structure (see figure 3.3). The Personnel Administration System has three levels of organization:

1. Normative and advisory level, in charge of the governing body of the Personnel Administration System.
2. Executive level, represented in each agency by its maximum executive authority.
3. Operative level, made up of the unit in charge of personnel administration.

The governing body is to issue and publish the basic norms of the Personnel Administration System, and has the authority to review them periodically and modernize them, based on the analysis of the experiences of their application, variations in the socioeconomic context, the administrative dynamic and the functioning of the other administration systems.

Added to this, the governing body, based on the norms in effect, is the one that regulates the administration of temporary personnel, including the conditions for recruiting, selecting, hiring, paying, evaluating and terminating the employee.

The Direction of the Public Function is the governing body's specialized unit that depends directly on the Ministry of National Revenue. Its powers are:

1. Introducing the Civil Service Program in the agencies of the central administration and of the decentralized administration, in the place indicated by the direction.
2. Monitor the Personnel Administration System.

3. Control and regulate the training of public servants.
4. Promote the research and development of topics related to personnel administration.
5. Lend technical assistance to the agencies of the public sector and systematized information to the governing body for the adoption of personnel policies.

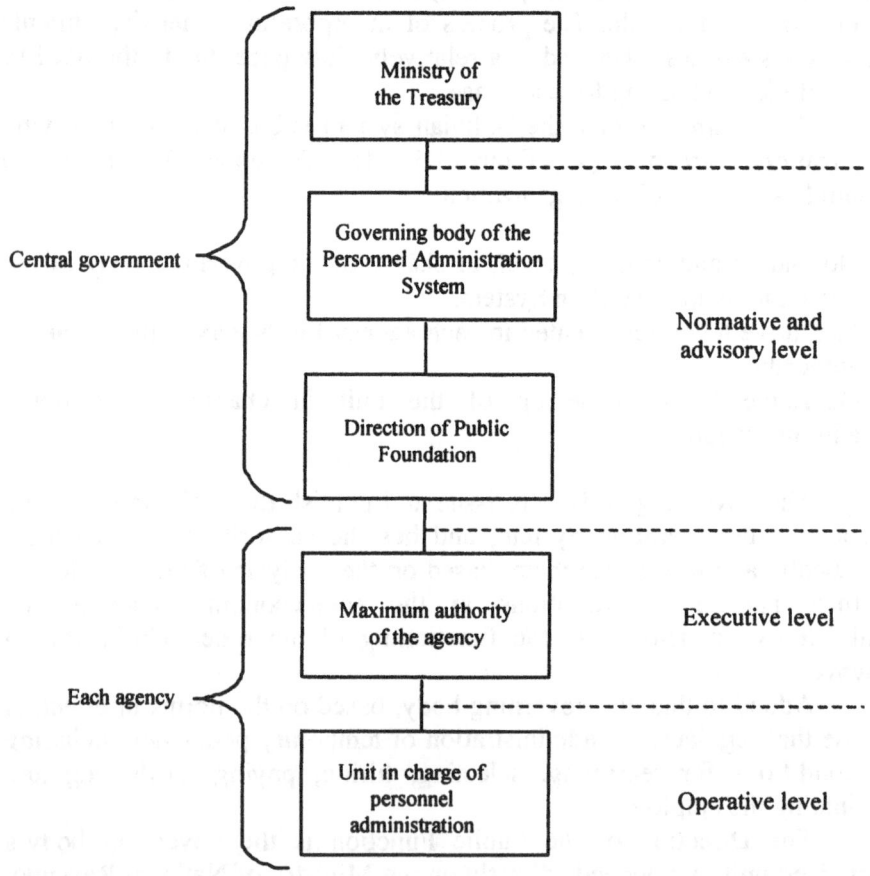

Figure 3.3 Structure

The unit in charge of Personnel Administration is made up in each agency by its heads of units (departments), and is responsible for preparing the specific regulations governing the agency. The governing body must review the regulations proposed by each agency to verify their compatibility with the law in force.

The scope of the Civil Service Act is for the personnel of all agencies of the public sector. Only those officials who are publicly elected or who are employees of the Legislature, the president of the Republic, the Executive or the Judiciary, are excluded.

In case of discriminatory or unjust treatment, or violation of the norms regarding the administration of human resources, the person concerned will be able to resort to an appeal to the Administrative Court, whose ruling will be of obligatory compliance.

The Personnel Administration System is divided into seven subsystems, each one referring to critical points identified in the bill of the Secretariat of the Treasury and Public Credit. The most important points in each subsystem are detailed below.

Selection, recruitment and revenues

Through the subsystem of Programming of Posts, Bolivian law establishes the definition of post, as well as the procedures to determine their objectives, evaluation and classification.

A post is the set of functions, powers and duties to be exercised by a person and that correspond to the specific objectives of each agency. A post is in effect as long as the conditions for which it was created still last, and a change in these can bring about its modification or elimination. The evaluation and classification of posts is based on their analysis and description. By analysis and description of posts we understand:

1. The designation, category and location of the post within the organizational structure of the agency.
2. The nature, norms to be observed, functions of the post and expected results, expressed in terms of quality and quantity.
3. The personal and professional qualifications required by the post.

The analysis and description of each post is drawn up or modified at the beginning of each administration based on the necessities of the agency and the community.

The categories for the classification of posts may be observed in Table 3.1.

Table 3.1 Classification of posts in order of importance

Level	Category	Posts	Responsibilities
1	Higher	Leadership and first level	Lead the agency
2	Advisory	Consulting positions	Advise the higher category
3	Managers	Heads of units	Head up units
4	Middle level	Posts that organize and supervise work teams	Organize and supervise work teams
5	Professional	Posts with specialized functions	Develop specialized functions, form work teams
6	Technical-administrative	Posts with specialized support functions	Develop specialized support functions
7	Auxiliary and services	Posts with non-specialized support functions	Develop non-specialized support functions

Staffing subsystem

The main objective of this subsystem is to provide suitable personnel to carry out the functions of each agency, guaranteeing transparency and objectivity in the selection and recruiting processes.

The personnel can be defined as regular or temporary. Regular personnel includes those employees who occupy the posts contemplated in the organic structure of the institution. Temporary personnel refers to those employees who are hired for a definite time interval or who are assigned directly by the agency authority and do not occupy a post in the civil service. Temporary personnel cannot automatically become regular personnel.

Hiring as regular personnel consists in going through a selection procedure that begins with the definition of the type of competition to be held. The competition can be by direct invitation or by public announcement.

Competition by direct invitation is held for people who have high personal and professional merits, for vacancies in the category immediately above. Also, direct invitations are made to people who are going to perform the functions of posts not included in the civil service, in any one of these categories.

Public announcement can be internal or external. Internal invitation functions as a promotion and is only for personnel belonging to that agency, whereas the external one is open to all people with the necessary qualifications for the position, whether or not they belong to the civil service.

Recruiting of temporary personnel is done through the procedure that each agency considers adequate in order to choose the right person to hold the position. Temporary personnel must always fulfil the minimum requirements stipulated in the job description.

Competitions to fill all the posts of top levels, middle echelons and professional levels, can only be held by public announcement, either internal or external.

The competition should be declared void if it does not attract enough applicants to ensure an adequate competition or if no applicant fulfills the minimum requirements for the vacant post.

The selection process includes the evaluation of three aspects: résumé, technical capacity and personal qualities. Each agency has a Selection Committee made up of a representative from the personnel administration unit of the agency and one from the unit making the request.

Bolivian law does not specify the mechanism for carrying out the technical evaluation, but rather gives freedom to each agency to define the methods that it considers pertinent. Obviously, this grants enough authority to the agency to incorporate specific criteria for its selection of personnel.

Once the evaluation of the three aspects has been carried out, the Selection Committee prepares a list with the results obtained by each candidate, in order to submit it to the authority authorized to make the selection. With the objective of "guaranteeing transparency", this report is also available to any person who has participated in the process.

With the list of results, the authority makes the corresponding selection and, unless there exists a fully supported appeal process, they may then proceed to possession, induction and evaluation of confirmation (probation period).

Evaluation and development

Performance evaluation in Bolivia has the following objectives:

1. To act as an element for judging the promotion of personnel who have shown the potential to perform more complex functions.
2. To give recognition of a monetary kind or with psychosocial content.
3. To rotate or transfer personnel in order to take greater advantage of their abilities.
4. To decide on the continuance of a public servant in the agency.
5. To give feedback to the diverse subsystems (i.e., training).

The programming of the performance evaluation is prepared in each agency according to the institutional policy defined for this. The programming defines objectives, scopes, evaluation factors, performance parameters, instruments to be used and intervals during which the performance evaluation is to be carried out.

The factors to be evaluated should take into consideration the employee's performance according to the description of his position in regard to three general aspects: efficiency, effectiveness and economy in achieving expected results. In the event the civil servants evaluated belong to the category of managers and middle levels, the aspect of the exercising of managerial abilities will be included.

The agency defines the evaluation procedure, which is to be carried out using any of the following methods: scales of points, checklists, methods of comparative evaluation and methods of field evaluation.

The execution of the performance evaluation of each official is the responsibility of his boss immediately above on the dates established by the agency and will be held at least once a year.

Based on the result obtained, the evaluator draws up a report where the performance of the official is marked as excellent, good, satisfactory, under observation or unsatisfactory (see table 3.2).

Table 3.2 Implications of results obtained

Mark	Work implications	Salary implications
Excellent	Horizontal step	Monetary incentive and salary increase given
Good	Horizontal step	Salary increase
Satisfactory	No change	No change
Under observation	Evaluation over the next six months: two consecutive grades of "under observation" give rise to dismissal of employee	No change
Unsatisfactory	Dismissal of employee	No change

Training and Salary Scale

Personnel training consists in favoring the acquisition of knowledge, skills and attitudes; to satisfy the public servants' needs for skills improvement and specialization in carrying out their duties; to prepare them for occupational needs of a higher rank; and to foster the development of ethical values compatible with the philosophy of the agency.

The Training subsystem includes the processes of needs detection, programming, execution and evaluation of the program and its results.

The detection of training needs is done through the evaluations of individual and group performance, and is the responsibility of the head of the unit.

The training programming is mainly based on needs detection and is the job of the unit responsible for personnel administration in coordination with the bosses immediately above. The program is part of the agency's budget, so that the agency will be able to cover its training needs every year.

Every time that a training program is executed, the unit in charge of personnel administration must make a training evaluation based on the objectives set for the program. The law does not stipulate any follow-up actions to be carried out based on this evaluation.

Each agency, depending on the budget assigned to the Training subsystem, is authorized to give study grants to the personnel that fulfill the stipulated merit requirements, provided the study topic is relevant to the agency. Those public servants whose performance evaluation is more than "satisfactory", and who possess development potential, will be given priority in participating in training programs, including grants.

The training programs will be obligatory when their goal is to attend to the needs detected through deficiencies in performance or to update the official's abilities. And they will be voluntary when they are intended to attend to needs for developing the personal potential of the public servants.

The public servants' remuneration consists of salary, benefits and recognition. Salary refers, mainly, to the basic salary determined by the value of the position, the salary scale and the payroll list approved for the agency.

The salary scale is a table that the agency proposes, subject to the salary policy, which includes the following information: level, job description, number of posts per level, monthly cost and annual cost. The budgetary schedule reflects the programmatic structure of the agency and the necessary resources for operating the agency.

The benefits are the same for all public servants, regardless of the post they occupy; they are of an obligatory nature and are established by the current legal provisions in the area of Bolivian social security.

Recognition is the agency's annual acknowledgment of outstanding performance or of the public servant's improvement as an incentive for maintaining levels of efficiency. It is granted according to the individual performance evaluation, the guidelines issued by the governing body, the agency's budgetary capacity and the stipulations in the specific regulations of each agency. The incentive can reach a maximum of the equivalent of one month's salary.

Promotion and separation from the civil service

The subsystem of Employee Mobility includes the processes of promotion, rotation, exchange, transfer and removal of the employee.

Promotion can be horizontal or vertical. Horizontal promotion implies a degree more within the same rank and the possibility of a salary increase. Each agency has autonomy to define the maximum number of grades at the same salary level. Vertical promotion is the change of the public servant from one position to another of a higher rank inside the same agency. For vertical promotion to be possible, there must be several factors:

1. There must be the clearly identified demand and corresponding vacancy.
2. The candidate should have the necessary qualifications for the position, obtain positive results in the performance evaluation and have the necessary potential to occupy the position to be filled.
3. Not have been promoted during the last twelve months.
4. Fulfill the confirmation evaluation satisfactorily.

Rotation is the moving of a public servant from one work unit to another in order to occupy a similar position. It does not imply a rise in salary. Each agency has the authority to program its personnel's internal rotation according to its necessities and in order to facilitate their indirect training and avoid work obsolescence.

Exchange is similar to rotation, but the difference lies in the fact that the public servant moves from one agency to another.

Removal is the conclusion of the work relationship between the agency and the servant. Grounds for removal are:

1. Written resignation.
2. Unsatisfactory result in any evaluation (either confirmation or performance).
3. Mandatory removal when there are grounds of incompatibility as established in the internal regulation of each agency.
4. Retirement.
5. Certified physical incapacity.
6. Elimination of the post due to change in agency's jurisdiction.
7. Conclusion or rescinding of contract of temporary personnel.
8. Decision of the maximum executive authority of the agency.
9. Imprisonment of the public servant, as a result of formal jail sentence.
10. Destitution.
11. The Act does not specify the rights that of government employees terminated from the civil service.

Records Subsystem

The objective of the records is to have reliable, agile and timely information in order to maintain and optimize the operation of the Personnel Administration System and to adopt institutional policy in this matter.

The information in the Records Subsystem is of two types: individual documents (such as performance evaluations) and documents characteristic of the system (such as evaluations of the processes developed inside each subsystem, salary tables, organizational structures, etc.). All the information contained inside this subsystem is of a confidential nature.

Each agency is obligated to provide information to the governing body of the Personnel Administration System or to the specialized unit when so requested.

Evaluation of the Bolivian civil service and recommendations for Mexico

The system of Bolivian recruitment leaves the weight of the subjective selection procedures to the discretion of the agencies, such as the evaluation of résumés and interviews. The potential problem is if the head of the agency makes up the evaluation of the selection criteria so as to benefit one person and so does not permit an atmosphere of equal opportunities. Mexico cannot run the risk of the implications inherent in this system: having non-transparent selection processes without equal opportunities, and not obtaining suitable persons for each position. The Mexican system should limit the weight granted to potentially discretionary processes, such as the interviews and résumé evaluation.

The Bolivian Training subsystem contains some points that are worth pointing out:

1. The training item in the budget guarantees the achievement of the subsystem's objectives.
2. The identification of the training needs is mainly based on performance evaluations.
3. The evaluation of the results of the training programs, measured by greater efficiency in the performance of the employees.

The training programs in Mexico would benefit by including these points. The main advantage that a similar plan would have is the more effective management of resources allocated to training personnel, programming courses that contribute greater benefits to the department (proven through the program evaluations) and the guarantee that there is a budget item allocated to this purpose.

Bolivian law does not grant any protection whatever to personnel dismissed from the public function, no matter what the grounds. This is not a mechanism that would be repeatable in Mexico because of the lack of security and the high risk that a person feels when entering the civil service.

The difficulty that has been observed in the Bolivian system due to making the civil service system depend on the Treasury Ministry, and not on an institution with clear impartiality and hierarchical authority over the other departments (e.g., Office of the President of the Republic or an autonomous institute), has not permitted the establishment of an operatively efficient civil service.

Finally, associating training with promotion (horizontal or vertical) must be avoided, because this can generate perverse incentives of "training in order to be promoted" and not training for reasons of productivity, as in the case of organizational problems, which do not allow all trained personnel to be promoted, thus causing demoralization of the members of the civil service.

Other cases in Latin America

The case of Ecuador

In 1991, Ecuador began a process of government modernization aimed at reducing the size of its public sector, increasing the efficiency of its civil service and orienting the management of the public administration toward obtaining results.

Unlike Bolivia, it sought to concentrate efforts and resources on generating "critical masses" in a limited group of departments or agencies right from the beginning of the process (at the suggestion of the multilateral organisms that offered technical assistance for the project). The process was carried out in a partial context of structural reforms aimed at improving the performance of the economy. This project was made up of two components: one for improving the systems of public financing management, and another for institutional strengthening or restructuring. This policy was supported by the State Modernization Act (R.O. no. 349

dated Dec. 31, 1993), by the general regulations and by the Budget Act of 1992.

In the administrative area, the objectives of the project translated into the restructuring of the departments of the 14 state ministries; and in the area of human resources, into the downsizing by about 50,000 civil servants, of the existing total of approximately 350,000. With the downsizing of personnel, a saving of about 20% of the total payroll was obtained. In this way, changes in personnel management would finance an increase of wages of up to 80% with the savings obtained from downsizing personnel in the restructured agencies.

In addition, a support infrastructure was also introduced, made up of an Integrated System of Financial Administration that allowed any advance or setback in disbursements to be recorded; and a system of Modernization Monitoring that registered any advance or setback in the process of restructuring agencies.

In order to focus efforts on a limited group of departments, the National Modernization Council (Conam, for its abbreviation in Spanish) and the National Secretariat for Administrative Development (Senda, abbreviation in Spanish), prepared a framework (the Agreements on Institutional Restructuring), which granted specific benefits to the agencies that were going through the process, in exchange for specific commitments undertaken by the departments. A guidebook for institutional restructuring contemplated both the benefits and the commitments that the departments could agree on. These agreements were carried out with the Ministry of Economy and Finances, with the General Comptrollership of the State, as well as with Senda; the Sigef allowed information concerning budgetary allocations to be monitored, as well as any delay in payments.

Initially, the organic and functional structures of the central government's four departments, and the policies for the reclassification of grades and wages, managed to be reformulated, compacting salary levels in order to improve them.

However, halfway through the process, a change in government leadership meant that the sequential process contained in the restructuring guides was rejected. In fact, no real change took place inside the system, because it lacked the resources needed to carry out an effective modernization inside the administration. Recent events in Ecuador have placed the initiated process on a back burner.

The case of Venezuela

Venezuela has one of the most elaborate systems of recruitment, evaluation and promotion.

The system is generically more competitive than the previous ones; but the instability of its middle, upper and lower echelons, the inability to attract and retain qualified personnel, and the impossibility of firing stable or unionized employees, has kept levels of efficiency and effectiveness very low, even worse that those of the countries mentioned above.

The problem has been worsened by the absence of a program of administrative restructuring. According to the Venezuelan Central Personnel Office (OCP, initials in Spanish), Venezuela had 417,000 civil servants in 1991, distributed throughout 71 agencias.[8] Of these, around 51% were included under the Administrative Career Act and had job stability.[9] However, 47% were hired, unionized workers, which in practice made them virtually non-removable. Only about 4,000 (less than 1%) were high-level, designated workers.[10]

However, unlike Chile, the highest posts in the administration were – and apparently continue to be – subject to a very high turnover, a fact which affects the stability of the upper echelons designated by them, just as it affects the general efficiency of the system. In fact, between 1988 and 1993, a Venezuelan minister lasted, on the average, only 11.5 months in the government, a very low figure compared with the nearly 40 months for a Mexican or 20 for a Chilean. This high turnover is a handicap for the higher levels of the career personnel.

This happens in spite of the fact that the system includes varied degrees of protection against unjustified dismissal.[11]

Formally, entry to the system is somewhat more competitive that in Chile and Argentina, inasmuch as it admits external and internal candidates; however, one of the latter is only chosen if there are none of the former, so that, in practice, it is very similar to the systems of closed competition.

Also, the aim is to avoid monopoly in recruitment, allowing each department to manage the process. In order to ensure general control, the list of personnel evaluated by each department must be submitted to the OCP, unlike the rest of the candidates. However, in spite of these requirements, there exist several channels for hiring "interim" personnel that become permanent.[12]

The civil service assigns few resources to personnel training: about 0.45% of the total expenditure for personnel of the central government's ministries, less than a third of that hired in the public sector for the same purpose.[13] The evidence from the early 90s suggests that these quantities are allocated mainly to specific courses with little training in direction. Finally, the service has an evaluation system that began in 1986. It is administered by the OCP and is applied to 34 of the 71 agencies supervised by this office. The system uses 12 standard categories to evaluate its employees, of which each dependence should use three specified by the OCP, and is free to determine five; the OCP will elect the remaining ones. In each category there are four marks, to which a specific weight is assigned. Their sum constitutes the final number of points. The evaluations of the employees are later ordered according to the points obtained and, by means of bonuses (discretionary spending from a fund allocated to each department for this purpose) and primes (spending from the current budget), a compensation is fixed. Promotions are also linked to these evaluations.

Nevertheless, the system suffers from problems similar to those of the other countries studied. The bosses who evaluate the employees have a strong incentive to evaluate them positively. Also in Venezuela most of the promotions tend to reflect seniority in the public service, more than any other criterion, such as that of merit, which has proved to be better for the administrative service.

In spite of the safeguards in the systems of recruitment, evaluation and promotion, different sources point out the complaints both of the upper echelons and of the immediately lower ones because of the inefficiency of the system. These range from the incapacity of the higher echelons for planning their operations, to the need to hire personnel from outside the system in order to maintain the shift administration operating, and including the rigidity of the lower unionized levels, and the inability to get rid of redundant personnel. However, beyond this "anecdotal" evidence (based on interviews), there exists, to date, no systematic evaluation of the Venezuelan civil service.

The case of Peru

The Peruvian government has concentrated its efforts on reducing the level of employment of the public sector and on improving the performance of agencies that it has considered vital for the development of the government's program. It also centered its efforts on the transfer to the private sector of many functions that had previously been in the hands of the State, on radical changes in the management of those who remained, and on the creation of special agencies to achieve specific objectives. As in the case of Chile, the process was based on a sequential structure that allowed credibility to be won with the initial cases, to then continue with other more difficult ones.

The process began with the creation of an autonomous overseer's office of tax administration, that was separated from the department that controlled the revenues in the Ministry of Economics and Finances. Transparent processes of personnel selection, recruitment and promotion were created, salaries were improved and the autonomy of the management of directive personnel of the department was extended. In addition, greater powers were given for accomplishing their work.

After the success in this sphere, agencies were created with similar characteristics in the areas of the fight against poverty (Foncodes, abbreviation in Spanish), privatization (Copri), market freedom and consumer defense (Indecopi), customs (Sunad), water (Sunas), electricity, and so forth. When an agency was not created, a restructuring process began that included its processes of recruitment, selection and promotion, and the management capacity of its top levels was increased (as in the case of the social security, housing, public records and justice systems).

These agencies appropriated a good number of the functions that had previously been in the hands of the central government. At the beginning of the second period of the régime, a similar process began in the direct-line departments of the central government, seeking to reduce personnel through packages of incentives, to increase the autonomy of management, and to alter the incentives offered to the employees. However, although the downsizing of personnel has been relatively successful, the program has been paralyzed by the changes in the cabinet established by the second period, and by the recurrent political crisis at different stages of Peru's contemporary history.

Final recommendations of the chapter

In a process of civil service reform, the way that this is achieved is as important as its content. Although the processes have had different objectives and contexts, they do have some elements in common. All the countries examined have included improvements in the systems and quality of their human resources in the processes of government modernization. None has reformed their civil service simultaneously in all the departments and agencies of the administration. The only attempt (that of Ecuador) ended in failure. This leads us to think that a civil service law for a process of modernization should be only a set of general provisions, sufficiently flexible as to be used as one more element in the reform process introduced consecutively into departments and agencies, in conjunction with others.

Mexico should learn from the Latin American experiences, from both the successes and the failures. The recommendations identified through this analysis of countries are summarized in the following key points.

Experiences in Latin America that Mexico should implement

1. A gradual process of introduction of the system with a certain time limit for transforming all the positions and posts into civil service places.
2. An organic structure with a single directing organization with a higher level than the departments, whose resolutions are of obligatory compliance.
3. A governing organization that carries out studies for establishing policies, that supervises compliance with the regulations and policies, that solves problems that arise on the subject and that objectively evaluates modifications in procedures that the departments suggest in order to make the system more efficient (including criteria of selection, promotion, training and salary, among others).
4. To establish minimum principles for the processes of selection, recruitment, training, promotion, performance evaluation and separation of public employees; based on competition by merit and with equal opportunities.
5. An information program and change in organizational culture by means of which all public servants are notified and participate in the changes in the processes of selection, recruitment, training, promotion, performance evaluation and termination of employment of public servants, as well as of their rights and obligations to create a true civil service career.

6. A compensation system that would attract the most competent individuals and whose attractiveness depends less on the possibility of receiving a bonus at the end of a period, than the fact that it is based on a basic salary that is competitive with respect to the private sector.

7. A database with information about the current officials and those recently terminated, in order to categorize the processes of selection and recruiting to fill vacant positions.

8. A system of *exceptional* designation by free appointment that would guarantee that the person named is the most qualified to serve in the position.

9. A well structured training program, with items of identification of needs linked to productivity.

10. A system of performance evaluation that forces the evaluators to carry out an objective and truthful evaluation of the duties performed by public servants in their position, associated with the mission of the area, department and established public policy.

11. A system of appropriate penalization to be implemented for people that break the laws, rules and norms governing the career civil service.

12. A flexible system that would permit each department to establish its own civil service system, subject to counterbalances of accountability, transparency and results in the services it offers.

13. Creating two organizational structures in the same agency is to be avoided: one of older, non-removable public servants and another of public servants "hired by honorariums" that do most of the work.

14. Nor is it advisable to give too much weight to discretionary actions in processes of selection, performance evaluation, and separation of public servants. This is in order to avoid falling into nepotism, cliques and similar forms of corruption.

Based on the above, we should emphasize the fact that introducing a career civil service requires a strategy and not only a law. In fact, to try to bring about changes simultaneously in the whole administration prevents concentrating the reform efforts into a limited, easily-handled number of objectives, and it endangers the credibility of the whole process.

The lessons learned from the experiences of the OECD and Latin America suggest that it is preferable to follow a sequence of reforms (that concentrate initially on strengthening the systems of personnel and budget management) in order to then incorporate, in successive stages, other departments and agencies into the process of reforming their personnel management, in conjunction with other elements of administrative modernization.[14]

In this context, a civil service law is only one more component in a reform. If this process is to be begun with a law, it is necessary that the law include only sufficiently flexible principles in order to follow a sequence in the changes that concentrate initially on the central bodies of the system, but that continue to decentralize as the process advances.

A law with these characteristics makes it possible to follow a strategy that considers only a small set of objectives at each stage. This increases the possibility of obtaining favorable results, makes it possible to learn from the process, diversifies the risks that may appear and creates credibility. Besides, it makes it possible to coordinate the reform activities both inside the upper echelons of the administration and at the lower levels. Thus, a civil service act should be not only a declaration of principles that are seldom observed in practice, but the regulation of a visionary, forward-looking reality as a comprehensive system in the public administration.

Notes

[1]   U.S. Government, Chiefs of State and Cabinet Members of Foreign Governments, editions corresponding to the years 1988 to 1993.

[2]   Between 1989 and 1993, the ministerial wages of the region fluctuated around $26,000 (US) annually, excluding Mexico, Colombia and Argentina, which had significantly higher wages – the lowest being that of Venezuela, $13,000 US, little more than what one receives in Bangladesh ($12,500 US) and the highest, that of Nicaragua ($38,000 US). The salaries of Argentina, Colombia and Mexico ranged from a high of $120,000 (almost the same as in the United States or Singapore) to $50,000 (a little less than in Taiwan). See above, note 1.

[3]   The absence of stability, the non-competitive wages and the rigidity of the lower levels, are what usually influence the effectiveness of the civil service system. Even with very elaborate civil service systems (as for example, in Venezuela), the lack of stable upper echelons significantly affects the administration's performance. The low productiveness of the Mexican public administration at its lower levels suggests that, in order to attain important improvements in the system, a treatment of the problems of non-removability and performance evaluation at the lower levels, should be included in a process of administration reform.

[4]   Examples of this are found in the following organizations: Chilean Superintendence of Banking and Insurance, Central Bank of Venezuela, National Superintendence of Peruvian Tributary Administration, etc. This competitiveness is almost nonexistent in the civil service systems regulated by law.

[5]   This figure is valid for 1989, and was calculated without including the personnel working in the health sector, because most of the posts are half-time positions. For further information, see Reid (1993, 1994).

6   See the case of the United Kingdom.
7   See chapter 3 of this book, "The Case of France".
8   Statistical report: Distribution of charges and costs in National Public Administration, 1991.
9   The Administrative Career Act dated May 13, 1975, omits, in article 5, employees of the Congress, Judiciary, Attorney General's Office (Venezuelan District Attorney's Office), Electoral Supreme Court, External Affairs, the Armed Forces and the university system. Each of these was regulated by its own norms.
10 A little over 1% more (about 5,000 people) were high-level consultants, hired in the administration, who entered and left with the designated personnel.
11 For an account of this phenomenon, see Moisés Naim, "Latin America's Post Adjustment Blues", *Foreign Affairs* no. 3, 1994; M. Naim, *Latin America's Journey to the Market: From Macroeconomic Shocks to Institutional Therapy*, International Center for Economic Growth, San Francisco, 1995; or Reid and Scott (1994).
12 If a candidate fails to pass a "competition", the department may hire an "interim" candidate for a trial period of 6 months, during which period the agency must give the candidate an exam. If they fail to do so, it is understood that there is tacit consent of the OCP, which guarantees stability.
13 This figure corresponds to the average for the period of 1989-1993, data of the OCP, 1994.
14 See on this topic, G. Shepherd et al., 1996; and also G. Reid, 1996.

4. The Experience of OECD Member Countries

Introduction

The most recent tendency in changes in the management of human resources systems in the OECD countries is characterized by the gradual decentralization of central elements of the service to their own departments. This has been experienced in countries with a long tradition in their civil service, such as the United States and the United Kingdom, and also in those with more recent systems, such as Australia, New Zealand, Sweden and other Scandinavian countries.[1] This has involved processes of selection, evaluation and determining of salaries, and so forth.

Decentralizing mechanisms include: the transfer of functions from the central bodies to departments or agencies, the substitution of prior controls for later controls, the use of lists of requirements instead of minimum standards, the definition of objectives instead of procedures, and other techniques that increase the autonomy of the departments and agencies without however diminishing the control to which they are subject.

On the other hand, most of the countries of the OECD have a meritocratic system for selecting their public servants. The form in which the principle of meritocracy is satisfied ranges from the application of centrally regulated exams, as in the case of France, to the discretion of the department heads, as happens in New Zealand. Studies carried out by the world forum in Davos, Switzerland, have demonstrated that certain countries that have an entry system based on merit and competition, have more competent civil servants than those that do not have meritocratic systems of selection.

For separation, the tendency is similar. In most of the OECD countries, continuance in the civil service depends on the individual's performance. The case of France is a clear exception.

Also, two types of performance evaluation may be distinguished: that of the department or section and that of the individual. The first type has proved to be more objective and easier to measure, since the second requires more subjective judgments in most cases. In the performance evaluation of a department, it is possible to involve the opinion of the citizenry, as in the case of the Citizens' Charter program in the United Kingdom, which has shown that public participation that is heeded contributes two unquestionable advantages: objectivity and low cost. Another case that is worth pointing out is that of New Zealand, where the performance of a department is not measured by the overall results of the department but by its operative results. For example, the performance of the Department of Health is not evaluated according to how much they have reduced the cases of polio (general results), but rather on the number of vaccines that have been administered. The reasoning behind this is that departments should only be evaluated on the basis of what they have control over. The evaluation of individual performance almost always involves the opinion of people who have worked with the one being evaluated. If there are few of them, the risk is that the evaluation may be partial; but, on the other hand, if the number of people involved in the evaluation process includes almost all the personnel (360° evaluation), it can become inoperative. It is crucial to reach a good balance of operativity and objectivity, since a civil service system based on merit without an objective, operable performance system combines the worst of two worlds: lack of meritocracy and excessive bureaucracy.

Experiences of administration and reform of human resources systems

General guidelines and fundamental principles

A revision of the most important changes in public administrations of countries representing developed and developing economies shows how the aspects of reform have been expressed both in countries with more advanced administrations, and in others that are still incipient. In both cases, the changes have responded to similar pressures for efficiency and economizing. The cases of the OECD countries are interesting because they show the scopes and specific tendencies of these changes on a vast scale. They also serve to illustrate the necessary prerequisites for making them effective: all these countries, at the beginning of the reform, had a professional staff of public servants and quite an advanced system of budgetary management.

Tendencies in the management of human resources administration in the OECD

Since the late 1980s, most OECD countries have been involved in the process of reforming their systems of personnel management. The main reason for this change has been similar in most cases: fiscal restrictions faced by the public sector increased the demand for more efficient services and programs, often with a smaller work force as a result. The need for accountability to society, for increasing the transparency in public expenditure and its own transparency, are other elements that have promoted these changes.

This pressure has produced diverse reactions among the countries that make up the organization. Foremost among them is a group of audacious reformers including in particular Australia, New Zealand and the United Kingdom (Sweden and the other Scandinavian countries are going through a similar process at the moment). Australia reformed the structure of the Prime Minister's cabinet, as well as its ministerial and departmental positions in order to create a stronger center of control, at the same time as they devolved discretionary authority to their direct-line departments. The United Kingdom so far has transferred over two thirds of its work force to autonomous agencies to separate the definition of execution of policies, and has thus given these agencies greater management autonomy.

The case of New Zealand is of special interest, since it is the one that has taken these reforms to the extreme. In this administration:

1. Budgets are defined by programs and results, rather than by activities and resources allocated. These programs are linked to performance indicators, and to more transparent practices in budgetary accounting.
2. The hierarchical forms of control and their corresponding regulations are replaced by a greater autonomy of management, a greater use of incentives and of contractual or quasi-contractual relationships between agencies.
3. To facilitate these relationships, the agencies are classified into policy-making and policy-executing agencies; into agencies that provide services and those that buy them. This implies, in most instances, a process of privatization and streamlining of the administration.
4. Finally, competition is encouraged among the suppliers of services, whether these be from private enterprise, the public sector or non-governmental organizations.

From a perspective of human resources management, in these countries the general lines that define the criteria to be followed in evaluating personnel, assigning primes and, in many cases, budgets and maximum rewards available, are established centrally. The flexibility of the administrative tradition in these countries has facilitated the change.[2] In fact, within the framework outlined by these reforms, the agencies are free to choose the method of evaluation, assign prizes and sanctions, and choose their type and amount.[3] A more detailed analysis of the constituent components of the civil service in these countries is developed more extensively throughout this chapter.

In general, these reforms have been successful and are providing many benefits to the administrations that introduced them, which has produced a tendency to change in a similar direction in other OECD member countries. However, the differences in the traditions of each country are decisive, so that the inherent difficulties in their operation have led them to introduce them in different ways.

In fact, most of the countries that have centralized civil service corps with a long tradition of operation (France, Germany, Spain, Switzerland, Japan, etc.) have not made radical reforms in their services, but rather have been gradually and partially decentralizing the functions related to selection, recruitment and evaluation; in an effort to seek a balance between the demands in the departments and agencies for greater flexibility in managing and administering, and the necessity to maintain functional criteria in the central bodies.

In spite of these differences, the systems follow a common tendency toward decentralization and autonomy by results in the administration of systems of human resources management. According to the most recent OECD evaluations, the main elements in this process are the following:

1. Decentralization of the responsibility for managing human resources, from the central management offices to the departments and agencies.
2. Devolving authority on human resources management to line managers in the departments and agencies.
3. The preference for policy frameworks and guidelines for action emphasizing the use of basic standards, and for guidelines on good practices, instead of detailed controls.
4. A devolution to the departments and agencies of the budgetary capacity, which consolidates salary and administrative costs.

5. Systems of payment, employment and more flexible recruitment.
6. Training and development systems intended to strengthen skills, competence and flexibility in the work force, for a better execution of the program's demands and thus reinforce reforms in the public sector.
7. Measures for budgetary saving designed in the form of payment reductions, reductions of employment level and pressures to produce gains in efficiency.[4]

Thus, for example, the oldest evaluation systems, which were installed centrally, were unique for the whole system and, above all, standardized. This happened in the United States, Canada and the United Kingdom. These countries mainly concentrated on the personnel in the middle or upper echelons. At the present time, the system in the United States covers approximately 140,000 middle level officials in the federal government.[5] However, the different sizes, functions and characteristics of the different departments meant that in practice they had to pursue very different goals or purposes in their evaluation.[6] The result was that the more recent systems (employed in Denmark, the Netherlands, New Zealand and Sweden) are not very standardized, allowing departments and agencies a greater latitude in designing and introducing the system.[7]

In fact, in countries such as Denmark, Sweden, the Netherlands and even France, who have a centralized system of human resources management, an effort to establish very centralized systems would be rejected. In fact, the most recent evaluation systems serve more to link the civil servants' performance to the mission and to the strategic ends of the department, than to reward or sanction them, since these links usually generate evaluations with marks significantly slanted toward the higher levels of marks, in which almost nobody does badly. Therefore they set limits, as in the United States or Venezuela, to the number of civil servants that can get very good marks, or as in the Scandinavian countries, where they are not linked to salary compensations or threats of dismissal.

Something similar happens with salary compensations. On one hand, in Latin America and in the OECD member countries, there is great pressure to reduce the work force due to fiscal restrictions, while there is a simultaneous demand by the administration for better performance. There has also been a need to make salaries more competitive with respect to the private sector, in order to be able to improve the quality of the administration staff.

On the other hand, in the countries that have carried out structural reforms recently, there has been a movement toward greater decentralization in order to face this dilemma. This has been the case of Australia, New Zealand, the United Kingdom, Sweden and other Scandinavian countries.

In these countries, the process has taken place in two areas: the central government, decides on increases in salary payments, trying to maintain an effective control on the total levels of expenditure; while the second, decentralized one, determines the distribution of resources allocated to efficiency programs, as well as those allocated to remunerating public servants as a result of their performance, or to covering the differences that arise when reclassifying their positions. Both areas can be connected. In fact, in Australia a "productivity fund" has been set up to which agencies contribute one-third of the savings obtained by their increases in efficiency, and which serves to contribute to improvements in other areas of the administration. In this way, the agency that manages to economize on specific results, keeps the remaining two-thirds.

In summary, one can affirm that the systems introduced recently are decentralized, flexible, autonomous, made up of evaluation counterbalances and with processes of transparent accountability.[8]

Common reform strategies in the civil service systems in OECD member countries

The varied contexts in OECD countries have led them to follow different reform strategies. In spite of their variety, the following common elements can be distinguished:

1. Countries that have achieved major beneficial changes are the ones that initially imposed the reforms from the highest levels in the administration (e.g. Office of the President of the Republic) onto the component departments and agencies. In fact, it is difficult to find cases in which reforms have come from the departments themselves.
2. When reforms are introduced and promoted initially by an agency or central dependence in the system, the success tends to be facilitated if the agency in charge of the process has both political support and leadership from the highest level.
3. A balance has still not been reached between the flexibility of the administration and control of the central bodies. However, most of the

countries insist on maintaining a set of general regulations for the civil service under the control of their governing bodies.

4. When the changes in the systems of human resources management are general and flexible, they tend to reinforce each other, generating processes that are favorable to the reform process.

As can be observed, in spite of the fact that there exists no unique tendency, some common elements can still be identified. These models show that, in their initial stages, it is better to concentrate resources and information in an institution in charge of the reforms that has clear political support. This process would be initially oriented toward changing the environment in which the departments and agencies operate. However, as the process advances, efforts will begin to decentralize into departments and agencies.

These facts suggest that, in order to regulate a result-oriented civil service, even in its most moderate version, it is necessary:

1. To have a flexible, effective and efficient system of budgetary and human resources management.
2. To separate the process of reform from the daily operation of the system, and centralize it in a department with political support, in charge of carrying out these changes.[9]
3. To regulate the process by means of flexible provisions, which allow for a gradual and strategic transfer of functions to departments and direct-line agencies.

One point that should be stressed is that, unlike the case of Mexico, the administrations of other OECD countries did have civil service systems at the time reforms were begun.

The civil service system in the United Kingdom

The Northcote and Trevelyan Report

In the case of Great Britain, civil service reform was the result of a long historical process. In the 19th century, the Treasury considered it necessary to make a diagnosis of the civil service, and put Charles Trevelyan and Stanford Northcote in charge. Their report harshly condemned the nepotism, incompetence and other defects of the system that were inherited from the 18th century. Several proposals came out of this report; those that were accepted include: regulating the selection of personnel by means of the establishment of the requirements of the position and the introduction of entrance tests; the setting up of two types of exams, one that regulated the entry of the candidates with university education for the high positions in the administration, and another for young people who took care of secondary tasks. Thus the Civil Service Commission was also created so that it would apply the selection exams independently. As a result of these reforms, there began what would be a long period of stability for the English public service.

The Fulton Report

Criticisms of the civil service increased toward the 1960s, giving rise to what we will call a "first crisis" that made the creation of an adjunct committee necessary. This commission was made up of five people, headed by Lord Fulton, whose task consisted in studying the public service in practice and drawing up a diagnosis with suggestions. The objective was to judge the structure, recruitment, administration and training of civil service personnel, and formulate recommendations. The result was a controversial report that was called the *Fulton Report*. The main proposals implemented were:

1. The creation of the Central Policy Review Staff (CPRS), at the initiative of the conservative government of Prime Minister Edward Heath (1970-1974), made up of officials, and some politicians and businessmen.
2. The creation of the Policy Unit at the initiative of the Labor government under the leadership of Prime Minister Callaghan (1976-1979), so that the government could have more consulting with the parties, which would reduce somewhat the tendency for policies to be determined by the interests of the government employees.

Other important consequences deriving from the suggestions of the report mentioned were:

1. The creation of a department of the public service that would have to do with selection, training and skills improvement; with the

compensations and personnel management, as well as with the organization of the central administration (to which department the Civil Service Commission belongs).
2. The creation of a Civil Service College with the mission of training government officials and perfecting their directorial techniques.
3. The unification of the hierarchical structure, eliminating classes and creating grades, in order to ensure the establishment of a system of promotion on merit.

A second crisis happened when the conservative government under the leadership of Margaret Thatcher came to power in 1979. She made several criticisms of the civil service, related to the great number of employees, their lack of autonomy and the privileged situation of the public service in times of economic recession.

The Next Steps and Citizens' Charter programs

Criticisms of the government on the part of the citizenry, combined with strong budgetary pressures and deficient public services, gave rise in 1988 to the *Next Steps* program, which imprinted another focus onto the British public service. Next Steps began as a result of interviews with managers of several levels in order to recognize the obstacles to improving the government's efficiency. The interviews revealed, among other things, the following results with respect to the situation of the public administration:

1. The ministers did not have time to take charge of policy making, because of the attention given to operational details.
2. Part of the government's functions included executing policy, so that the separation of the public policy making and policy execution would help each part do its job efficiently.
3. If the government is not homogeneous, it should not be administered as though it were.
4. The civil service is resistant to change. Therefore, a reform program should be brought in from the top of the administration, involving all key elements and designating a high-level project manager.

The first step in this direction was to separate the policy making from the provision of services. This was achieved by delegating the operative work to more autonomous agencies would that guarantee higher levels of efficiency by being outside of the area of the central agencies. These agencies were given financial and technical autonomy, besides freedom in designing operations and establishing salaries for their employees based on their productivity. Also, in order for this system to function well, the guidelines of the program imposed perspectives typical of the private sector, such as that of "attention to the customer", on the public service. Each of these agencies was placed under a minister's department. The Ministry retained the authority to dictate what points should be included in the agenda, namely in what areas actions should be taken, and in policy-making, but the agency was authorized to choose the paths that it considered most efficient for their implementation. At the moment, over 72% of civil service personnel works in executive agencies of the Next Steps program.[10]

Parallel to Next Steps, the Citizens' Charter program was created, aimed not only at evaluating the performance of these agencies, but at having the general population participate in these evaluations. At the beginning of every period, the agency commits itself to certain operational objectives that it publishes in the newspapers, such as processing any license in not more than two days (Department of Transport). At the end of that interval, the statistics of the real results are published and compared with the commitments established. Based on this, the population chooses which agency should win the annual prize of excellence. The interesting point of this system is that, apart from having a high degree of objectivity (it is the citizenry, not the government, who makes the evaluations), there are no high transaction costs for its introduction.[11]

The reform of the civil service

At first, with the autonomy granted by the Next Steps program and the rigorous Citizens' Charter's evaluations of the public servants' performance, the chief executives in charge of the agencies faced a responsibility to produce results accompanied by an inflexibility to recruit, give incentives and manage their personnel. In other words, they were responsible for the products and the results, but they did not have control over their agencies' inputs. Consequently, in 1991, the human resources administration was decentralized, a process that was carried out gradually by the Cabinet Office, the organization responsible for public service efficiency. The devolution of autonomy occurred strategically and gradually, department by department.

There are those who claim that the reforms introduced by Thatcher led to bewilderment and demotivation in the public servants; they argue that by implying a significant reduction, if not disappearance, of the traditional civil service, the reforms weakened the esprit de corps and public mission of the civil servants and affected the uniformity of the merit system. On the other hand, there are those who believe that the reform was timely and, besides, necessary, since the old civil service system never produced the benefits that it promised, whereas it did involve rigidity and excessive autonomy of the bureaucracy.

Present public administration system

The current public administration structure in the United Kingdom is formed mainly by six governing bodies and overseers of the public service: Parliament, the Privy Council, the Cabinet, the Treasury, their own departments and the Cabinet Office (Efficiency Unit).

1. Parliament is, perhaps, the one that has the least intervention. It intervenes mainly through ministerial responsibility.
2. The Privy Council is an auxiliary organ of the crown. It exercises its authority insofar as it advises it in the regulations issued. These regulations are in fulfillment of the prerogative and statutory powers of the crown.
3. The cabinet is made up of the ministers of the departments and is responsible for advising the Prime Minister on policy.
4. The Treasury is in charge of all issues to do with budgetary regulation. It is in charge of checking that the departments comply with the principles and conditions that it establishes.
5. The departments are bodies that are subordinate to the minister. The undersecretary or director of Personnel is the one who is in charge of supervising that the guidelines of the Cabinet Office are observed in regard to the personnel of his department.
6. The Cabinet Office, under the direction of the Prime Minister, has several functions:

a) Development of the Citizens' Charter program.
b) Promotion of competitiveness in the central government.
c) Implementation of the Next Steps program.
d) Promotion of better practices.

e) Delegation of human resources responsibilities.
f) Monitoring of delegated pay practices.
g) Promotion of high standards of integrity, efficiency and merit.

After the reform, the Cabinet Office became a unit for consulting and support, transferring its "human assets" with the best practices to the different departments.

At the present time, the specific regulation of the conditions for service, and of the principles and policy holding sway in the departments, are dictated by the Cabinet Office; budgetary policy, by the Treasury. For example, "Civil Service Pay and Condition of Service Code" is issued by the Treasury and describes the decisions taken regarding remuneration of civil servants, and of politicians, and general normative criteria issued by the Cabinet Office.

Present civil service system

It is necessary, as a first step, to clarify the scope of the Career Civil Service System (CCSS). In Britain, the workers that are under the régime are known as civil servants. The classic definition distinguishes them from other workers as a function of several criteria: they are servants of the crown, their salary is paid with the budget approved by Parliament and they are hired as civilians.

The civil service in the United Kingdom has a minimalist criterion. That is to say, it grants authority to the departments to manage the administration of human resources, with all that this implies, but subject to certain general guidelines that prevent nepotism and injustice. The Civil Service Code that regulated the administration of human resources, became a code that establishes applicable guidelines to all departments and leaves the form or details to their discretion.

One might say that the service is divided into two major groups: the Senior Civil Service and the Civil Service. The former includes the highest levels of the service, specifically the seven highest grades, and although their members are managed by their departments, they form a cohesive group at the top of the service pyramid. The main characteristics of this group are:

1. A central catalog with nine overlapping salary levels, plus that of the permanent secretary. The departments have the autonomy to place their officials (of the Senior Civil Service) in the ranks established.
2. A personal, formal contract based on a standard model that can be adjusted to the needs of each department. This contract stipulates the terms of employment.
3. A common system of evaluation.

In charge of recruitment for the Senior Civil Service is the Senior Civil Commission, which, in justified cases, approves the appointment of a civil servant without going through the normal competition process. When there are vacancies at the highest levels within this group, the commission decides if the position is placed under open competition (including people from outside the service), inside the Civil Service only, or inside the department. Between 1996 and 1997, 48% of these vacancies were offered in open competition, and 69% of these posts were won by people that did not belong to the service.

Grade ladder in the Senior Civil Service
Grade 1 Permanent Secretary
1st Second Permanent Secretary
2nd Deputy Secretary
3rd Under Secretary
4th Executive Directing Bands
5th Assistant Secretary
6th Senior Principal
7th Principal

The second group of the civil service includes all the other degrees (lower than degree seven). In this group, the departments are those that have the autonomy for recruitment, selection, promotion and management of human resources in general. The Civil Service Commission[12] is the one in charge, primarily, of upholding the general principles of justice and merit of the service.

Recruitment and selection process Recruitment of the civil service of the United Kingdom is based on the principle that it is more costly to choose the wrong person than to spend time looking for him/her.

The recruitment and selection process has as its fundamental principle, equality and merit, and the Civil Service Commission oversees the observance of these principles. Accordingly, the civil service code establishes that the selection process of all departments should include an evaluation and that the competitions should be open, with a few exceptions.

The objectives in having this system of open competition and meritocracy, in spite of the resources consumed, are:

1. To obtain the best person for the post regardless of ethnic group or gender.
2. To avoid suspicions of favoritism.
3. To make sure that the recruitment procedures reinforce the political impartiality of the civil service.

In order to achieve this it is necessary that:

a) Work opportunities be published under parameters of equality and merit.
b) The selection of personnel be transparent, objective and flexible in each department.
c) The evaluations make it possible to verify that those designated have the necessary aptitudes for the job and, consequently, the best candidate be chosen for the position.

For example, article 1.1.1 of the Code establishes the following:

1.1.1   In the system presented by the Consul of the order of the Civil Service 1995 and the Recruitment Code issued by commissioners of the Civil Service, the departments and agencies have the authority to:
a) determine practices and procedures for personnel recruitment for the home civil service; and
b) determine the requirements regarding age, knowledge, ability, professional merit, attitude and potential, for the selection of those who will occupy positions in their organizations.

These delegations are subject to the following conditions:

1.1.2 Departments and agencies should:

a) make sure that their recruitment systems generate appropriate candidates for their necessities and that they are able to perform the required tasks; and
b) retain records of at least three years of the recruitment criterion and the performance of those hired.

This article reflects the minimalist form and the basis of the Civil Service Code very well.

One aspect that should be pointed out here, is the way a vacant position can be filled in this structure. The recruitment process is an autonomous, flexible process based on sound evaluations, if one is to judge by the following:

1. The recruitment of personnel is done by open competition (with the exception of the applicants to the *fast stream* program, which will be explained in more detail in the section on promotion).
2. The academic requirements depend on the level being applied to.
3. And lastly, but very importantly, an individual can compete to enter at any grade of the structure even if it is not the level immediately above, provided they satisfy the requirements of the competition.

To fulfill their recruitment function for the Senior Civil Service, the Senior Civil Commission has been organized, since 1981, into four divisions:

a) *The Administration Group Division*: responsible for the process of candidate recruitment to fill positions in the administration group and positions in the diplomatic civil service and tax inspection.
b) *The Science Division*: responsible for the recruitment process for positions for scientists, doctors, veterinarians and similar.
c) *The Technology Division*: responsible for recruiting engineers, architects and similar.
d) *The General Competitions Division*: responsible for recruitment in the social and humanities areas.

These divisions concentrate their attention on recruiting personnel to fill vacant positions in the open structure, that is to say, at the seven highest levels.

The selection is composed of three stages:

First stage: the applicant undergoes evaluations oriented toward examining his common sense; they are evaluations of analysis of statistical information, numerical ability, precision and comprehension. The tests last a day and a half and are both written and oral. Among the most important is the writing of a summary of a text that offers solutions to an imaginary problem presented.

Second stage: in the first phase, the candidate is given a simulated file and must provide a solution by writing a diplomatic letter. In the second, there is an oral exam, referring to an informal discussion in small groups, simulating a committee that is to adopt a resolution. Lastly, there is an interview with members of the team in charge of the selection process.

Third stage: consists of an interview with the Final Selection Council that consists of three people, with whom the applicant will speak individually. This last stage is decisive and largely decides whether or not he obtains the position.

A general principle of the recruitment process is that when a vacancy is announced, sufficient time should be given for the applicants to submit their application. For higher positions, three weeks approximately should be allowed and for lower positions, a shorter time period.

Exceptions to recruitment principles The system permits certain exceptions to the selection by open competition and the agencies and departments are the ones who decide how and when these exceptions can be made, but taking care not to show favoritism or political preference. The object of allowing certain exceptions is to give flexibility when necessary.

The agencies should provide information about these exceptions to the Civil Service Commission, except in cases of appointments for less than twelve months. The situations in which these exceptions can be made are:

Short-term assignments. For an assignment of less than twelve months it is not necessary to go through the competition process, but when the twelve months are up; if the person wants to continue in the position, a competition is opened and the employee can compete for it.

In exceptional cases, for example if the project in question has only a few more months until it ends, the term of the appointment can be extended to 24 months.

Specific aptitudes. If very specific aptitudes are needed for a position, and thus the universe of candidates is very limited, it may not be cost-effective to open it to competition. In these cases the exception is allowed, provided the following cases occur:

1. The required aptitudes are very specific and can be justified if necessary.
2. The position is for a term of up to five years only.

Rehiring former civil servants The purpose of this is for the agencies and departments to capitalize on the investment that they have made in qualifying people who then left the service. This does not mean that an individual is entitled to being rehired; it is only justified if there is a clear benefit for the agency or department.

Training As for training, after the Civil Service College was formed, it began to operate in 1970 with three centers: London, Sunningdale and Edinburgh. Three functions were mainly entrusted to them:

1. To provide better training courses in the areas of administration and management, designed to support the specialists in their aspirations to be promoted, as well as to improve their productivity in the performance of the administration as a whole.
2. To provide a set of short courses aimed at "junior civil servants" (levels of administrative assistant and official assistant).
3. To carry out research tasks on topics in administration and management.

However, in 1976 the administration of Callaghan took another turn. The standing of the College declined and it became part of the Civil Service Department, as a new training group. The rank of the director of the College was also lowered (from Deputy Secretary to Under Secretary). In 1977 the center in Edinburgh was closed and the length of the courses reduced, to be finally abandoned in 1980.

The College still exists, but it has been privatized. Now only those departments that have the necessary resources can train their staff. In answer to this situation, some departments have carried out their own efforts to fill that gap. Thus, in the period of 1983-1984, 73.8% of the training was covered by their own departments; 21.2% by outside instructors and only 5% by the College.

Promotions Those in charge of deciding on the promotion systems are the promotion committees within each department. These committees analyze and establish an order of merits among the candidates to fill a vacancy. The process is the following:

1. A yearly report is carried out. The one in charge of preparing it is the immediate superior.
2. An exam to assess the work of the personnel is given. This exam consists of an annual interview with the boss who carried out the employee's annual evaluation.
3. Interviews related to the career of the public servant are held to sound out his perspectives. These are carried out every four years and personal projects are discussed, as well as the type of work that the civil servant would like to carry out in the future.

One can speak of a variant in this promotion process: the Fast Stream, by means of which small groups of specialized personnel who are interested in attending a training program in order to enter the multifunctional class, are selected.[13]

There are two ways in which the applicant is selected to belong to one of these groups. The first is to be nominated by the agency or department to which he/she belongs. The second, to have the necessary academic qualifications specified, or to already have a position inside the civil service (almost always in the specialist group). Once the mentioned requirements are met, the selection process is similar to the one described above. Once the applicants are accepted, they should undergo a probation period that usually lasts two years. The promotions of Senior Civil Servants corresponds to the Senior Civil Commission.

Remuneration Each department and agency designs its pay scale, observing its necessities and the general government's pay policies in the public sector. These arrangements should reflect the following key principles:

1. The greatest benefit for the payroll money.
2. Financial control of the payroll.
3. Flexibility in the payment systems.
4. A close, effective relationship between payment and performance.

If an agency wants to make significant changes in its payment structure, it must submit the case to the Cabinet Office. The new payment outlines are to be evaluated after three years of being in effect, comparing them with the principles mentioned above and sending a copy of this evaluation to the Cabinet Office.

Separation Beginning with the arrival of Thatcher in the government, and mainly in the 1980s, the possibility of linking the stability of the civil servants to their performance began to be considered. The consideration was taken as a serious proposal after 1982; that was the year in which the report on effectiveness and efficiency in the civil service was published, harshly criticizing the absence of a clear orientation toward achieving efficiency and effectiveness at the higher levels of the organism.

There now exists the possibility of dismissing civil servants who are rated as inefficient or of limited efficiency. Somebody is rated as inefficient when his/her work has deteriorated to an unacceptable level or when his/her frequent absence affects the efficiency of the office to which (s)he belongs. Also, someone is declared of limited efficiency when his/her performance is not that required for the position, but neither is it such that can be rated as inefficient, or when (s)he is absent and does not attend to his/her duties satisfactorily.

To be able to discharge somebody on grounds of inefficiency, if the individual has been rated as inefficient or of limited efficiency on at least one normal evaluation, it will be suggested that (s)he resign voluntarily; the agent has the right not to resign, in which case, (s)he has the obligation to improve his/her performance. If the individual has been assessed the same way on at least two normal evaluations, then the agency can dismiss him.

In both cases the employee is entitled to be warned in advance and also to appeal against the decision when it can be shown that the process or the evaluation was not made in the specified way.

Mandatory early or flexible early retirement Departments and agencies can lay off personnel for structural reasons. That is to say, for severe conflicts of administration caused by blocked promotions or other situations creating organizational problems that hamper the efficient operation of the department. Obligatory early retirement for structural reasons is applied mainly to Senior Civil Servants.

There can also be obligatory early retirement if the employee's performance has been declining in the last two report periods and improvement is not likely. This also applies, mainly, to members of the Senior Civil Service. In all cases downgrading can be an alternative option to mandatory retirement.

Recommendations for Mexico

Without a doubt, the civil service model adopted by the United Kingdom as a result of the reform has proved to be beneficial. The meritocratic, transparent and sound character of the code regulating the Civil Service has converted an inefficient, costly government into one of the best qualified ones in the world without significant budgetary increases. In any case, one must not forget that added to an administration system based on the autonomy of the departments, there are mechanisms in the United Kingdom such as the Citizens' Charter that demand and evaluate their good performance.

Based on the best practices in the United Kingdom, the following is recommended for Mexico in regard to recruitment, selection, performance evaluation and salary.

Recruitment and selection

1. To implant a recruitment and selection system that pursues the following goals:
   a) To acquire the best person for the position regardless of ethnic group or gender.
   b) To avoid suspicions of favoritism.
   c) To ensure that the recruitment procedures reinforce the political impartiality of the civil service.
2. To take into account that it is more expensive to choose the wrong person than to spend time looking for the right one.
3. To have a system in which, provided the requirements of the competition are met, an individual can compete to enter at any grade of the structure although it is not the one immediately above.
4. To allow certain *exceptions* to the selection, clearly justified and legitimately agreed on by consensus, and based on merit, in order to give flexibility in cases of necessity.
5. To have the option of rehiring personnel previously in the civil service without going through the normal process of recruitment and selection, provided seniority is not a priority principle to merit and excellence in performance, and so as to capitalize on the investment made in training said personnel.

Performance evaluation

1. To create a program such as the Citizens' Charter involving the citizenry in the evaluation of the public service performance and which, at the same time, brings the public services in line with the needs of the citizenry.
2. To establish dismissal principles based on transparent, legitimate periodic evaluations, offering job security for efficient public servants committed to the performance of their functions.

Remuneration

1. To give autonomy to the departments to establish salaries for the different positions according to their necessities and the general pay policies in the public sector.

The civil service system in New Zealand

The reform of the civil service in New Zealand should not be considered an isolated change, but rather part and consequence of an overall reform that embraces both public sector and private. Without a doubt, the administrative reform of New Zealand has not only been one of the most drastic, but also one of the more oriented toward market economy. As a result of this reform, this country has a public administration scheme that is quite similar to the private sector.

There are two systems that govern public administration in New Zealand: the formal and the informal. The formal includes all written norms, codes and institutions that regulate the behavior of the officials, whereas the informal one covers the effect of all the unwritten, culturally implicit norms in a tradition of values, such as ethics and loyalty, combined with the effect of the size of the country's population.

Being a country of approximately three million inhabitants generates a group pressure toward ethical behavior and excellent performance on the part of the officials. It is important to keep in mind this particular advantage of New Zealand's when comparing its practices and policies with those of other countries.

Background

Before the reform, New Zealand had one of the most protectionist economies in the western world. Government regulations, such as price and wage controls, were notorious both in the public sector and in the private. Public administration was quite centralized and, as a reflection of this, so was the human resources management of the public service.

In 1973 a strong economic crisis began in New Zealand. In the first place, the entry of Great Britain into the European Common Market caused a decrease in imports from New Zealand; in the second place, the "OPEC crisis" of the Organization of Petroleum Exporting Countries caused an abrupt rise in the prices of oil, which imposed serious costs on New Zealand. By 1984 the situation in New Zealand was critical: high inflation, a fiscal deficit, increasing interest rates, plummeting currency and a highly inefficient government. Economic and administrative reform was essential.

Reform

In 1984, the reform began in three overlapping stages. First the private sector was liberated from excessive government regulation; then the government's commercial operations were restructured, bringing them into line with market mechanisms; and, finally, the public sector and job market were deregulated. Later, the State Owned Enterprise Act 1986 changed the structure and operation of parastatal companies, eliminating government control of the operations and separating them from the central government. These parastatal companies became what are now called Crown Entities, which are legally separated from the central government, although in many cases they belong to the crown, and act under the responsibility of one or more ministers. The Crown Entities are responsible for giving service and for operation, while the minister (or central government) is the one who establishes policy and fixes the prices and production volume of the Crown Entities. The relationship between the ministers and the Crown Entities is contractual, so that, in many cases, these compete with private sector companies, generating a pressure toward efficiency, which is typical of competitive, private industry.

These organizations were created to provide services that can be carried out more efficiently outside of the central government. Consequently, this reform brought an increase in the productivity and the competitiveness of the parastatals. Many of these parastatal companies (now Crown Entities) have been privatized, others are still public and others are mixed capital.

It was this success which motivated the guiding principle of the Crown Entities to expand to other departments of the central government, following a model similar to Next Steps; with the difference that the case of New Zealand is contractual and the Crown Entities are outside of the central government. At the present time, they represent one-third of public expenditure.

Another effect of the success of the principle that governs the Crown Entities was the emphasis on accountability to the central government. The reform of the human resources administration was similarly based on the maxim that managers cannot be held responsible for results if they are not granted freedom of action.

Structure of the public service

Figure 4.1 shows the public structure in New Zealand; here it can be appreciated that the main actors in the public service are:

1. Parliament
2. Governor General
3. Prime Minister
4. Cabinet
5. Secretariats
6. State Services Commission

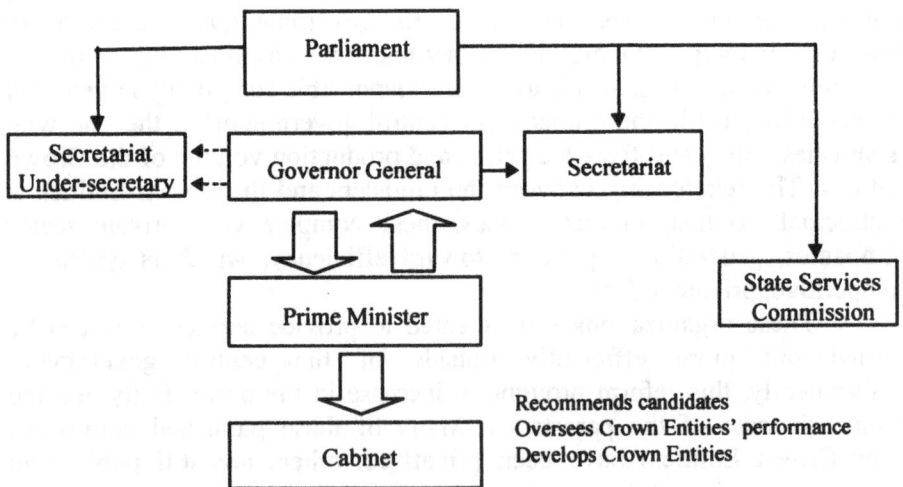

Figure 4.1   Public structure in New Zealand Parliament

In New Zealand, the public sector is organized into departments that depend on ministers, while the ministers are responsible to Parliament. The departments are the units and the level where managerial discretion and accountability are exercised, but not the contractual scheme. That is to say that the departments are the responsibility of the ministers and, therefore, also of the central government. The operation of these departments, according to the individual case, can be the responsibility of the chief executives of a department, of Crown Entities or of private industry.

In the first case, the chief executive of the department depends on a minister based on a contract of not more than five years. Although the chief executive is under contract, the functions of the department fall within the central government's jurisdiction. In the second case, the operations are the responsibility of Crown Entities agencies, which are not governed by the central government but whose function it is to provide services or public products. And in the third and last case, the minister hires these products or services in the marketplace.

Although the structure in general is similar to that of Next Steps in the United Kingdom with respect to the division of policy making and operations planning, the case of New Zealand is contractual. The contractual nature is what generates more pressure to improve efficiency.

In the case of New Zealand there are many more departments than ministers, so that it is common for a minister to be in charge of several departments and sometimes for a department to have two ministers. In this latter case, for each function of the department there is a minister who is the one with responsibility, who clearly defines who is accountable and must produce results.

Functions of the minister The minister is the one responsible for policy making and the one who decides if he will buy the services or products from a Crown Entity, or from his department, or if he will buy the product or service in question in the marketplace.

Functions of the department chief executive The chief executive has practically total control of the operative administration and human resources of his department. The heads of department are hired for a period of not more than five years, and at the end of this time it is possible for them to be rehired depending on the evaluation of the results. For a boss to be rehired, it is not enough for him to have done good work; his performance must be outstanding. In practice, it is difficult for the commission (who, as explained below, is the one that negotiates the contracts of the chief executives) to decide whether to renew a contract or not, when a boss has given good performance, but not excellent.

Unlike the situation before the reform, these chiefs are responsible for dismissing inefficient managers, removing redundant workers, recruiting people outside the government, negotiating salaries with high-level managers, taking responsibility for the quantity and quality of products. In short, they are responsible for the efficiency and effectiveness of the department, but enjoy autonomy in the management of resources, subject to general normative principles as indicated in the State Service Commission.

State Services Commission (SSC) The State Services Commission would be similar to the Cabinet Office in the United Kingdom.

This department, which was drastically reduced with the reform, has the following functions:

1. To review the government's functioning, including:
   a) The assignment of functions of each department, as well as their structure.
   b) The necessity or advisability of creating new departments and the dissolution of existing departments.
   c) The coordination of activities of the departments.
2. To review the efficiency, effectiveness and economy of each department, including the performance of the chief executive of the agency.
3. To negotiate employees' work conditions in the civil service.
4. To promote, develop and monitor personnel policies and standards of personnel administration in the department, as well as merit and equal opportunities programs.
5. To advise and attend to each department with respect to personnel training and development.
6. To provide assistance to each department regarding systems, structures and organization.
7. To exercise functions with respect to the public service administration on behalf of the Prime Minister, when functions not included in this law are involved.

It also has the function of recruiting, promoting and negotiating contracts of the chief executives of departments. The commission, with the approval of the cabinet, can dismiss heads of agencies.

Reform of the human resources administration

Before the reform of the human resources administration in 1988, New Zealand had a centralized system. The State Services Commission was the employer of all civil servants, that is to say it regulated recruitment, selection, salaries and organizational structures, and although the selection was based on merit, seniority was also considered merit. Elaborate appeal and revision systems existed to ensure that appointments and promotions followed the law to the letter. This made the processes very slow and, on occasions, it seemed that the system was designed not to reward efficiency. The employees, when entering the civil service, had work assured for 40 years, which produced inefficiency, as well as a feeling of injustice in people who were not in the civil service and who, though offering better results, obtained lesser salary than those servants within the service, for reasons of seniority and regulations, but not efficiency.

Present civil service system

At the moment the employees of the departments, in spite of continuing to be employees of the crown, are subject to the administration of the chief executive of the department. That is to say, he has the power to represent the crown as employer to the public servants. And as employer, he is responsible for the recruitment, selection, dismissals, salaries and management of personnel in general. The chief executives in turn have a contract with the minister for not more than five years. If there is a dispute (or conciliation problem) in the public sector, it is resolved in the arbitration commission or in the labor court in charge of conciliating in problems of the private sector. Also, the labor law that is applied to the private sector is the same one that concerns public servants.

According to the reform, instead of human resources administration being regulated by a law, it is regulated by principles of equality and merit. The reason why the administration functions under these principles is due to the informal system of group pressure and the unwritten rules mentioned previously.

Article 56, part V, of the State Sector Act of New Zealand reflects the degree of control of the civil service code over the human resources administration:

56. General principles:

1. The chief executive of a department is to operate under a personnel policy that is consistent with the principle of being a good employer.
2. For the purposes of this section, a "good employer" is one who operates a personnel policy that contains provisions generally accepted as necessary for fair, proper treatment of employees in all aspects of their work; it includes provisions that require:
   a) Good, secure working conditions.
   b) Equal opportunities program.
   c) Impartial selection of people suitable for appointment.
   d) Recognition of
      - Requirements for employment of personnel.
      - Civil servants' goals and aspirations.
   e) Opportunities for enriching individual employees' abilities.
   f) Recognition of the goals, aspirations and cultural differences of ethnic groups.
   g) Recognition of employment requirements for women.
   h) Recognition of employment requirements for the disabled.

3. In addition to these requirements, each chief executive will ensure that all employees maintain characteristic standards of integrity, behavior and concern for the public service.

Recruitment, selection and separation of public servants The chief executives have total autonomy over these functions. For example, with respect to selection, the only thing that the State Sector Act establishes is:

60. *Appointment on merit.* A chief executive, when making an appointment under this act (State Sector Act) is to give preference to the most appropriate person for the position.
    If a person inside the department does not agree with the chief executive's decision, for example, in choosing a friend or relative, (s)he can ask for this selection process to be reviewed and, if there is a dispute, for the State Services Commission to review it.

As for recruitment, the code establishes that if there is a vacant post, it must be announced publicly and well in advance:

61. *Obligation to notify of vacant positions.* When the chief executive of a department seeks to fill a vacant position or one about to be vacant, the chief executive is to notify extensively while applicable, to allow qualified candidates to compete for the position.

Performance evaluation There is a process of performance evaluation for the department, and another for its chief executive. Both are annual and are the responsibility of the State Services Commission.

The evaluations of the chief executives are based on three principles of accountability:

1. The chief executive is personally responsible for the performance of the department.
2. Performance expectations should be specified in advance.
3. Performance should be compared with previously determined objectives.

As a rule, for the chief executive's evaluation, the self-evaluation of the person being evaluated is analyzed, as well as one or more evaluations from the minister or ministers concerned, central agencies and external judges. In some cases, the Prime Minister participates in the appraisal. The results of the assessment of the chief executives are reported to the corresponding minister.

The performance evaluation of the rest of the civil servants depends on the chief executive of the department.

Negotiations of employment conditions In the past (before 1988), all officials were employees of the State Services Commission, and this was the one in charge of negotiating employment terms with the unions. At the present time, the chief executive is the one in charge of these negotiations; however, the chief executive consults with this department before closing a negotiation in order to have information of the terms that are being arranged in other departments.

Thus the negotiations of contracts between chief executives and ministers are the responsibility of the State Services Commission.

Recommendations for Mexico

The reform of New Zealand had two directions: the devolution of autonomy combined with accountability and restructuring based on contractual economy. Although it is clear that this reform brought benefits to the country, one must not forget that in the case of New Zealand there were circumstances that are not present in Mexico or, at least, not to the same extent: an informal system of unwritten norms, based on traditional values of ethics and loyalty and a phenomenon of group pressure caused by the size of the population.

This does not mean that it is not recommendable for Mexico to proceed in the direction of the devolution of power, accountability and contractual market economy; on the contrary, this case suggests that it would be beneficial. However, it would be advisable to do so gradually, since it lacks an informal system that could serve as a substitute for a civil service law.

Thus it would be possible to implement a meritocratic civil service, in which the efficient performance of the top levels is a factor that in different ways stimulates this same characteristic in all areas of the public administration.

The civil service system in France

The French civil service model is one of the most centralized and controlled in existence. At the beginning of the 19th century the system arose to remedy a situation of injustices and inequality, as well as to face a growing unionism. Hence their centralism and excessive control. Nowadays, the population's necessities have become more heterogeneous, public services need to be closer to the users and with the advances in technology, changes must be swifter. For this reason, the civil service system that worked in the past, today makes for inflexibility. The public service is considered remote and authoritarian, with quite complex rules and procedures. This is why there have been reform attempts lately in the French civil service system.

Background

In France, the characteristics of the Napoleonic administration gave rise to a model of the public service characterized by economy, hierarchy and competence. This model underlines three elements primarily: 1) the government employee's mission as representative of the State; 2) the importance of the guarantees with respect to status and continuance in the position, and 3) the prevalent contribution of the public service to the continuity and stability of the administration.

This does not mean that there is no politicizing of appointments; this phenomenon is seen in the formation and appointment of cabinet ministers, where there exists total freedom of selection.

In the past few years, the civil service in France has undergone problems that have given rise to a rethinking of the public service. Mainly they face a loss of legitimacy, professional uneasiness and a need for modernization.

As for the first aspect, one can say that the public service has been characterized by stability of employment, which has helped compensate for government instability brought about by constant, and sometimes surprising, government changes, as well as by tensions between government and Parliament. The importance and role of the high French administration is derived from the way that government's élites established a virtual monopoly based on the way they were educated and selected.

This has meant that the image of the bureaucracy has been devalued and appears as a privileged group (since even in times of unemployment, their positions and salaries are guaranteed by the legislation) that is not equal to the new demands of the citizens for more participation, better quality in the services and greater accountability.

As for the crisis or professional uneasiness of the French government employee, the feeling persists that the training of public servants should be more specific, unlike what is happening at the moment, since the selection of the individuals is made by means of exams based on general knowledge. This means, for French bureaucrats, the need to acquire specialized knowledge in order to develop new abilities that will allow them to adapt to the necessities really required by the position.

In France there exists a strong linking of university education to the possibilities of acceding to public positions. In this respect, the competitions held by the École Nationale d'Administration are the most important means for ministerial recruitment with the patronage of the Ministry of Public Administration. Among other big institutions that have channeled important individuals into the administration for several generations, are the École Normale Supérieure, the Polytechnique, the École des Mines and the École des Ponts et Chaussées.

The modernization of the French public service, just as in other cases studied, has meant the need to reduce dissatisfaction regarding the performance of bureaucratic organizations and the civil service system behind them. In order to attend to the protest of many politicians and citizens who demand more flexible and more responsible public organizations, the French government has carried out reforms in which the civil service is one of the main points. Among the measures that have been put into operation are the new approaches oriented toward user satisfaction, especially regarding the provision of services, in which case the individual ministries establish the systems of performance measurement.

The current objectives of modernization of the civil service in France are also associated with the criticisms of the high degree of centralization and authoritarianism. In order to achieve its goals in this respect, the government has revived social dialogue and negotiations with the unions; it has begun programs to develop the autonomy and credibility of the agencies and, consequently, there has been a greater opening up toward the public.

Civil service system

In France there are three civil services: that of the central government, that of the local government and that of the Ministry of Health. The process of entry, promotion and termination of employment in these three services can have as a common denominator the following characteristics:

The French civil service is governed by two meritocratic principles: access to the service by means of competitions, as well as equal opportunities. However, the government has the ability to exercise certain discretion in naming officials, especially higher officials of whom absolute loyalty is demanded to those who appointed them. Also, in certain cases, people are hired for three-year contracts, without being in the service.

The competition consists basically in presenting an exam. For each corps there is an evaluation and, depending on the mark obtained by the applicant, (s)he is assigned to the corresponding ministry. There are ministries whose work situation is more attractive than others, such as Finance, and therefore they have much more demand (from the point of view of labor). For that reason, according to the mark one obtains, one is assigned to a ministry of greater or lesser prestige: those with the highest percentage enter the Finance Ministry, and so on down to those of lesser demand. These exams are designed jointly by the *corps*,[14] or ministry (if this corps exists only in a ministry), and the Ministry of the Public Service, which forms part of the General Direction of Administration and Public Service. When entering the service one begins from the bottom of the civil service promotion ladder; by having certain studies or relevant experience does not mean that somebody can enter at higher levels. In fact, in each corps there is an age limit after which it is impossible to apply for a position in the service. One exception for the exam competition, are the people who have graduated from the École Nationale d'Administration (ENA). In order to enter this school it is necessary to compete by means of an exam, but after graduating, it is not necessary to compete to enter the service.

Once a person enters the service, (s)he has guaranteed tenure for life. The civil servants that did not enter by means of the ENA spend a period of one year before they are given the work guaranteed for life, but in practice, 99% of the employees weather this probation period successfully.

As can be observed, the element of competition through *quasi-market* mechanisms, in which the most solicited jobs demand greater competitiveness in the mark required for acceptance (e.g. the finance department), generates positive incentives in the departments (who compete for the best candidates), as well as for the applicants for the positions (due to the status and performance information indicated by the mark in the exam).

On the other hand, as was already mentioned, the incentive of having a "job for life", after passing certain exams or probation periods, produces perverse stimuli that can lead to mediocrity in the public service.

Recent reforms

At the moment, France is in a process of administrative modernization. One of the government's initiatives is to deconcentrate the administration in order to improve the efficiency both of policy decisions (the central government's responsibility), as well as of their implementation. For example, the reform in controlling expenses of deconcentrated services began as a pilot experiment in two regions in 1995, and there are now plans to expand it to all of France. Another initiative is to make the public services more adapted to the citizens' needs.

It is expected that this type of administrative reform will lead to a deconcentration of human resources administration, which, to a lesser degree, would be the sequence observed in New Zealand and the United Kingdom.

Recommendations for Mexico

The study of this case shows that the current civil service system in France arose out of circumstances very different from those at present and there is consequently inefficiency and rigidity in the public administration. For that reason, initiatives have recently been proposed that point toward autonomy and flexibility.

From France's experience, we can take as a recommendation for Mexico the practice of requiring exams for entry to the service. As there is a common exam for each corps, and a corps can include many departments, the departments compete to recruit candidates with the highest points in this exam. This creates an incentive to the applicants to obtain the highest possible mark and to the departments to offer the best working conditions and attract the best candidates.

Based on negative results that have produced inefficiency and inflexibility in France, we shall make the following recommendations:

1. Not to centralize the catalogs of positions and salaries, but to have common norms for their operation established by a governing department.
2. Not to make public servants non-removable, since this generates inefficiency and inflexibility.

Conclusion: the tendency toward the devolution of autonomy in human resources administration

The devolution of the responsibility for human resources management from central organizations to departments, and inside the departments to middle managers, has been the priority of the reforms of the last decade. This devolution of autonomy has proved to be beneficial in the promotion of more efficient and more effective administrations in the public sector. The benefits have also been remarkable in the reforms aimed at improving the motivation and performance of the civil servants, especially managerial.

To achieve a more efficient and effective use of human resources, devolving autonomy to their administration has had the priority of granting middle managers flexibility in recruitment, selection and reallocation of personnel and, very importantly: tools that permit the recruitment of ideal people for the appropriate positions and the measurement of their performance in this way.

Most of the OECD member countries have certain basic central principles in common to ensure the proper operation of the civil service system:

1. Equality of opportunities in entry and promotion.
2. Selection of public servants based on merit, by open competition.
3. Accountability to the citizenry of the public servants' (and public service's) performance.
4. Transparent, respected laws and procedures, to govern the citizenry.
5. Clarity in the rights and obligations of civil servants.
6. A clear role of management with a pertinent division between political and administrative functions.
7. Professional independence and a certain degree of job security, based on impartial evaluations and confined to performance toward the established objectives.
8. A predetermined level of payment.
9. Transparency and communication with the citizenry.

Figure 4.2 compares how close the different countries come to what are considered ideal elements for establishing an efficient civil service within a context of visionary, responsible public administration, aimed at achieving results.

Best practices ●
Worst practices ○

	United Kingdom	France	New Zealand	Argentina	Colombia	Chile	Bolivia
Autonomy	●	○	◑	○	○	◑	○
Income	●	◑	◕	◔	○	○	◕
Separation	◕	●	◕	◑	◑	●	◕
Promotion	◕	●	◑	●	◑	◑	◑
Performance evaluation	●	◑	◕	●	●	●	●
Remuneration systems	●	◑	◕	◔	◑	◕	◕
Support organizations	●	◕	◕	◕	◕	◔	◕
Introduction	◕	◑	◑	●	◑	●	◑
Scope of the civil service	●	◑	◕	◑	◔	◕	◕

Source: Booz Allen and Hamilton de México and the Strategy and Development Center

Figure 4.2 Efficiency of civil service in public administration

Notes

[1] See an evaluation of these reforms in R. Laking, Public *Management Lessons for Developing Countries and The World Bank,* 1996, mimeo. A review of countries that have made more radical reforms is to be found in G. Scott, P. Bushnell and N. Sallee, "Reform of the Core Public Sector: The New Zealand Experience", *Governance,* vol. 3, no. 2, pp. 138-167.

[2] See annex B.2 for more information about the Citizen's Charter program.

[3] Australia, New Zealand, the United Kingdom, Holland and the Scandinavian countries use performance agreements between the central bodies and the departments intensively. They have greatly decentralized the budgetary and personnel management systems, in order to allow the departments a more effective administration by goals. The system of agreements at the same time guarantees a transparent structure of accountability.

[4] See *Organization for Economic Co-Operation and Development,,* "Integrating People Management into Public Service Reform", 1996, pp. 9-11. In addition, previous publications of the OECD reported the appearance of parallel management structures outside of the civil service. See *OECD Public Pay Dispersion,* 1993.

[5] See OECD (Desk Copy), *Performance Evaluation: Experiences in Ten OECD Countries,* 1997. Note, on the other hand, that size is not an indicator of how standardized it is. In France, for example, with an administration of a relatively large

size, few rules are used to specify the nature and characteristics of the prizes that are allocated.

6   The New Zealand civil service, for example, which perhaps uses performance evaluation more generally within its system, is made up of 39 different departments, ranging from departments with 7,000 to 8,000 people (their social security system) to others of only six (those that administer the island territories).

7   Different studies agree that the problem of evaluating performance is, to a large extent, due to the difficulty of measuring the effort and results obtained by the department in question (inputs/products). The systems are more effective when it is possible to measure both (for example, the productive departments that issue licenses or permits, or the mail). In some departments the effort can be measured, but not the product (many functions of the Judiciary, of the Comptrollership or of the Army in a barracks); and in others, the product, but not the effort (the Department of the Interior, the army at war). On this topic, see James Q. Wilson, *Bureaucracy*, 1994, pp. 154-157; or R. Klitgaard, *Information and Incentives in Institutional Reform,* IRIS Center, Maryland, 1995.

8   OECD, Private Pay for Public Work: Performance Related Pay for Public Sector Managers, 1993, pp. 9-11.

9   This is achieved by creating a "Cabinet Office" dependent on the Federal Executive.

10 Issues and Developments in Public Management: Survey 1996-1997 on the United Kingdom-Internet. For a detailed analysis of the Next Steps program, see annex B. 1.

11 See annexes B. 1 y B.2 for a more detailed analysis of the issue.

12 This commission is part of the Cabinet Office.

13 Class made up of employees capable of performing different functions in different areas.

14 A *corps* is a group of civil servants with the same function. For example, the corps of accountants, the corps of lawyers, the medical corps, etc. There are cases in which a corps exists in only one department, such as the corps of firemen.

5. Experiences of the Civil Service in Mexico

Introduction

Within the framework of the modernization programs of the Mexican State that seek greater efficiency and effectiveness in the execution of institutional objectives, as well as in public administration, the career civil service occupies a fundamental place. The career civil service is a method of administering public personnel whose main characteristics are entry by competition or exam, promotion for merits and seniority, political neutrality, professionalization and job stability.

Mexico has for many years had legal and institutional provisions to regulate the functions of the public servants. However, these provisions have not always been linked systematically to form an overall, coherent schema, but rather have been presented in a disjointed, sporadic way, with few results as far as the establishment of a career civil service throughout the whole government is concerned. This has its origin in the historical characteristics of the Mexican political system, which has meant that the processes of selection of public officials are dominated by clientelist policies.[1] Nowadays it is common to see areas of government where the recruitment and selection of civil servants is done through contacts, recommendations and political obligations.

The existing system of loyalties in Mexican bureaucracy, among other factors, has generated a significant decline in the confidence that society places in state and bureaucratic institutions, as shown in the World Development Report 1997, of the World Bank.

As mentioned in the introductory chapter, this loss of confidence in government institutions and policies has meant that throughout the present century there have been diverse laws aimed at revitalizing the public function.

The first attempt to professionalize the public administration was made in 1923 in the state of San Luis Potosí, with the Civil Service Law. In 1931, President Pascual Ortiz Rubio approved the Federal Labor Act, and in 1932 the Agrarian Officials and Employees' Responsibilities Act.

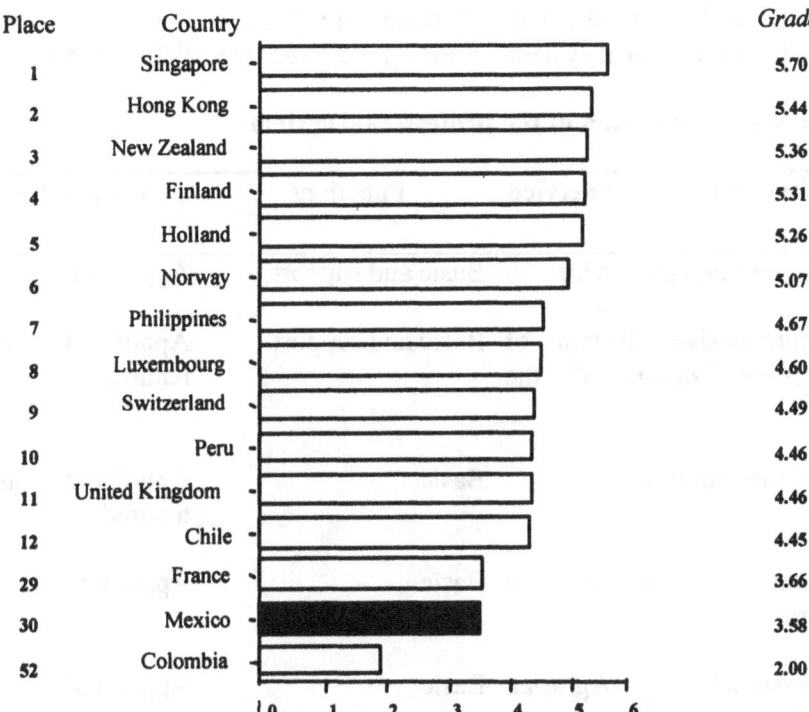

Source: The global Competitiveness Report 1997, World Economic Forum

Figure 5.1 Are government policies transparent and impartial? (Maximum grade, 6; minimum, 0)

In 1934, President Abelardo Rodríguez, aware that the main cause for uncertainty and inefficiency in the public administration was the mass exodus of workers of the State with each change of government, promoted the Agreement on the Organization and Operation of the Civil Service Act, which considerably influenced the administration of Lázaro Cárdenas, who in 1938, in the Statute of Workers in the Service of the Powers of the Union, already distinguished between tenured and appointed employees.

To these efforts was added in 1940 the Civil Servants' Responsibilities Act; in 1957, the Incentives and Extras for Officials and Employees of the Federation Act; in 1963, the Federal Law for Workers in the Service of the State; in 1975, the Law for Civil Servants' Bonuses, Incentives and Extras; in 1979, the Law of Responsibilities of Officials and Employees of the Federation, of the Federal District and of the high Officials of the States; and in 1983, the Federal Law of Public Servants'

Responsibilities and the Civil Service Inter-secretarial Commission, in which the professional systems in force today were established (table 5.1).

Table 5.1 Composition of the professional systems

Professional or Civil Service	Functions	Work status
Mexican Foreign Service	Basic and support	Appointed
Comprehensive System of Professionalization of the INEGI	Basic and support	Appointed and tenured
Teaching profession	Basic	Appointed and tenured
System of Specialists in Hydraulics	Basic	Appointed
Professional Agrarian Service	Basic	Appointed
Career Civil Service of the PGR	Basic	Appointed
Career Civil Service of the PGJDF	Basic	Appointed
Military profession	Basic	Appointed
Legal profession	Basic	Appointed

What is known today as the State Reform had its beginnings during the presidency of Miguel de la Madrid. In the field of public administration, and especially related to the civil service, three concrete actions were carried out: the reform of Section IV of the constitution (the term "public officials" was changed to "public servants"); the Federal Law of Responsibilities of Public Servants and the establishment of the Inter-secretarial Civil Service Commission. These actions marked the beginning of a true reconstruction of the national public administration, which was part of what was known at the time as *the moral renewal of society.*

At the present time, advances in the implementation of the Career Civil Service are reflected in the Program of Public Administration Modernization 1995-2000, which establishes, by means of the Program of Public Administration Modernization (Promap, its abbreviation in Spanish), that Mexico should have a professional career civil service that would guarantee an appropriate selection, professional development and retirement worthy of public servants, in order for the public administration to be transformed into an organization with a culture of service that favors honesty, efficiency and integrity.

In spite of the efforts made, the current model of human resources administration in Mexico still retains deficiencies that prevent the government from offering better services at the lowest possible costs. Among the costs implicit in the model now in effect are:

1. Increase in the operation costs of the public machinery, as well as in transaction costs and delay in government administration.
2. The erroneous message that what is important is to carry out procedures, not to produce results.
3. It inhibits the complete development of public officials due to the lack of incentives that promote their professionalization and training.

Mexico does not have an appropriate recruitment system nor professionalization and development system for public officials. That is to say, there is no system that enables the performance of public officials to be measured, which prevents there being a meritocratic system that would promote the professional development of the officials that are outstanding in their administrative functions, thereby resulting in an inequitable promotion system.

Due to these problems, the need arises in Mexico to establish a Career Civil Service that would allow clear, concise expectations to be created, with sound, practicable evaluations, and a promotion system based on merit and results (figure 5. 2).

The clear, concise expectations in the career civil service system are important for a productive behavior of public servants. A system that offers competitive salaries, bonuses, benefits or training, when the resources to make them effective do not exist, cannot attain the desired result and ends up demoralizing the personnel that supposedly ought to be encouraged. A promotion system based on training, when the administrative structure has insufficient positions to promote people, will not give results either. The necessary change in models requires a cultural revolution and a basic change in the way the public service is understood.

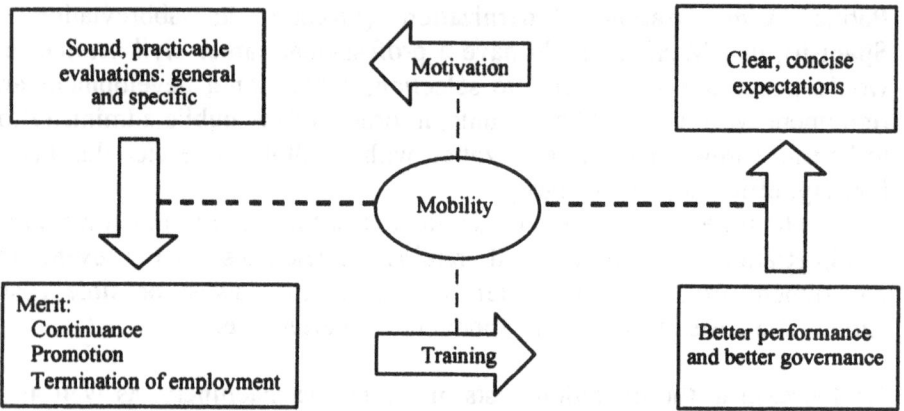

Figure 5.2 The name of the model: evaluations of merit to be carried out, clear expectations to be announced and offers that can be made

The objectives of the new culture should be clearly defined. The personnel must be motivated by means of sound evaluations. The intention is for these evaluations to be of two types:

1. On general knowledge that any public servant should possess (for example, the minimum levels of writing and vocabulary).
2. Specific evaluations related to the results to which the public servants are committed.

The model of public administration of which we are speaking is based on personal contracts, with definite, easily measured results – an administrative model based on an evaluation system that would allow feedback in order for public officials to generate better tools for job development.

A system of public administration with a career civil service that does not have a good evaluation system cannot work efficiently. If people are non-removable, the system deteriorates and becomes obsolete. The results of the evaluations should be considered, in due time, to decide on the future of the public servants. These should be the input source of information and, of course, the motivating force for acquiring the personnel that deserve the position. This appraisal is completely relevant for people's mobility.

Clear, concise expectations, as well as general and specific evaluations aimed at public servants, should have principles of merit as a basis. Merit is what makes someone worthy of something. This does not necessarily have to do with the length of time a public servant has performed his functions (although a correlation generally exists between good performance and seniority, justified by the possible experience acquired). Merit is important in order for people to remain, be promoted or, when appropriate, have their employment terminated in the public function. Merit is the opposite of clientelism, string-pulling, nepotism and corruption. Merit means that the one who offers results deserves the job and greater opportunities; it allows the system to offer better conditions and opportunities, with the mission of better performance, a fundamental part of which is that training which generates a better government and a country with fair, equal and efficient development.

A comprehensive system is required that has a very clear definition of what modernization in the public administration is; that has no problem of excessive control or authority; that has the minimum human, financial and material resources required; and that really functions in streamlining so that missions can be correlated with results, and these with better services for the citizenry.

In conclusion, an efficient career civil service should be based on a continuous modernization of public administration, in which human resources are a fundamental cogwheel (but not the only one) for a better performance on the part of public servants; a government to serve, made up of correct incentives and institutions that define property rights efficiently. This is a fair, transparent system that will generate a greater development and better distribution of wealth over the middle and long term.

In order to achieve an efficient career civil service with processes of equity in the Mexican context, some cases are analyzed that have been pioneers in Mexico in establishing it. This is the case of the Secretary of External Affairs, the National Institute of Statistics, Geography and Computer Science (INEGI), the National Water Commission and the Secretary of Public Education (teaching profession).

At the end of the chapter, conclusions are presented, including a synthesis of the main lessons and implications for public policy derived from the analysis of the case of Mexico.

Current situation

Governing bodies

The appointment and termination of employment of public servants has been carried out in our country by means of the system of vertical designation (*spoils system*). However, unlike other countries (mainly the United States), the apportioning of positions in Mexico has been made among factions and groups of a single party; the posts inside the public administration have been the prizes and rewards (or punishments) for those who have shown "loyalty" to the boss or leader of the group, or for those who, having lost in a political contest, maintain discipline and accept defeat without openly questioning the system.

Based on this, the national administrative machinery has, for over 20 years, suffered a gradual period of delegitimization, provoked partly by the distrust of the citizens with respect to public resources management. They have noticed a waste of economic, financial, technical and human resources, especially the last-mentioned, as a consequence of the prevailing recruitment and selection systems, where the fundamental criterion is the personal commitment that presupposes individual or group loyalty, rather than institutional and from merit.

The economic crisis that affected the country at the beginning of the decade, together with the worldwide tendencies toward administrative modernization of the public machinery, was the basis for the new ruling élite to promote a process of streamlining the federal bureaucratic machinery. This élite faced a greater civic demand for services, a demand on one hand for transparency in the public administration, but also faced a reduction in the amount of financial resources managed by the country. The government was at a crossroads whose only solution was a reform of the public machinery that would translate into greater quality in services and better attention to citizens; this would imply efficiency, transparency and effectiveness in the use of public resources.

To have an approximate idea of the importance of the implementation of the career civil service, it is useful to turn to the number of workers of the State that are now subject to some mode of this method of administration of public offices (table 5.2).

At the present time the career civil service is governed by the Inter-secretarial Commission of the Civil Service, which will be analyzed in more depth below. Although the civil service systems are generally administered by the operative area of human resources of the departments, the activity of the heads of these departments is usually regulated by a joint commission that evaluates the system and issues the general criteria.

These joint commissions allow discretion to be mitigated in the decision-making and, in most cases, those who preside over them are the heads of the institutions themselves – such as the INEGI, the PGR, the PGJDF, the IFE, the Agrarian Attorney's office, the Judiciary Council – or some other high-level public servant to whom the corresponding authority is delegated, as for example the case of a career ambassador in the Foreign Service, or of the national coordinator of the teaching profession.

Although the integration of a joint commission does not totally guarantee that the professionalization systems will be developed effectively, impartially and transparently, it does constitute an excellent instrument in mitigating discretion.

At the present time, inside the Promap, the Secretary of the Comptrollership and Administrative Development proposes that the civil service be adjusted to the needs and characteristics of the rest of the government offices; for its part, the Secretariat of National Revenue and Public Credit proposes a scheme with a greater tendency to centralize the normativity in more detail so that the departments will only act as implementers of the same system.

Normativity

The legal-normative situation of the diverse professionalization systems that have been implemented in our country can be observed in table 5.3. In these cases each institution that has implemented the career civil service also possesses its own normative framework.

Composition

The career services or professionalization that exist in Mexico have mostly been structured exclusively for the personnel that carry out fundamental functions, except for the Foreign Service and that of the INEGI. The former was formed starting in 1994, in two branches; the diplomatic-consular and the technical-administrative. In the INEGI five branches exist: statistics, geography, computer science, publication and administrative. The fundamental functions are developed in first three branches, and the two remaining branches cover the support functions. In this framework, the Comprehensive Professionalization System is divided into three subsystems: Professionalization of Appointed Personnel, of Tenured Personnel and Appointed Personnel engaged under the general norms of the federal public sector. The personnel of this last subsystem makes up the basic structure of the institution and is not subject to the rules of the Subsystem of Professionalization of Appointed Personnel, although possibly it could belong to it, following the form of access established in the subsystem indicated.

The structure of the teaching profession includes three aspects for carrying out the fundamental functions of basic education; classroom teachers, educators in directorial and supervisory functions and educators in technical-pedagogical activities. In the CNA, the system is made up preferably of specialists in the area such as agronomists, chemists, etc.; although there is also a place for graduates in economy, business administration, law, computer and actuarial sciences, among other specialties.

As for the professional agrarian service, it is composed mainly of lawyers who are specialists in agrarian studies, in order to support the different stages of the Program of Certification of Legal Rights of Ejidos (Procede, abbreviation in Spanish).

On the other hand, the Military School offers technical-professional, military training based on the observance of laws and military regulations, with a high sense of the honor, discipline and morals, which are the fundamental principles of the National Defense. In the PGR and the PGJDF, the career for agents of the Federal Public Ministry, Judicial Police and experts who basically take care of the investigation and persecution of crimes of the federal jurisdiction or common order in the Federal District, respectively, has been regulated. Also, the law profession of the Judiciary Council only includes those public servants with jurisdictional and not administrative activities.

Table 5.2 Number of members of the professional services

Civil service or professional	Federal Public Administration			
	Centralized	Parastatal	*Autonomous*	*Judicial Power*
Mexican Foreign Service	1,352			
Comprehensive System of Professionalization of the INEGI	11,000			
Teaching profession	580,908 [a] (plazas)			
System of Specialists in Hydraulics	2,986			
Professional Electoral Service			2,336	
Professional Agrarian Service		1,300		
Career Civil Service of the PGJDF	376			
Military profession	120,000 [b]			
Legal profession				3,400
Total	16,622	1,300	2,336	3,400

[a] As a consequence of the process of decentralization that has taken place in the educational sector, most of these places are administrated by state governments. Besides, a teacher can have two postitions.
[b] Of which 10% are in the schools.

The above-mentioned shows that the personnel that carry out the support or non-basic functions, which are of a common, general type in all departments and agencies of the federal public administration, have been somewhat on the fringes of the current professionalization systems.

Table 5.3 Normative supports for professionalization systems

Institution	Normative aid
Mexican Foreign Service	Mexican Foreign Service Law and Regulations
Comprehensive System of Professionalization of the INEGI	Falta "acuerdo del sistema integral de profesionalización"
Teaching profession	National Agreement on Modernization of Basic Education
System of Specialists in Hydraulics	None exists
Professional Agrarian Service	Statute of the Professional Agrarian Service
Career Civil Service of the PGR	Organic Law of the PGR and Regulations
Career Civil Service of the PGJDF	Organic Law of the PGJDF and Regulations*
Military profession	Organic Law of the Army and Armed Forces and Regulations
Legal profession	Organic Law of the Judicial Power and Regulation of the Legal Profession.*

*Publication pending

Except for the INEGI and SEP, the systems include only appointed workers. This is largely due to the fact that this personnel lacks regulation, legal protection, job stability and specific rules for promotion and advancement regulated by joint committees on the promotion ladder which the unionized personnel has; but also to the resistance shown by the union organizations, whose scheme of privileges would be limited by the introduction of a system of professionalization which implies, among other things, the incorporation of evaluation models that can, as a last resort, decide on the public servant's continuance in the institutions.

As for absolute numbers, and excluding the members of the military (120,000, approximately) and teachers' (more than 580,000 places) professions, the members of the remaining profesionalización systems number about 30,000 in the federal public administration, and 3,400 in the Judicial Power. This emphasizes how thinly spread the human resources are so that, although the number has increased in recent years, it is still minimal with respect to the size of the public administration.

Hiring

The procedures for entry into the professional service in the institutions analyzed show similarities in filling vacancies, which is generally done by means of competitive examinations. It is common for them to announce public (open) or internal (closed) competitions. The former are published in the newspapers with largest national circulation, or in the *Diario Oficial de la Federación* (Official Journal of the Federation) as the Foreign Service and the Judiciary Council do, and both people from outside as well as applicants from their own institution can participate. For internal competitions, candidates from the corresponding institution only, are invited.

Recruitment and selection are carried out in a centralized way by the corresponding joint commission, although in some cases the process may be carried out in the same place where the vacancies are located, following the general guidelines issued by this body.

As a rule, applicants are subjected to a series of interviews and exams. However, these results are not definitive, since other internal factors, such as the opinion of the corresponding authorities, have an influence. In general, once the personnel have been selected and a trial period lapsed in most of the departments mentioned, they are hired definitively.

The analysis of these aspects implies that in forming the professionalization systems, greater emphasis has been placed on entry, to a great extent because of the importance of hiring the appropriate personnel worthy of being offered job security and continuance. This last consideration is fundamental for all the institutions; however, the necessity to maintain honorable, efficient public servants is accentuated in institutions such as the PGR, the PGJDF, the military profession or the legal profession, due to the relevance and social sensitivity of the functions under its responsibility.

Induction is a relevant element in the national systems in order for newly entering public servants to integrate, to identify with the mission and objectives of their respective institutions and to be encouraged in the vocation of service. In the departments studied, the length of the induction courses differs significantly: in the INEGI it is four hours long, in the Military School two months, one day in the CNA, one week in the Agrarian Court and five weeks long in the professional agrarian service, or else forms part of the studies previous to entry, such as the one-year master's in the Foreign Service, the nine months' basic training course for the PGJDF, or the basic training of the PGR and Judiciary Council.

Evaluation and training

Two excellent aspects of the Career Civil Service are evaluation and training. As mentioned above, these items represent two of the most important advantages offered by this method of public servant administration. The evaluation can take diverse forms depending on the institution concerned (Table 5.4); these range from one's academic degree to individual psychology.

As far as training is concerned, this is basically presented in two forms: centralized or non-centralized (Table 5.5).

Promotion

For advancement or promotion, the vertical structure is predominant, where the public servant's only option for higher income is if he moves to a higher category or level. This is the case of the Foreign Service, the CNA, the Agrarian Attorney's office, the PGR, and the PGJDF. As far as the INEGI is concerned, it has a specific structure that allows rises in salary to be obtained in the same post; and in the teaching profession there exists a system of horizontal promotion in five levels for obtaining economic improvements. In the Bank of Mexico, out of the five wage scales that are handled, those known as "development" scales have 18 levels that allow the personnel to obtain raises in salary periodically at the immediate boss's proposal or, when pertinent, with the authorization of the Committee of Promotion Management, depending on the category and level.

Table 5.4 Performance evaluation

Institution	Evaluation Parameters									
	AD	P	S	O	G	T	Per	E	Q	Psy
Mexican Foreign Service	x		x				x			
Comprehensive Professionalization System of the INEGI	x		x	x	x	x	x			
Teaching profession	x		x			x	x			
System of Specialists in Hydraulics	x		x		x	x	x			
Professional Electoral Service	x	x	x	x	x					
Professional Agrarian Service	x	x	x	x	x		x			
Career Civil Service of the PGR		x	x			x		x	x	
Career Civil Service of the PGJDF										x
Military profession	x		x				x			
Legal profession	x		x				x			

AD = Academic degrees
P = Profile
S = Seniority
O = Attainment of immediate objectives
G = Attainment of ultimate goals
T = Acquired training
Per = Performance
E = Efficiency
Q = Quality
Psy = Psychology

Table 5.5 Centralized and non-centralized training

Institution	Centralized	Non-centralized
Mexican Foreign Service	Matías Romero Institute	
Comprehensive System of Professionalization of the INEGI	INEGI	
Teaching profession	SEP	
System of Specialists in Hydraulics	CNA	
Servicio Profesional Electoral		Learning education
Professional Agrarian Service	Agrarian Attorney's Office	Regional offices
Career Civil Service of the PGR	Training Institute	
Career Civil Service of the PGJDF	Professional Qualification Institute	
Military profession	General Direction for Military Education	
Legal profession	Judiciary Institute	
Tribunal Superior Agrario	Center for Studies in Agrarian Justice	

In order to guarantee a line of promotion, as in other countries, the corresponding procedures are regulated by a joint commission according to the normativity for this purpose. Consequently, positions inside the system can only be held temporarily by people from outside, as in the case of members of the foreign service, agents in the Attorney General's Office, agents of the Federal Judicial Police or experts of the PGR. An exception to this is found in the professional agrarian service, which indicates that the attorney general can make engagements directly in category "G" (deputy or general director) provided these do not represent more than half of the total number of positions in this category.

Incentives

In spite of being recognized in most of the systems of professionalization, incentives and rewards have suffered from design problems, by not taking into account the budgetary availability. It is important to point out the case of the teaching profession, since although this system offers rises ranging from 28%, starting with the initial position of level "A", to 219% for level "E", taking as reference point the same initial position, it is common for educators deserving of incentives for satisfactory evaluations not to receive them promptly. There is a lack of available budget partly due to the fact that the system grants economic stimuli that are permanently assimilated to the salary, even when the educator subsequently lowers his level of performance, which makes it impossible for others to obtain them. A specific example of the problems generated by faulty design is that of the Agrarian Attorney's office, where the Professional Service Commission had decided in 1995, with the authorization of the Secretary of National Revenue and Public Credit that, according to the evaluations of the members of the system, they would be granted quantities equivalent to one month's salary for a grading of "satisfactory" and two months for "excellent"; but they could not completely cover these amounts because the latter department did not liberate the funds agreed on. Neither the Agrarian Attorney's office nor the SHCP foresaw that this incentive could not be offered to *all* public servants without incurring budgetary deficits. The system should have reserved an amount or fund set apart for incentives and awarded them to a certain number of personnel per rank.

   In contrast, the situation of the PGR is peculiar, since there is a system of economic incentives distributed in four levels in which 20% of the total personnel that makes up the staff participates, according to evaluations of its productivity, initiative, value, loyalty and honesty in the performance of its functions. These incentives can be granted by virtue of the fact that funds for this purpose are obtained by alienating goods insured by the institution and are granted according to the availability of resources.

Retirement

Retirement conditions for causes out of the public servants' hands are generally unfavorable, since there is no severance pay. An example of this was witnessed in the IFE, where personnel of the professional service were terminated from that organization, as a consequence of measures of organizational downsizing that took place in 1995 and early 1996, prompted by budgetary adjustments, without any compensation being involved.

The Foreign Service constitutes an exceptional case, since if the removal is not due to sanction, severance pay is invariably granted that is equivalent to one month's salary for every year of services, calculated on the basis of the last salary received by the public servant, up to a maximum of twelve months. In this service, retirement age is 60.

Having generally described and compared some of the different institutional systems existing in Mexico, these institutions are now described, analyzed and evaluated - in more detail.

Inter-secretarial Commission of the Career Civil Service

As was mentioned in the introduction to this chapter, the Inter-Secretarial Commission of the Career Civil Service was created in 1983, and made up of the Departments of the Interior, Programming and Budget, General Comptrollership of the Federation, Public Education, and of Labor and Social Prevision, as well as of the general secretary of the CEN of the FSTSE, whose main functions are: to promote the execution of specific programs of the Career Civil Service, to the departments and agencies of the federal public administration; to promote coordination mechanisms among the departments and agencies in order to standardize and systematize methods of personnel administration and development, aimed at implementing the Career Civil Service; to determine and propose elements that would permit the adaptation and integration of the legal and administrative framework that the setting-up of the Career Civil Service would require; to promote mechanisms of permanent participation to integrate and unify the postures of the departments and agencies, as well as what corresponds to the union representations in the implementation of the

Career Civil Service, as well as studying and issuing the necessary recommendations to ensure consistency in the norms, systems and procedures of the Career Civil Service with the instruments of the National System of Democratic Planning, ensuring their compatibility with the National Development Plan.

The Inter-Secretarial Commission of the Civil Service was created as a pioneer instrument in the coordination and consulting of the Federal Executive Power for setting up the Career Civil Service in the federal public administration. The work committees advise the Technical Subcommittee in the establishment of norms, the area of labor law and in carrying out studies in the departments and agencies that belong to their specific area. These committees are coordinated by auxiliary secretaries of the technical subcommittee.

The auxiliary secretaries are the official channel for informing the general coordinator on opinions, verdicts or projects of the work committees. The auxiliary secretary convenes meetings, takes minutes of the sessions and informs the general coordinator of the subcommittee on advances in the tasks; lastly, he/she submits a bimonthly report to the subcommittee.

The Technical Subcommittee meets every month in ordinary session, which is summoned with three days' advance notice by the general coordinator. In order for the session to be held, a quorum of two thirds of its members is required.

The general coordinator of the Technical Subcommittee convenes sessions of a preparatory nature for members of the subcommittee, and by means of the auxiliary secretaries convenes general sessions for the work committees. He/she is also to take charge of the normativity of the operation of the work committees, and requests the reports necessary for preparing their studies from the departments and agencies of the federal government, according to the goals of the subcommittee.

The general coordinator takes the minutes of the sessions, collects the necessary signatures in order to legally requisition the documents of the subcommittee and submits a bimonthly report to the commission of the progress in the work being carried out.

As for the technical secretary of the Inter-Secretarial Commission, (s)he convenes the heads of the commission with three days advance notice to the ordinary sessions, which are carried out every two months. To hold a session a quorum of two-thirds of their members is required.

At the conclusion of the sessions, the technical secretary takes the corresponding minutes, and the president of the commission is in charge of notifying the competent bodies of the agreements, for their general observance, and is to keep the president of the Republic informed, at all times, about advances in the work commissioned.

For reasons of logistics and incentives among the institutions, the commission in question has been normative (existing on paper) rather than real. As shown by the international cases evaluated in this work, a "supra-secretarial" organism is required, invested with enough authority to reconcile interests between departments, in order to reach satisfactory results.

National Institute of Statistics, Geography and Computing

Comprehensive system of Professionalization

The normative framework that regulates the functioning of the Comprehensive System of Professionalization (SIP) is in the agreement issued by the Internal Revenue Department on November 11, 1994, and published in the *Official Journal of the Federation*. The system is coordinated by a commission called the SIP-INEGI Commission, made up of:

1. The president of the Institute
2. The administrative coordinator of the Institute
3. The directors general of the Institute
4. The regional directors for the Northern and North Central areas
5. The director of the Administration and Services to Personnel Unit
6. The director of Planning and Training
7. The director of the Integration and Budgetary Analysis Unit
8. The director of the Unit of Integration and Budgetary Analysis
9. The technical director of Geography headquarters
10. The director of National Censuses of Statistics headquarters
11. The director of Systems Development of Computing Policy headquarters
12. The director of Normativity and Editorial Production of the Integration and Information Analysis headquarters
13. The director of Legal Aid

14. The director of Auditing

In this commission, the president of the institute has the deciding vote in the event of a tie and is the one who presides over the commission. As for the regional directors for the Northern and North Central areas, they are included as representatives of the other regional offices, which add up to ten altogether. The director of the Administration and Services to Personnel Unit acts as technical secretary for the commission; this unit is responsible at the same time for the operation and control of the system. When the commission addresses matters related to tenured workers, then the general secretary of the National Union of Workers of the INEGI must be incorporated.

The SIP-INEGI Commission is the maximum decision-making body in the system and its functions include:

1. Coordinating and overseeing the operation of the system.
2. Approving the norms and limits for the operation of the system.
3. Determining the creation of subcommittees and the members that should participate in them.
4. Giving verdicts regarding the competitive exams and competitions, and application for rises in salary.
5. Preparing proposals for modifying, adding to or repealing the SIP agreement.
6. Authorizing the dismissal from the public services through the Administrative Coordination.
7. Approving the design and content of the evaluation instruments for purposes of rises in salary level.
8. Resolving the applications for revisions of the verdicts given in competitive exams or competitions.

Also, the SIP-INEGI Commission has two subcommittees: one for preparing exams, and the budgetary subcommittee.

The former is responsible for the preparation and design of technical exams for personnel entering, or those whose job it is to apply for promotions for the internal personnel; also, it is responsible for updating these exams and for coordinating study guides for the competitive exams and competitions. The second commission is in charge of managing the budget in regard to rises, aids and promotions. The agreement establishes a catalog of ten positions for the personnel:

1. Services and support
2. Technician
3. Specialist/secretarial
4. Head of project
5. Assistant head of department
6. Assistant area director
7. Area director
8. Regional director
9. General director and coordinators
10. President of the INEGI

These positions are classified in turn into three subsystems, with regard to the mode of hiring:

1. Subsystem of personnel with tenure: support service, technician, specialist.
2. Subsystem of professionalization of appointed personnel: secretary, project head, assistant head of department, head of department, assistant area director, area director.
3. Subsystem of personnel engaged under general norms of the federal public sector: regional director, director general, coordinators, president of the INEGI, equivalent positions according to regulations (staff).

Operation of the SIP

In 1991 the design began of what is now the Comprehensive System of Professionalization, which began functioning as of January, 1994; to date, there are approximately 35,000 INEGI employees in this system.

The principles established institutionally that orient the SIP are:

1. The best situation for personnel according to their capacities and potential, as well as the needs of the institution.
2. Designs of the "challenging" worker, which means that the work should be rewarding in itself and with possibilities for growth.
3. Clarity in the work objectives, functions and programs.
4. Learning in the job itself, based on the carrying out, evaluation and feedback of the performance.

5. Co-responsibility at all levels of the organization in the different phases and activities, to promote continuous improvement in work processes and personnel development.
6. Enlarge the range of options for training and refresher courses.

The SIP is made up of six basic programs:

1. *Human resources requirements*. The program objective is to provide the necessary information on the requirements for personnel and their characteristics in order to support the process of decision-making in regard to personnel through the integration and updating of the catalog of positions, as well as the inventory of human resources.

2. *Recruitment, selection and hiring of personnel*. In this program, procedures are developed that allow the ideal or best qualified personnel to be identified and incorporated to satisfy the needs for personnel or to fill existing vacancies.

3. *Induction*. In this program activities are carried out by means of which the personnel are provided with information and orientation about the institution and about their work area, so as to facilitate their integration and adaptation into the job environment.

4. *Directing and evaluating performance*. This is more directed to the bosses than to the personnel of lower hierarchical levels, since what is wanted is for the boss to achieve an appropriate programming of the work, for him to orient, direct, evaluate and get feedback on the work of the personnel in his charge.

5. *Planning and development of personnel*. The objective of this program is, above all, to promote the individual betterment of the personnel by means of training and development of human resources.

6. *Remuneration and movement of personnel*. The activities that are developed under this program are those oriented toward establishing the mechanisms for recognizing and stimulating outstanding performance, experience and capacity of the employees, and at the same time establish the mechanisms for providing opportunities for access to other positions or salary raises in the same position.

Process of entry and promotion

The process begins formally with the application to fill a vacant post, which is authorized for competition in the central Administrative Sub-direction through the Administration and Services to Personnel Unit, which, after authorization, proceeds to issue the corresponding competition announcement. The announcement issued indicates the professional specialization that is required, the type and number of places in the competition, the specific position being competed for, the corresponding attachment, work schedules and general requirements (academic level, age, experience, etc.). Interested parties are also informed of the procedure and deadline for fulfilling the requirements. It should be mentioned that the competitions may be open or closed; generally, the announcements are posted in appropriate places inside the facilities of the INEGI, not in the mass media.

Once the candidates have gathered the documentation required for the competition and handed it in to the corresponding authorities, it is checked to determine whether the candidate has the necessary qualifications. By analyzing the documents it is established whether the applicant has the required profile or not. If (s)he passes this phase, the candidate is then registered to present the evaluation (technical exam for heads of department and lower, and competition for assistant director and higher). At this point in the process, the applicant is supplied with a study guide with the main topics and concepts dealt with on the exam. The exam is prepared from a database, through a computing system that produces different exams for each participant; each exam contains, of course, the same concepts and the same level of difficulty.

The subcommittee for preparing and updating exams applies the technical evaluation, marks it and hands in the results to the technical secretary of the Administration and Services to Personnel Unit. The applicants who have obtained satisfactory marks move on to the phase of psychometric evaluation, in which a comprehensive evaluation of the person's skills, capacities and interests is made. Those who have obtained satisfactory evaluations are given a technical interview by the boss of the petitioning area of personnel, who selects the candidate and makes the proposal to the corresponding subcommittee.

The subcommittee evaluates the petitioning area's proposal and submits it for consideration to the SIP-INEGI Commission, which decides finally on the proposal to hire or promote the candidate.

Promotion refers not only to the possibility of acceding to a position of a higher hierarchical level, but also to the possibility of achieving a salary increase in the same position owing to the seven ranks in the salary scale for the same position. This means that the rise in salary does not depend on the position itself, nor on a change of activity, nor on the retirement of the person who holds the position immediately above.

The process for achieving a rise in salary begins with a proposal that should be made by the immediate boss, justifying the worker's excellent performance. This performance must be characterized by the achievement of goals and contribution to the work. This proposal is sent to the corresponding subcommittee, which must validate the proposal and send it to the SIP-INEGI Commission, which makes the final verdict. If a worker is not being fairly evaluated by his boss, the system has a mechanism that allows the worker to "justify himself" in his performance and thus seek promotion. The worker must draw up the justification for appealing his case to be handed in to the corresponding subcommittee, and then to the SIP-INEGI Commission for the final decision.

Training

Training and professional development are carried out by means of courses, workshops and classes, although this does not prevent other mechanisms for betterment from being established, such as the facilities offered to the personnel who want to take specialization or graduate studies in other educational institutions. The INEGI has a building for training activities. The courses are not established systematically for all the personnel, and besides are not of an obligatory nature.

Termination of employment

The public servant that has not had a rise in salary, promotion or satisfactory evaluation over a period of three years will have to undergo an evaluation and exam for updating. If he obtains the minimum marks, the SIP-INEGI Commission will grant him six months to improve his mark, during which time he will be able to attend training courses. At the end of this interval he will be evaluated again and will be given an exam; if he does not achieve positive results, the commission will decide on his dismissal.

Conclusions

The INEGI implemented a professionalization system that covers all its employees (in three subsystems), although the service only includes *de facto* one subsystem; the other two are for tenured and freely engaged personnel.

Although the system of professionalization of the INEGI shows undeniable achievements over most of the cases presented in this book, it undeniably has some limitations also.

On one hand, the expectations of the employees that entered the system have not been fulfilled because the system was perceived as a mechanism for increasing salary permanently and not as a way of rewarding excellent performance (according to budgetary availability).

On the other hand, as in other systems, the evaluation and termination of employment of the officials is a complicated aspect to implement. In fact, the annual evaluation stipulated in the agreement of the creation of the professionalization service has not been able to be carried out systematically. The causes for this are very diverse and have to do with the impossibility of creating a profile for each position, but also with the *organizational culture itself* of the institution. To the extent that evaluation is not determined as a point in time, but rather requires a systematic monitoring of the activities of each of the officials (which is the responsibility of the different bosses), applying the evaluation annually would require an important percentage of the bosses' time in the respective areas. Consequently, the employment termination mechanisms based on performance have hardly ever operated in practice.

Regarding advantages that should be emphasized, it is important to mention that the SIP resolves the duality of systems (free engagement and tenure vs. career personnel) through the subsystems. In this way it was possible to solve the problems of the freely designated officials inside the professionalization service, without sacrificing too much the flexibility that this type of engagement implies.

Another of the advantages of the system is that the training of the officials - by not being obligatory and not being a formal part of the system of performance evaluation - acts as a means (as so it should) for officials to be trained and have greater opportunities for promotion without accumulating points *per se*.

SIP, unlike other systems (such as that of External Relations or the teaching profession), is not a self-contained system in its own promotion ladder, that is to say, the entry to any post is open, in such a way that it is not necessary to be in the position immediately below; in fact, it is not even necessary to be an official of the institution in order to compete. Of course, this has the logic of selecting the most able officials for the performance of the duties of a specific position, thus extending the range of options. Of course, it is assumed that employees of the INEGI, and especially those linked to the areas where the vacancy was opened, have an advantage because of the knowledge acquired in the performance of their functions, but this is implicit and must be demonstrated in the exams.

Department of External Affairs

The Career Foreign Service is the permanent body of officials of the State, specifically in charge of representing it abroad and responsible for executing the foreign policy of Mexico. Since 1922, entry to the Mexican Career Foreign Service has been effected by means of public competitions.[2]

The Mexican Foreign Service is made up of career personnel, temporary personnel and assimilated personnel. Career personnel is permanent and includes two branches:

1. Diplomatic-consular branch.
   Diplomatic-consular corps:

   Ambassador
   Minister
   Counselor
   First secretary
   Second secretary
   Third secretary
   Diplomatic attaché

2. Technical-administrative Branch.
   Technical-administrative body:

   Administrative coordinator
   Administrative attaché "A"
   Administrative attaché "B"
   Administrative attaché "C"
   Administrative technician "A"
   Administrative technician "B"
   Administrative technician "C"

Temporary personnel. Designated by agreement with the president. Carries out specific functions in a certain attachment and for a definite term, at the end of which their functions cease automatically. Therefore, these personnel do not form part of the Career Foreign Service and the respective promotion ladders, but are subject to the same obligations as career personnel.

Assimilated personnel. Made up of officials and attachés to diplomatic missions and consular representations, whose engagement has been negotiated by another dependence or competent authority of the federal public administration. Their assimilation only has effect while the commission lasts and is credited with the rank determined by the ministry.

The secretariat tries to make sure that the structure of posts in the different categories allows for appropriate mobilization on the promotion ladder, thus obtaining a pyramid between the categories of diplomatic attaché and minister.

The secretariat proposes to the Income Tax authorities (SHCP), the scales of the salaries of the members of the foreign service abroad, according to the cost of living of each place. For this reason, every year the Personnel Commission revises the pay formula according to the information it has on the cost of living periodically published by two international institutions (one of which is the United Nations Organization), in order to adapt the criteria of payment of the Foreign Service personnel's fees and to propose adjustments in the salary scale authorized by the Secretariat of Internal Revenue and Public Credit.

Normativity for selecting personnel

Entry as a career official into the diplomatic-consular and technical-administrative branches is carried out by opposition, by means of public competitions that are organized into eliminatory stages.

Diplomatic-consular branch

1. Exams and courses.
2. Exam of general culture oriented toward international relations.
3. Spanish exam.
4. Exams to check the mastery of a foreign language and the capacity to translate another.
5. Preparation of an essay on a current topic in foreign policy.

6. Interviews with officials of the Secretariat and, when appropriate, specialized courses lasting a minimum of six months at the Matías Romero Institute of Diplomatic Studies plus an additional year of practical experience in the Secretariat.

Entry as career personnel into the technical-administrative branch will be by means of a public exam whose modes will be determined by the department for entry at the level of administrative technician "C".

The requirements for entering the Career Foreign Service are the following:

1. To be Mexican by birth.
2. To be under 30 years of age (in exceptional cases, due to academic and professional profile, the entry commission could dispense with this requirement).
3. To have a good background.
4. To be suitable physically and mentally for the duties of the foreign service.
5. Not to be a member of the clergy.
6. Tó have at least a Bachelor's degree. (For the technical-administrative branch, the crediting of senior high school and the mastery of a foreign language is sufficient.)

Application and evaluation of exams

The exams are applied by the same department and evaluated by a body called the "Personnel Committee", presided over by the director general of the Matías Romero Institute, and made up of representatives of institutions of higher learning who have their degree in International Relations, as well as the director general in charge of Foreign Service affairs.

After an interval of one year, those admitted are evaluated by the Personnel Commission to determine if their engagement and definitive entry into the Foreign Service and, where applicable, the corresponding promotion, are recommended.

Performance evaluation

The commission carries out recommendations to the secretary of External Affairs for the entry, re-incorporation, promotions, transfers, commissions, sanctions, retirement, etc. The secretary also proposes the internal regulations of the department. The evaluations of the performance of the officials is carried out through competitive exams in order to promote up the ladder, in branches included in the Career Foreign Service and to encourage the mobility of positions inside the Foreign Service itself.

The Personnel Commission is made up of a career ambassador, the head official in the Department, the director general of Human Resources Affairs, the director general of Legal Affairs and three officials designated by the secretary of External Relations.

Promotion evaluation for career personnel

In the positions of second and first secretary, counselor and minister of the diplomatic-consular branch; in the technical-administrative branch, the positions of administrative-attaché "C" and administrative coordinator; the promotion competitions are organized by the Personnel Commission. In the other categories, the External Relations minister agrees to the promotions on the recommendation of the commission. The evaluation of the personal files will be made known to interested parties in advance of the exams dates, and the final result of the competitions will be public domain.

1. Evaluation of the applicants' file:
   a) Merits and efficiency demonstrated in the performance of his duties and commissions.
   b) Greater seniority in the category and service.
2. Written and oral exams:
   a) Additional points for published works and studies.
   b) Studies completed.

For the positions, in the diplomatic-consular branch, as minister, counselor, first and second secretaries; and in the technical-administrative branch, positions of administrative coordinator and administrative attaché "C", the secretary of the department is to hold promotion competitions annually.

The seniority requirements for promotion to positions subject to competition are:

1. Entry as third secretary: minimum two years' seniority and participation in the entry competition.

2. Entry as second secretary: minimum four years' seniority and participation in the entry and promotion competitions.
3. Entry as first secretary: minimum six years' seniority and participation in entrance and promotion competitions.
4. Entry as counselor: minimum eight years' seniority and participation in entrance and promotion competitions.

For the technical-administrative branch, the employees that have four years' seniority will be able to enter at technical-administrative category "B" and those who accumulate seven years, at technical-administrative category "A".

Cases of immobility in promotion ladder and causes for termination of employment from the Career Foreign Service

If a third secretary, second secretary, first secretary or counselor from the career personnel of the diplomatic-consular branch has not been promoted to the category immediately above over a seven year period, the Personnel Commission must give a report to the secretary of External Affairs, explaining if the official passed the corresponding exams, but there have not been enough positions for his promotion. If this is not the cause of lack of mobility in the promotion ladder, the commission will determine whether it is due to lack of sufficient merits for promotion, according to the evaluation made of the record of the official in question or for not passing the promotion exams on three consecutive occasions. If one of these is the cause, then the secretary of External Affairs can agree to one of the following decisions:

1. To invite the official to the next promotion competition. This measure can only be authorized on one single occasion during his career.
2. To grant the official a post in the technical-administrative branch, provided he/she has a good record.
3. To terminate his/her employment from the Foreign Service. In any event, he/she will be given the severance pay indicated by the terms in the regulation of the Foreign Service Act.
4. Resignation, retirement or having incurred some administrative sanction will be cause for termination of employment.

Incentives and rewards

The secretary, according to budget availability and previous authorization from the SHCP, has a program of incentives and rewards for the auxiliary employees who have given outstanding service, or who have distinguished themselves for their loyalty and length of service to their country.

Free engagement

Inside the Career Foreign Service there exist levels at which free engagement of officials is used.

The designation of ambassadors and general consuls is determined by the president of the Republic, preferably from among the career officials displaying greater competence, category and seniority in the diplomatic-consular branch. The External Affairs secretary submits the names and background of the ministers in the career personnel who, in his opinion, have the necessary merits, to the president of the Republic for consideration. Those who are designated in this way do not lose their status as members of the career personnel of the Foreign Service.

Conclusions

The Secretariat of External Affairs in fact has two parallel systems of personnel: one attached to the career service and the officials named according to the norms for appointed personnel in the public sector.

Officials belonging to the career service may or may not have a commission (specifically those of the consular branch). In this system there is a clear division between the position (the functions that the official is carrying out at that moment) and the post (hierarchical level inside the career service).

The apparent problem in this situation is that both systems are dispersed horizontally and vertically inside the organizational structure of the secretariat. For example, a director general may or may not belong to the career service (ambassadors are the ones who have this salary level), but if inside the secretariat it is decided not to assign career personnel, the payroll expenses increase considerably.

Another of the problems in this duality of systems is that the commissions of higher rank (such as the embassies) can be held by temporary personnel (presidential appointment), as in fact happens with the main embassies. To the extent that these engagements have been systematic and not justified by reasons of merit, this has damaged the functionality of the system itself.

On the other hand, the career service is a self-contained system (such as the teachers' profession) where it is necessary to start from the bottom and work up. This hampers the achievement of one of the main objectives of the career service: to hire more qualified people to exercise functions specific to a position. In fact, this restriction is a barrier for entry to these positions so that, if an individual wants to accede to a minister's position, for example, he must first move up through the whole scale (which represents eight years of seniority in the average scenario).

As for the evaluation and termination of employment of the officials within the system of career service, there is a personnel commission in charge of these functions. However, concerning the evaluation, the criterion of seniority is a factor that weighs heavily. It is also specified that those officials who fail three promotion exams consecutively, or who have not been promoted over a period of seven years, will be able to present the next promotion exam only once, or they will be given the possibility of holding a position in the technical-administrative system, or else their employment may be terminated from the Foreign Service (with the corresponding severance pay). The serious problem with this termination mechanism is its applicability, the incentives involved and the expensive installation process to make them effective.

On the other hand, as one reaches the positions of higher rank (such as consul or ambassador), there are no evaluation or termination mechanisms for these officials.

National Water Commission

According to the concepts established in the Public Administration Modernization Program (Promap, abbreviation in Spanish), and generated by the Secretary of the Comptrollership and Administrative Development (Secodam abbreviation in Spanish), the National Water Commission (CNA, initials in Spanish) has implemented the Program of Personnel Development (PDP, initials in Spanish). This consists basically of the implementation of individual actions that are however related to each other, that help to create plans for the professionalization of public servants, up to a certain level of the institution, establishing the necessary methodology for recapturing and revitalizing a Career Civil Service (SCC, initials in Spanish).

To this end, the CNA has three main branches of personnel, of which - depending on the situation of the public servant, the most appropriate plan for its development is established (see figure 5.3).

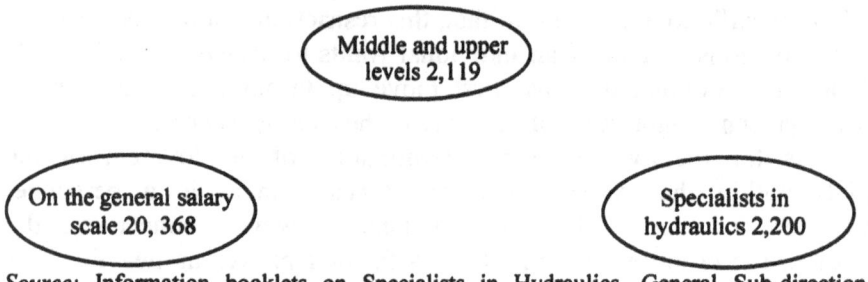

Source: Information booklets on Specialists in Hydraulics, General Sub-direction of Personnel Administration and Management.

Figure 5.3   Personnel of the National Water Commission

Derived from this, and in accordance with the situation of the personnel inside these branches, a plan is established according to the universe in which they are developing, seeking the best options for their development and growth inside the institution. This is done gradually, over the middle and long term, for them to move into a position of greater responsibility inside the same occupational group or in another branch, as the case may be, depending on their performance, career direction, etc.

For the PDP the intervention of the different administrative units of Personnel Management is required, within their respective spheres of action, without this distracting from their habitual functions or their established objectives and goals, these being:

1. The Salaries Sub-management, in charge of controlling and generating authorizations for movements of rises and/or promotion that are granted to personnel, including kardex and payroll data, in which the basic data of the work force of the National Water Commission are registered, in their databases.
2. The Administrative Modernization Sub-management, an area in charge of coordinating the Promap on the inside of the institution, also runs programs of training, organization, recruitment, selection and of specialists in hydraulics; also having basic information about the

personnel in middle management and equivalent positions of consulting and of specialists.

3. The Work Reconciliation Sub-management has information on personnel on the general payroll list for tenured and appointed personnel. It is a key link of the PDP with the union, since knowing the promotion system of the latter will make it possible to establish a plan for the life and career of their personnel,, in such a way that it is not opposed - at any given moment - to that established by the union.

For the appropriate comprehensive management of all the information, this program proposes its unification into a single computing system that allows monitoring of personnel that are getting ready to cover the different positions, without this signifying the discarding of the current bases; on the contrary, it will consolidate the establishment of uniform criteria for capturing data in each of them for information feedback through the program.

The PDP establishes that the Life and Career Plans should be initiated, with the objective of providing public servants with the training required in technical aspects and in skills development, which is necessary to occupy new positions within their level of development in order to move to the following branch with the minimum of knowledge and skills established for performing the new duties. Also established are the systems of monitoring and evaluation, the programs of incentives and training, the evaluation of posts and especially a close link with the areas involved in the process of personnel incorporation.

Personnel Management is the only area empowered to grant authorizations for movements, for which purpose it has a database in which it is possible to consult immediately the legitimacy or otherwise of the applications for filling vacancies. By verifying and authorizing the filling of the vacancy, this is intended to generate a format to notify the corresponding movement both to the petitioning area and to the Administrative Modernization Submanagement. The former must issue the application for substitution and propose candidates, and the latter is to provide the information required about viable internal candidates, according to the substitution tables.

The system is oriented toward the training of candidates for the position immediately above them inside the universe in which he/she works or for entering another occupational branch.

With the establishment of a database that monitors personnel and in which the individual achievements are registered, it is possible to choose the appropriate candidate promptly and to have the elements necessary for making decisions in the recruitment and promotion of personnel. According to this, when a vacancy is created, internal candidates who fulfill the established requirements for the position are to be proposed.

In the specific case of personnel on the general payroll, promotion is negotiated according to the stepwise promotion program of the union, in order to avoid divergences with respect to movements approved within this occupational branch.

This establishes the controls required for the introduction of the PDP, whose aim is to have the information permanently up to date on the movements originating in the standard turnover of the institution, without stimulating growth proportionally to its work force. By establishing a stepwise promotion of all personnel, the vacant positions will correspond to the lowest levels in the general salary scale.

The achievement over the middle and long term is the professionalization and creation of a true public career within the CNA that will enable there to be replacement tables of candidates suitable to cover the next level of responsibility, thus making it possible to achieve the objectives and goals established for the institution.

Advantages

1. It allows for orienting the training of personnel with characteristics and skills required to occupy positions of greater responsibility.
2. It increases the identification of the personnel with the objectives of the institution.
3. The process to be followed for filling vacancies is institutionalized.
4. Replacement tables with qualified internal personnel are generated.
5. Matching of methods for capturing information among the internal units of Personnel Management.
6. Expedites the information system for authorizing the filling of vacancies.

Scope

Appointed employees At the present time a system of career civil service is being established, starting from the level of heads of unit to assistant managers. The positions of managers, general assistant directors and director general are granted by means of free engagement.

As part of the career civil service, the category of Specialists in Hydraulics was created, incorporating qualified professionals capable of being developed over the middle and long term, as active participants in carrying out the fundamental programs of the CNA. At the same time as they improve their execution capacity inside the institution, they guarantee future continuity of the programs. This category forms an intermediate level between appointed and tenured personnel that gives rise to technical support personnel (analysts), and is made up of 16 levels. This program originated in 1989 through the installation of efficient methods of recruitment, selection, evaluation and development of personnel.

Among aids to personnel of Specialists in Hydraulics are:

1. Establishment of the Graduation Program based on different agreements established with institutions of higher education. This program contemplates aid in the administration of academic-administrative procedures: seminars given in thesis-writing and courses in investigation methodology; validation of social service; reimbursement of expenses incurred by completing the degree, contemplating the printing of up to 25 copies of the thesis, payment of degree registration and professional identification; payment for right to professional exam, payment to jury members, payment of document of professional exam and payment of degree document.
2. Continuous training. Training courses are constantly being designed and developed, emphasizing aspects such as technical knowledge and managerial skills.
3. Training of a qualified cadre of employees to cover vacant posts in the event they satisfy the profile demanded by the flow-chart or position.

Tenured employees Different measures have been implemented to permit the entry of tenured workers into the program of career civil service; among these measures are training and instruction programs for a selected cadre of personnel.

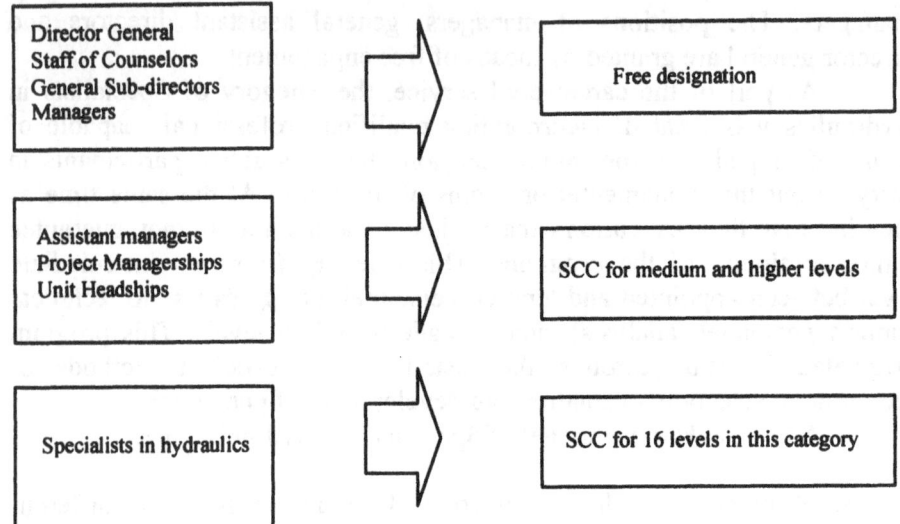

Figure 5.4 Structure

Salary Scale

1. There are 20,368 employees on the general payroll; this category personnel considers all operative, tenured or unionized personnel.
2. There are 2,119 personnel in the middle and higher leves, of which 10% are freely engaged. The salary scale for this group of employees is designed by the Secodam in coordination with the SHCP.

About 2,220 posts have been created for specialists in hydraulics, around whom the core of the career civil service program is centered. This program has a specific salary scale authorized by the SHCP, and has been designed so that the CNA will be competitive in the job market for qualified personnel. The salary scale contemplates the following levels:

Table 5.6 Salary scale

Level	Amount
I S	1,647
II S	2,087
III S	2,632
IV S	2,998
V S	3,362
VI S	3,466
VII S	3,994
VIII S	4,202
IX S	4,463
X S	4,737
XI S	5,269
XII S	6,006
XIII S	6,575
XIV S	7,168
XV S	7,455
XVI S	8,036

Source: Information pamphlets on Specialists in hydraulics. General Sub-direction of Personnel Administration and Management.

Entry and evaluation Entry takes place through open or closed competitions. In the former case, two groups are considered:

1. Those lending social service, through different agreements with the institutions of higher learning.
2. External candidates, through agreements with associations of professionals, companies and private.

As in the case of closed competitions, only employees of the National Water Commission are considered candidates.

The Personnel Management defines the selection criteria through the corresponding area. The CNA observes the normativity of the National Commission of the SCC, but establishes more specific criteria given the technical characteristics that are required in a great number of these positions.

The aspects to be evaluated are:

1. Curricular analysis:

    a) Education level
    b) Experience
    c) Comparison of profile with mission of the position
2. Initial interview:
    a) Personal and professional background
3. Technical interview:
    a) Level of technical knowledge about the area he/she wishes to enter

Performance evaluation The evaluation system is yearly and is made up of four marks:

1. A self-evaluation that implies a reflection on the achievement, development, attitude and behavior of the individual in question during the previous period.
2. Evaluation made by the head of the area.
3. Immediate boss's evaluation.
4. Manager's evaluation.

Termination of employment and incentives In case the evaluation is not satisfactory on two consecutive occasions, the employee being evaluated will be dismissed or reallocated.

    The economic incentives are conditional on SHCP authorization so that an internal program of incentives has been implemented that considers:

1. *Graduation.* This program offers both academic and administrative support.
2. *Training.* It allows access to constant updating.
3. *Scholarships for graduate studies.*

Conclusions The Program of Personnel Development (PDP) of the National Water Commission only includes appointed employees, and under this heading are those attached to the PDP and those freely designated, which in real terms means that less than 20% of the total number of employees of the Commission are attached to this system.

    One of the main problems facing the system is centered on the evaluation and termination mechanisms; especially, in the latter it is stipulated that in the event of not obtaining two satisfactory evaluations, the official will be fired or reallocated.

The problem with a system of this type are the "cultural" costs and the costs of correct methodological evaluations. On the other hand, although the evaluation system is extraordinarily precise in the weighting of each of the factors to be evaluated, the way these points are assigned to each of the factors is subject to the appreciation (mainly) of the employee's bosses and there are no clear mechanisms of appeal.

The evaluation system permits the worker's rise in the salary scale. But the system itself (unlike others, such as the teaching profession or the INEGI) specifies a minimum of points in order to achieve the rise. This gives the opportunity over the middle and long term if the CNA does not have sufficient budgetary funds to continue with the system.

Table 5.7 Evaluation scheme

Sections	Headings evaluated	Maximum points	Additional
Academic modifications	Refresher courses, Diploma courses	40 points	
Achievement of goals	Achievement of goals	64 points	Specialization 40 points
Performance	Performance in job and behavior of specialist	176 points	Master's 70 points
Technical capacity	Quality and promptness in handing in work and exploiting of resources	21 points	Doctorate 90 points
Communication	Interaction and communication, Boss-subordinate	6 points	Experience 54 points

Teaching Profession

The teaching profession was created in 1992 within the National Agreement for the Modernization of Basic Education.

The teaching profession is a stepwise system of horizontal promotion for teaching personnel of the subsystems of basic education, with its own rules and modes, that responds to the demand of teachers and their union organization for a mechanism that would allow for mobility within their own category, maintaining the current promotion ladder in effect without affecting the worker's labor rights.

In the National Agreement for the Modernization of Basic Education, the teaching profession aims at answering two necessities of the teaching activity in the country: to stimulate the quality of education and to establish a clear means of professional and material improvement of the teacher's social condition.

Thus the establishment of a mechanism for horizontal promotion is agreed on for teaching personnel. Its purpose is for teachers to accede, within the same function, to higher salary levels based on their academic education, efforts to take refresher courses, professional performance, and seniority in the service and in the levels of the teaching profession.

The general objective of the teaching profession is to improve the quality of Mexican education through recognizing and promoting the professionalization of teachers, and through improving the living, as well as working, conditions of the educators. Their specific objectives are:

1. To reinforce interest in the teachers' professional performance, by offering higher levels of payment for better educational quality.
2. To recognize teachers' performance and continuance in the teaching service, as well as their academic background, knowledge and attendance at refresher courses.
3. To promote the professional and work commitment of teachers at the educational level.
4. To carry out plans that promote a general participation of the teacher in the school and in the community, favoring greater recognition for the teaching activity.

Scope

Within the teaching profession all educators of basic education that have the following requirements can participate:

1. If they have tenured engagement (code 10).
2. If they have provisional engagement without graduating (code 95).
3. If they have the minimum seniority requirements.
4. If they have completed the academic degree required for each type of educational mode.

Modes

There are three modes of participation within the teaching profession, which depend on the functions or work carried out by the educator; namely:
1=AA Aspect- Classroom educators.
2=AA Aspect- Educators in functions of direction and supervision.
3=AA Aspect- Educators, directors and supervisors in technical-pedagogic functions.

These three modes of participation are to be evaluated according to the same parameters, first for entering the teaching profession and later for purposes of promotion at the five levels ("A", "B", "C", "D" and "E").

Table 5.8 Educational levels participating

1.	Initial	7.	Televised junior high
2.	Pre-school	8.	Physics
3.	Primary	9.	Special
4.	Indigenous	10.	Extra-mural
5.	Junior high	11.	Boarding
6.	Technical junior high	12.	Training centers

Each level of the teaching profession proposes its own requirements, so as to encourage the incorporation or promotion of those teachers who are most capable, have the best background, give the best performance, and can obtain the highest points in the evaluation system.

The differences in remunerations are covered by payment of compensation with the following characteristics:

1. It is modified in proportion to the increases registered in the associated positions.
2. It is taken into consideration for the Christmas bonus and vacation pay.
3. Compensation is subject to reasonable deductions according to the law.

Normativity for personnel selection

1. Procedure for registration in the teaching profession includes the following:
a) The educator hands in the following documents to the Academic* Evaluation Body (OEE):
   – Registration application
   – Certification of seniority
   – Last level of studies
   – Certification of refresher courses
b) The OEE reviews it and adds it to the file.
c) The OEE gives it to the supervisor, who passes it on to the central office for the corresponding educational level.
d) The database office receives the certifications and prepares the census of teachers participating in the teaching profession.
e) Once incorporated into the teaching profession, they are promoted to higher levels:
f) -The educators who receive most points in the five factors.
g) -Who cover the years of continuance indicated in the program's general guidelines.
h) -Who obtain the corresponding favorable verdict.
i) Evaluation and application are the responsibility of:
j) The Joint SEP-SNTE Commission.
k) The Academic Evaluation Body.

Table 5.9 Members of the Academic Evaluation Body (OEE, initials in Spanish)

In the case of complete schools	In the case of schools with one, two types of education, and incomplete
All members of the School's Technical Council.	All members of the Technical Council of the sectorized zone.
A representative of the SNTE.	A representative of the SNTE.
The director presides over the OEE.	The inspector or supervisor presides over the OEE.

Performance evaluation

The performance criteria for evaluation have been set by the Joint SEP-SNTE Commission:

1. *Seniority.* This is equal to the years of educational service performed in the basic education of the federal, state or municipal educational systems (10 points).
2. *Academic degree.* Documented certification of the academic degrees (15 points).
3. *Professional background.* Exam of basic knowledge for educational practices, mastery of the subject corresponding to the function carried out (25 points).
4. *Credited refresher courses.* Courses that the educational authority determines or authorizes (certification).
5. *Professional performance.* The sum of actions that the teacher carries out from day to day in interacting with his/her students in the educational process and in achieving significant results in terms of learning products.

The evaluation of professional performance is understood as the sum of actions that the teacher carries out from day to day in interacting with his students, with the school community and the community in general during the educational process, in order to obtain significant results in terms of learning products and changes in behavior.

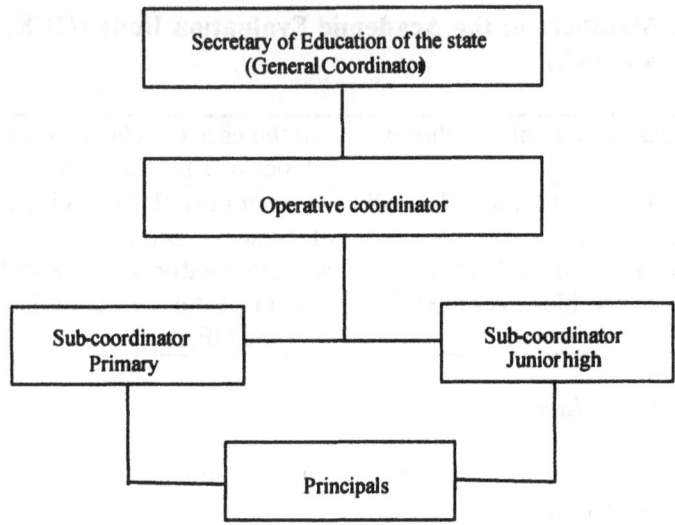

Figure 5.5   Operative structure in the joint SEP/SNTE commission

Table 5.10 Seniority

Years of service	Points	Years of service	Points
1	5	16	7.8
2	5	17	8
3	5.2	18	8.2
4	5.4	19	8.4
5	5.6	20	8.6
6	5.8	21	8.8
7	6	22	9
8	6.2	23	9.2
9	6.4	24	9.4
10	6.6	25	9.6
11	6.8	26	9.8
12	7	27	10
13	7.2	28	10
14	7.4	29	10
15	7.6	30	10

Table 5.11 Academic degree

Maximum level of studies	Points
Normal – basic	9
Normal – basic – Bachelor's degree	11
UPN Bachelor's (thesis not terminated)	10
UPN Bachelor's (thesis terminated)	11
Normal – higher – 75% of courses	9
Normal – higher – thesis not terminated	10
Normal – higher – thesis terminated	11
Master's – thesis not terminated	12
Master's – thesis terminated	13
Doctorate – candidate	14
Doctorate – terminated	15

The fundamental basis of this evaluation is the honest, committed participation of the professors who make up the Academic Evaluation Body (OEE, initials in Spanish), who are to consider the evaluation made by the principal of the school and the self-evaluation made by the educator of his/her own teaching work.

This evaluation is based on the following factors: planning of the teaching-learning process; development of the teaching-learning process; participation in the functioning of the school; participation in the school-community interaction.

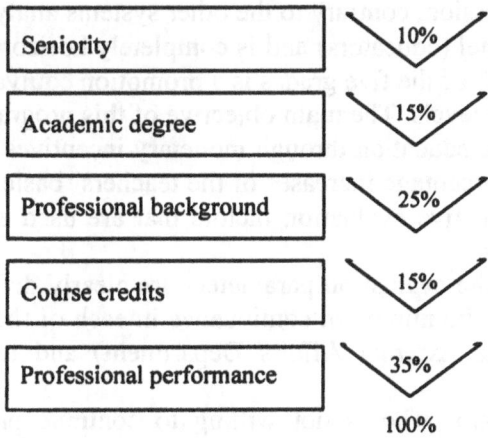

Figure 5.6   Factors to be evaluated

In order to belong to the teaching profession, the evaluation is made in three stages during a year (the first one at the beginning, the second halfway through and the last when the school year finishes). Once accepted, it is not possible to lose the position, unless there is a serious fault committed.

For promotion, it is necessary to have been at least two years in the previous category in marginalized areas, and three years in non-marginalized areas.

Benefits

In the guidelines for the teaching profession, there are series of benefits granted by this type of promotion, which can be summarized in the following way:

1. It guarantees horizontal promotion.
2. It does not modify the current promotion ladder.
3. The incentive granted is an economic one.
4. It recognizes the teacher's efficiency.
5. It improves the teacher's status.
6. It is flexible in regard to the number of hours a teacher teaches.

Conclusions

The teaching profession, contrary to the other systems analyzed, is centered on tenured personnel (educators) and is completely horizontal. In this way, a promotion at each of the five grades is a promotion equivalent to what the INEGI calls salary levels. The main objective of this program is to improve the quality of basic education through monetary incentives (the five levels, which represent percentage increases of the teachers' basic income). These levels are linked to five evaluation factors that are used as parameters of educational quality.

Although the evaluation parameters are clearly defined, promotion requires linking to the minimum continuance in each of the levels (such as in the case of the External Affairs Department) and to the budgetary availability.

Any educator who is not willing to continue profesionalization within the system in order to improve his/her performance will be sanctioned by not continuing to move up the scale (in any case moving up is not guaranteed). On the other hand, once the last level of the promotion ladder is reached, there no longer exists any incentive or removal mechanism.

In spite of this, the teaching profession is mainly a system that has contributed to encouraging and recognizing the training of classroom teachers, especially if compared with the promotion system described above that depended only on seniority, but whose economic recompense was minimal.

The greatest strength of this system is perhaps the clarity in the evaluation mechanisms. Certainly it should be recognized that this is thus due to the nature of the educational function itself, since it is difficult to find an organization where the functions of the individuals are so heterogeneous. It is necessary to qualify this observation, since the factor that has most weight in the evaluation process (professional performance 35%) is perhaps the most subjective.

Conclusions of the chapter

The present chapter has shown that the modern State must be characterized as requiring the mastery of professional knowledge. This is how the professionalization of the government and administrative function implies a condition that needs to be consolidated in Mexico, so that matters concerning the common interest can be attended to effectively, efficiently and fairly.

In this sense, unfortunately, the professional development of public servants in Mexico still lacks a strategic, long-term vision. As can be observed in this chapter, merit criteria are almost null or nonexistent. If somebody is looking for an administrative, secretarial, janitorial, or elementary technical job, he/she turns to the union of the bureaucratic unit in question, and gets this labor organization to propose him/her for the position when there is a vacancy corresponding to this type of activity. On the other hand, if one is seeking an opportunity involving greater responsibility based on one's professional background or capacity, then he/she looks for someone who knows someone, with a middle or high position, and tries to inveigle him into "please" giving him a chance to occupy the position. That is to say, a good recommendation is wanted. A human resources system with these institutional mechanisms cannot be efficient, or fair.

What has been stated should be qualified, since a law already exists for professionalizing workers serving the State; a system of social security that guides them, and even norms with incentives and rewards for those who are outstanding in the service. Let us be clear: the point is for officials to reach their position as a consequence of their merit, based on institutional arrangements that generate low transaction costs, that correctly define rights and obligations, that allow for the achievement of more with less (or of more with the same thing); this is, of a system that allows their ability, honesty, dedication to service and effectiveness to be proven.

In certain cases, the institutional arrangements are not only far from ideal regarding recruitment of public servants; neither are the training systems, in the way they promote and remunerate the public employees, in the mechanisms for controlling their performance nor in the organizational culture of demanding responsibilities of them.

In summary, the present chapter has shown that an important part of Mexican public administration suffers from the lack of clear mechanisms and selection objectives, as well as of middle- and long-term institutional programs that strengthen the training of human and professional resources.

What is required is a system for developing professional, responsible and first-rate human "assets" linked to a transparent, efficiently-run public administration, which considers contexts and is sensitive to the particular necessities of each department;[3] a system that is minimalist in bureaucratic demands, flexible, and strict in its demand for results.

The public service, as its name indicates, is a vocation, a sense of responsibility and honesty. It is necessary for the public servant to be productive, creative, with a sense of innovation, reflection and self-criticism in his work; who feels and knows that what he is contributing, leads to solutions demanded by the country. The new public problems require innovative solutions, and unconventional, creative treatment.

What is required is a System that establishes clear rules for income and promotions; transparent competitions; irreproachable juries, and experts; severe requirements both for entering and for remaining in the service; salaries that depend on performance; induction into the posts according to the institutional mission and the real necessities of the citizens.

It is clear that the design of the professionalization systems involves a series of decisions that are far from being optimum; on the contrary, it is necessary to take stock and shoulder the costs that are invariably bound to each of the options. The weighing of costs and benefits depends on the particular characteristics of each organization, but without a doubt the guiding objective will be better service to the citizenry.

In other words, given that the design of the systems of professionalization (especially in the critical points)[4] is a function of the characteristics proper to each organization; a homogeneous, centralized system would greatly hinder the possibilities of success in the design of mechanisms of evaluation (and, therefore, of termination of employment) from the system (to mention one example).

On the other hand, a flexible, mostly heterogeneous system would hamper the evaluation and control of the system as a whole, and would create the possibility of diminishing the impartiality and transparency of the promotion and recruitment mechanisms. At the same time, increasing the element of discretion would endanger the effectiveness of the internal mechanisms of the departments in order for their officials to act transparently and honestly (accountability).

The challenge is then in establishing the balances between control, on one hand, and flexibility, on the other. In terms of the professionalization systems, this balance could be established by identifying those critical points tending to homogenization and those that ought to be the responsibility of the organisms themselves (in this case, setting up mechanisms for auditing that, if they do not reduce the autonomy of the departments, do force them to be accountable to a regulating institution).

In this sense, the investigation has laid emphasis on the fact that the institutional structure (both formal and informal) should be minimalist in bureaucratic requirements. Flexible according to the particular necessities of each organ of the government. Firm in defining and introducing criteria of merit and equal opportunities, and severe in the requirements of accountability according to the mission established.[5]

Therefore it will be necessary to establish a gradual plan of introduction, where each of the departments defines its mission, establishes its indicators of performance, makes up the organizational structure that best suits it and applies a comprehensive system of human resources consistent with merit and the criteria described above.[6] In order to achieve this, the axioms emphasized by the evidence of the best practices analyzed are summarized in the following criteria: 1) orientation of performance indicators by means of evaluation of the positions; 2) sense of competition and cooperation within the institution and between departments; 3) formation of efficient institutional arrangements; 4) transparency in the design and implementation of public policies. These four are clearly bound to the constituent elements of the system of professionalization and evaluation of the performance of the public servants: recruitment, entry, development, training, evaluation and retirement.

As a function of the recruitment, entry and appointment of public servants, the critical elements evaluated in this chapter show that in general, except for some cases analyzed in our work and others,[7] in our country recruitment is carried out by knowing certain people, through political commitments between public servants, by recommendations, or simply because there is no better choice. In short, for the most part there is a lack of an adequate system of recruitment, entry and appointment of public servants.

In this respect, the case of Mexico has made clear the need for a rational and democratic entry system for the public service; institutional mechanisms that make it possible to respond – plainly and simply – to the following questions that any individual can formulate: what steps should I follow to enter the public administration?, how can I become a professional public servant?

Thus, professionalizing the public service presupposes, in principle, redesigning the recruitment system at the levels of administrative direction, based on a new functional catalog of the public administration that is no longer exclusively built on criteria of a budgetary nature, but in the search for the ideal among public tasks and aptitudes and skills required for its performance.[8] A recruitment system that would also have to be public from its conception to its capacity to convene all of Mexican society, so that the positions no longer depend on the good will of the authorities of the departments and of the administrative organs, but on the exam open to those who want to make a career in the professional public service. All this through procedures that are so clear and transparent that is really impossible to interfere with the selection competitions in favor of personal political interests.[9]

This does not mean that all positions in a department, right from the first to the very last, should be reached by scale.[10] It means that once it has been determined which are the positions of free designation - be they few or many, high or low, and not counting those of an exclusively political nature that there are in every administration -, those are occupied according to a procedure of permanent preparation, selection, promotion and updating.[11] And also the unions, in regard to their capacity to make postulations to fill certain positions, should introduce both selection and induction mechanisms to the corresponding jobs,[12] in both cases according to clear rules known by those who participate in the process, in order to create a professional body of civil servants that will be continuously evaluated, and that based on that will be permitted continuance, promotion or retirement from the service.

What is proposed are criteria that justify the reason for the ranks of the positions with the character of administrative and political servants.[13] Each department, both at the federal and state levels, has its own necessities; however, the criteria (institutional arrangements) in all cases should be governed by suitable incentives and principles of equality.[14]

In regard to training, the study has emphasized that it should be closely related to the present performance and the future of the official in question. That is to say, training aims at the professionalization and development of public servants, giving them new knowledge and skills so as to increase their productivity, efficiency and quality. This training should take into account needs detection based on position, development and evaluation of one's own training.

The cases analyzed have made it possible to recognize the fact that for the most part there is a lack of a system of comprehensive, forward-looking development and training of the public servant within the institutions. This implies that there is no system that makes it possible to measure whether the public servant has acquired greater knowledge or skills in the public function that he performs, in order to be able to offer better results in his respective responsibilities.

Also, the evidence of the best national and international practices shows the advisability of making up training programs linked to agreements with institutions of high school and higher education, and with the institutes of scientific and technological research, that would make it possible to economize with the existing human "assets", and that by the same token allow the universities involved in the area of public policy, administration and government to know and to have an up-to-date diagnosis of "what's missing" and, based on this, prepare the students adequately for the needs of the prevailing job market.

Lastly, one important consideration: expectations should not be created that cannot be fulfilled. To link training as a condition or mechanism for scale-wise promotion generates a perverse incentive in two senses: 1) civil servants are trained (or overtrained) as a way to be promoted, and not with the purpose of being trained for the intrinsic value of the training itself (to be more efficient in their present and future responsibilities), and 2) linking training as an incentive for growth in the organization with a limited, pyramidal structure (such as those existing in the public sector), generates compromising expectations of promotion that the institutions, in many cases, will not be able to fulfill and that, in the end, demoralize the system and undermine its credibility.

Consequently, the development of the public employee should not only be made up of formal institutional elements (courses, scholarships, seminars, etc.),[15] but also of informal institutional elements (formation of sound expectations and establishment of a new organizational culture).

Regarding the evaluations, it should be reiterated that an efficient evaluation system is a *necessary condition* for the formation of a professional human resources system.

The performance evaluation has a *prioritary* role in any professionalization system, and has two purposes: to encourage an excellent performance, and to identify and separate the members whose performance does not cover the required minimum levels. This second aspect could be considered the "bottleneck" of the current systems, and if there were no satisfactory solution - just as has happened in the cases analyzed - this would result in bureaucratic non-removability. It is established in the study that to exercise this ability to terminate employment when there exists clear, transparent, verifiable justification, is essential in preventing the perversion of the professionalization system and thereby contribute to the bureaucratic rigidity of the public service.[16]

In this framework of action, it is imperative that the evaluation be linked directly to the results actually obtained by the professional public servant (as a function of the requirements of the citizenry), to the areas or units to which he corresponds and to the institution of which he forms part.[17] In this respect, the areas or units must design mechanisms that help ensure that the grading of each of the civil servants in the administrative career does not *only* depend on the biased judgment of their bosses, nor on neutral commissions in charge of carrying out the evaluations, *but also* on the society that receives the benefits (or suffers them).

Regarding the system of compensations (e.g., salary, incentives, benefits), these are to be determined in each of the respective departments as a function of their needs[18] (principles of autonomy and flexibility) based on axioms of equal opportunity, impartiality, transparency and linking with results.[19]

Finally, a professionalization system as proposed here would not be complete if it avoided the need to have guarantees in order to give security to public servants who dedicated themselves with excellence and devotion to their work, both during their work and as a function of their retirement (or when the work relationship is concluded due to causes attributable to the institution).

That is to say, termination of employment for causes foreign to the excellent public servants, should mean having them receive a decent retirement through a severance pay that the system can commit itself to offering. On the other hand, those officials who are removed from their positions for reasons of bad behavior or poor performance, should not receive any severance pay.

In summary, the elements proposed in our study are: to establish a system that defines clear missions and is subject to performance indicators oriented toward results; to constitute recruitment programs that make it possible to attract qualified people; to develop a selection scheme by means of a rigorous, impartial process that guarantees the entry of the most capable people; to have a system of compensations that allows the most qualified personnel to be attracted and retained; to form efficient mechanisms for mobilizing and relieving officials with poor evaluation from their posts; to encourage the development of the public servant, strengthening his commitment to the institution; to contribute to the development of an effective and honest culture of service; to dignify the public function, and establish the continuance of the public servant as a function of merit.

Notes

[1]   See Roderic Ai Camp, Politics in Mexico, 2nd ed., Oxford University Press, 1996; and Merilee S. Grindle, "Patrons and Clients in the Bureaucracy: Career Networks in Mexico", Latin American Research Review, vol. 12, pp. 37-61, 1977.

[2]   Regulation of the Mexican Foreign Service Act, SRE, 1994.

[3]   Every six years 5,500 directive positions approximately are filled, in the range from technical coordinators to area directors alone. Every time it is more complex to fill these positions effectively without a comprehensive professional system.

[4]   See appendix C at the back of the book.

[5]   Based on these axioms, the cases analyzed prove that establishing the civil service is not unavoidably equivalent to professionalization, honesty or efficiency. To fulfill those aims a complex institutional design is required to accompany its establishment.

[6]   To give viability to completed professionalization projects, it is necessary to work on a strategy that makes it possible to select administrative areas that become the object of the professionalization; to imagine how to convert the theoretical proposal into decisions that put it into operation; to determine the selected hierarchical levels; to clearly define

the scopes of the professionalization programs and labor rights; to decide in a practical sense what rules shall govern these systems, all this in order to begin working with the idea of not covering everything, but only covering what is possible hierarchically, taking into account the characteristics of each department and the resources available for this task.

7 Added to the cases analyzed in this work, see the advances achieved in this matter by the Federal Electoral Institute, as well as by the Secretary of Social Development.

8 Induction is an element of utmost relevance in order for the *best* public servants to be incorporated, identified with their respective institutions and have the vocation of service inspired in them.

9 The investigation has stated that to enter a meritocratic system, in general the following two requirements are demanded: an exam of general minimum knowledge (under the responsibility of an external institution, where the applicant pays the cost) and a technical exam that should be applied by the department which he wishes to enter. Finally, an interview under the responsibility of the agency or contracting dependence is anticipated.

10 With respect to the hierarchical levels that should be integrated into this scheme, it is advisable to recognize the need to reserve certain posts that, due to the nature of the function to be carried out, require free designation by the head of the department or corresponding agency. This ability would mean that these positions could vary not only from one institution to another, but also from one administrative area to another in the same government.

11 Professionalization will be inclusive with regard to human resources, and include unionized workers as well as appointed ones. Segregating the former group would mean leaving out the majority, insofar as the participation of this personnel is fundamental in improving the quality of public services and, consequently, the image of the government as a whole. In this respect, the system should be made up of unionized personnel that voluntarily decide to join the system as a result of the promotion in the hands of the respective administrations; they would be trained and authorized to take on greater responsibilities and be able to be evaluated based on tangible results (just like other members in the system). These responsibilities would be associated, certainly, with fair remuneration. Therefore, the professionalization of the unionized public servants, consistent with a comprehensive approach to human resources, is essential for an authentic transformation and modernization of the public administration.

12 It is necessary to take into account that in order to make a change that would suddenly eliminate free designation, when this has been standard in the government environment, would surely face strong opposition, which would reduce its viability. Therefore, the specific strategy as to which administrative areas are to be selected for professionalization, how to proceed in their implementation and which hierarchical levels will be selected as maximum in the system, is of the greatest importance and, given the diversity of the public administration, cannot be instituted uniformly.

13 In this respect, the recommended approach is to establish the principle that every post that is not technical-administrative will be subject to free designation; that is to say, free designation will be justified as long as it clearly has a political function and is treated as the exception. Contracts "by honorariums" by free designation will also be regulated; if not, they can end up becoming a "parallel system" to the system and the "Achilles heel" of the civil service, due to their increase.

14 Of course this work has reiterated the importance of the system's being based on principles of equal opportunities and merit, but at the same time there should be no hesitation in promoting prioritarily the less privileged groups of society, so as to achieve thereby an *authentic equality of opportunities.*

15 The withdrawal of an official from his position for training reasons (e.g., a scholarship) should imply that the unoccupied position will not be reoccupied by another public servant for more than the time of absence of the one granted a scholarship, so as to avoid exponential (and uncontrollable) growth of personnel in the institutions.

16 In the case of tenured workers, the diagnosis is very clear: the worker is non-removable. This generates inadequate incentives that (in many cases) involve the wasting of resources and inefficient practices.

17 In this order of ideas, the evaluation of professional performance must be carried out through two complementary aspects: one that would be directed toward each of the public servants periodically so that he/she can be competitive in his/her area, and that of the unit as a whole, so as to generate mechanisms of collaboration among the different public servants of the area in question.

18 Therefore criteria are required to be agreed on in conjunction with the Secretariat of National Revenue and Public Credit.

19 As for the budgetary funds, the viability of any plan for professionalization will depend on the extent to which it is possible to stay within the financial ceiling that traditionally has been set for each department or agency. Therefore, the corresponding proposals will have to be structured on a basis of lump sum, that is to say that the total value of promotions and incentives are compensated by means of mechanisms that maintain the expenditures approximately at their current level.

6. Final Considerations

The objective of these considerations is to situate the main contributions of the study in a framework, with respect to their theoretical (new economic institutionalism and public choice), pragmatic (international and national cases), and strategic elements (concrete recommendations for the comprehensive establishment of a system for professionalizing the development, and evaluating the performance, of public servants in Mexico). The purpose is not to reiterate the critical elements set out in this book, but to recognize some of the essential axioms that are considered of vital importance for establishing a system of efficient public administration oriented toward offering results.

The explicit mission of the present book has been to show excellent arguments in favor of the professionalization of the Mexican public service, in the light of the guiding principles of merit, equal opportunities, sound expectations for the development of public servants, impartial evaluations, besides principles of development and training that promise stability and opportunities for promotion for officials showing excellence. However, principally, the purpose of the book forms part of a much broader discussion about the new role that the Mexican public administration should play in the future, looking toward the new millennium.

The work has explained the problems of institutional credibility in both developed and developing countries, of the legitimacy of the State, and of the importance of administrative efficiency as an instrument of credibility, economic development and a means of generating social capital.

In this regard, this study shows that one of the fundamental reasons for the crisis of legitimacy of the contemporary State is, in fact, the crisis of legitimacy in the public administration.[1] The exhaustion of an administrative structure that has grown with the explosive complexity of the social, economic and political systems (besides the increasing organizational complexity of the state apparatus) is what led to inefficiency, being able to fulfill the results demanded by the citizenry.

As well as efficiency, there exists another relevant reason that calls for administrative modernization in our country, and that is that an effective administration is the way to guarantee an effective democracy. As an example of this, and the topic of this book, is the introduction of a career civil service based on merit, as a necessary step toward administrative modernization. A system based on opportunities open to all, with clear, well-known rules for entry, consolidates the democratic system by providing equal opportunities to the different social strata.

This book has underlined the fact that administrative modernization acquires great importance by forming a fundamental element in contributing to the increase in productivity and the requirements of the advance of democracy. Therefore, modernization of the public administration should not be a goal in itself nor a passing fashion, but a continuous, comprehensive, long-term process, a condition of permanence and perfecting of government institutions and a guarantee of better service to the society that supports it and in which it finds its raison d'être.

The work has also remarked that the administrative inefficiency is translated into a "regressive tax", according to which the most disadvantaged classes are those most affected inasmuch as they have fewer opportunities to establish "connections in high places" in order to occupy positions of responsibility. In addition to this, they are the ones who have fewest resources with which to stand up to the mishandling of administrative authority.

On the other hand, the theoretical evidence and the cases presented in this book recognize that administrative modernization should be implemented in a comprehensive way and with a forward-looking intention; for this reason emphasis was placed, among other things, on consideration of the following purposes: 1) thematic purpose: to base valid objectives on the mission of the State and its institutions, 2) a transparent institutional purpose: to generate efficient incentives and clear, credible, sound, applicable rules; 3) territorial purpose: to take advantage of benefits according to region and population centers, and 4) administrative purpose: to match budgetary, administrative, cultural, financial, technological and human elements.

The purposes in question will be implanted gradually and many of them will surely pass through several stages of development. But if carried out comprehensively, a true administrative modernization will be achieved.

In these lines, the book has reiterated that it is essential to have a modern, efficient administration in order to make the transition from the administrative subculture of individual loyalties toward a civil service based on merit; from the discontinuity of public policies toward the formation of State policies; from corrupt, inefficient and clientelistic practices toward efficient administrations concerned with collective interests; from conflicts between and within bureaucracies toward common languages of cooperation.

In this respect, the work has maintained that in order to give direction and vision, it is just as important to establish a way to regulate the struggle for power (a democratic-institutional concern) as it is to regulate the exercise of acquired power. One efficient way is the existence of an effective public administration, with clear, transparent rules and with professional public servants.

In summary, today more than ever, in the here and now, a meritocratic career civil service as a function of a result-oriented administrative reform, acts as an institutional bridge from the country we come from, to the country we need to reach (see figure 6.1).

In conclusion, it is necessary to emphasize the importance of answering the initial question of the book: How can public institutions recover their credibility, that *sine qua non* tool for development? This work has made it clear that this is achieved with *results*, which are not given by decree, nor by magic formulas. They are achieved with vision, with clear missions, pragmatic proposals, useful, innovative ideas, with efficient institutional arrangements, with criteria of flexibility, of equal opportunities, of accountability to the citizenry, with unyielding principles of merit. Results are achieved with a professional system of public servants, ready to be useful, proud to form part of a public administration that serves society as a whole – and *that offers results*.

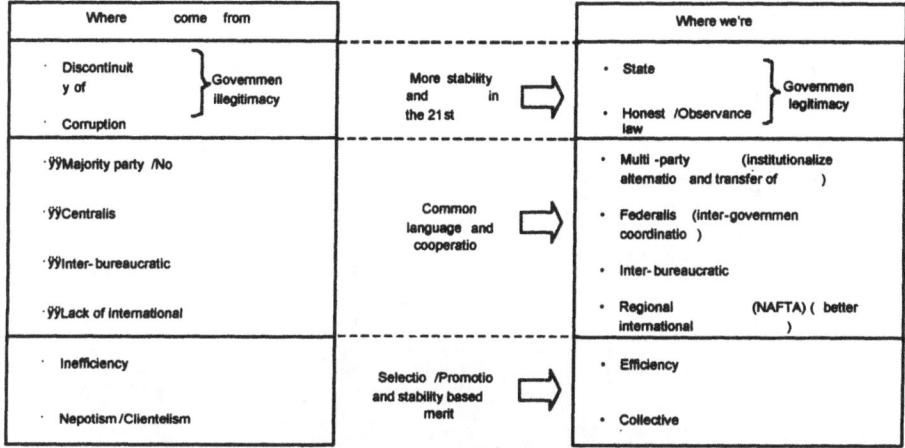

Figure 6.1   Administrative modernization. Professional career service

Notes

[1]   See A. Wolfe, Los límites de legitimidad. Contradicciones políticas del capitalismo contemporáneo, Siglo XXI, Mexico, 1980.

APPENDICES

APPENDICES

Appendix A

OECD recommendations on the content of civil service legislation[1]

This checklist is intended to provide a means of ascertaining whether matters commonly included in OECD civil service legislation have been considered for inclusion in a particular statute under preparation. It is not intended as a direction as to what must be included in such a statute, nor how particular matters should be dealt with. Choices in those respects must reflect local circumstances. In this checklist, "the Act" refers to the primary legislative instrument governing the civil service; "the legislation" refers to the Act together with the secondary legislation made to supplement it.

Objectives

Note: The usual purposes for enacting civil service legislation include the following -- to:

(a) establish a professional and politically neutral civil service which provides public services promptly and efficiently in response to the needs of the nation, free of bias, corruption and misuse of power, but loyal to the requirements of the government;

(b) define the institutions that are empowered to manage civil servants or to monitor their management when carried out by the ministries/agencies;

(c) provide for selection of civil servants on merit after fair and open competition;

(d) provide for equality of opportunity for entry and promotion in the civil service and for a career in the service;

(e) create a regime of duties for civil servants directed to producing quality, continuity and impartiality in, and accountability for, the performance of their functions; and

(f) guarantee a range of rights, benefits and other conditions of employment that will attract high quality civil servants.

179

1.1. Will the legislation satisfactorily secure the objectives? In particular –

(a) is the correct balance struck between the constraints upon civil servants that arise from the regime of duties and the special status and positive privileges that they are given in return?
(b) is adequate protection given for job security or tenure of office that will provide protection to civil servants from politicization of the service and abuse of political power?
(c) are the benefits provided (e.g., in terms of working conditions, leave, promotion opportunities, allowances, health care and pensions) sufficient to attract and retain the desired quality of personnel needed?

1.2. Is the Act itself to contain a statement of the objectives which it is designed to achieve? Or will the actual rules in the Act or its accompanying commentary make the objectives sufficiently clear to parliament and to users of the legislation?

Scope of the Legislation

2.1. What categories of persons performing public functions are to be subject to this legislation?
Does the Act contain clear definitions or descriptions of the categories that it covers?

2.2. In particular, does the Act make clear whether the legislation --

(a) is to be confined to those officials who perform executive and administrative functions for the state ("state officials")?[2]
(b) also extends to those who perform similar functions for local governments?

State Officials

2.3. If the legislation is confined to state officials, does the Act make clear whether the legislation is intended to apply to officials concerned with the administration of distinct state authorities, such as:

(i)   the office of the state president?
(ii)   parliament?
(iii)   the office of the ombudsman or similar authorities?
(iv)   the courts?

2.4. If the legislation is confined to state officials, is it concerned with those who discharge functions of some responsibility ("high functionaries")?, or does it also extend to support staff ("industrial state employees", such as secretaries, computer operators, drivers, messengers and security guards, etc.)?

2.5. If the legislation is principally concerned with high functionaries, does the Act make clear:

(a) how those officials are to be identified (e.g., holding a post in an authorized list of such posts or particular class or grade in the service)?
(b) what legal rules govern industrial state employees?

2.6. If the legislation is confined to high functionaries, does it include provisions that enable industrial state employees to enter the ranks of high functionaries by some form of internal promotion (e.g., by gaining necessary qualifications or passing a special examination)?

2.7. If the legislation is confined to state officials, is it intended to apply to other categories in addition to those stated above? If so, does it apply to --

(a) members of the judiciary (i.e., judges or magistrates who perform judicial functions)?
(b) members of the disciplined forces (e.g., armed forces, police, customs and border guards, prison officers)?
(c) employees in state-provided medical services (e.g., doctors and nurses)?
(d) employees in state-provided educational services (e.g., university and school teachers)?
(e) employees in the national transport and communication services?
(f) employees of parastatal authorities or agencies?

Note: The more categories included, the greater the necessity for ascertaining whether the general provisions in the legislation (e.g., duties and rights) can be applied equally to each category, and, if not, for making provision to modify those provisions appropriately. In many cases, it may be better to undertake the enactment of separate legislation which deals explicitly with the special needs of the category (although matters in common with those in the Act can be dealt with in the same way or by reference to the Act).

2.8. If the legislation is not intended to apply to all or any of these other categories, does the Act make that clear (e.g., by excluding words), and does the Act indicate by which other law or legislation those categories are governed?

Categories Other than State Employees

2.9. If the legislation is intended to apply to other categories of persons in addition to state officials, do these include --

(a) employees in local government?
(b) elected members of the state government or of local governments?

2.10. If the legislation deals with elected persons, does it take account of the fact that such persons cannot be given tenure?

Political, Fixed-term or Contract Officials

2.11. Is the legislation to be concerned only with those in full-time and enduring service ? If so, has consideration been given to the legal position of those who:

(a) are appointed by ministers or other elected persons to provide them with political or policy-making services during the term of office of the minister or such other person?
(b) are brought in under a personal contract to perform a civil service function for a fixed-term or for a precise purpose?

2.12. If such cases are to be permitted, should the Act --

(a) indicate how, when and by whom such appointments and contracts are to be made, how those cases are to be regulated and the extent to which the general provisions of the legislation are to apply to them?
(b) provide safeguards against the wide-scale use of these powers in ways that are incompatible with the objectives of the Act in providing a permanent civil service?

Cross-Government Management

3.1. Is the legislation built upon a system for the cross-governmental management of the whole civil service? If one is not already provided for, is this Act (or other legislation) to establish such a system?

Note: the objectives in providing such a system are usually to ensure that there is some body responsible for securing:

(a) equity of treatment between different parts of the civil service and between different regions;
(b) a guarantee of standards of quality throughout the public service;
(c) fair treatment for all civil servants;
(d) professional and loyal execution of government policy decisions throughout the public service;
(e) conditions that permit mobility of civil servants within the service (which are necessary if the civil servants are given tenure and cannot be dismissed);
(f) proper oversight of the economic costs of the civil service and some central control over its size and distribution; and
(g) independent monitoring of the implementation of the civil service legislation.

3.2. If no cross-governmental management function is to be provided, how are these objectives to be secured? If management is to be undertaken separately by each ministry/agency, how are their management activities to be collectively coordinated and monitored so that common standards are applied?

3.3. If a cross-government management system is to be provided --

(a) is it to be a central management authority (e.g., a commission or directorate), with policy-making and secondary legislation powers for the whole civil service?
(b) Or is there to be some central unit, with its own human resource management expertise, charged with the duty of coordinating ministry/agency management, and entitled to set common standards by issuing secondary legislation and guidelines?
(c) To which minister or body in central government will such a body or unit be responsible (e.g., prime minister, council of ministers, minister for the civil service)?

Secondary Legislation

4.1. Does the Act take fully into account the inevitable need for supplementary, secondary legislation?

Note: Secondary legislation is inevitable for a number of reasons --

(a) it is not logistically practicable for all the details of the new arrangements to be decided by parliament;
(b) details will have to be changed quite frequently, especially during the period of reform; it is improbable that Parliament will have time for this;
(c) much of the detail is of little interest to parliament and can be dealt with better by a more expert body (e.g., civil service commission or directorate, or council of ministers); ·
(d) much of the detail depends on principles decided upon by parliament, and may need to be implemented at short notice and speedily; this is a task better suited to a government body.

4.2. Does the Act identify the authorities that are empowered to make secondary legislation to give effect to the various general requirements of the Act?

4.3. Where there is the need for common standards or practices or for the regulation of issues that affect the civil service as a whole, is it made clear that the making of secondary legislation is to be by, or should involve, a central body of authority (e.g., the council of ministers, ministry of finance)?

4.4. Is it feasible for the draft secondary legislation to be prepared alongside the Act so that the entire legislative scheme can be presented to parliament and considered at the same time?

Contents of Secondary Legislation

4.5. Has a sound balance been struck between the contents of the Act (in terms of basic structures and principles) and those of secondary legislation (in terms of detail, and procedural and administrative provisions)?

4.6. In Particular --

(a) is the Act concerned in the main with establishing the broad framework of principle and in settling the essentials of the new arrangements and resolving those issues that are likely to be controversial – i.e., matters in which parliament has an interest?

(b) does the Act authorize matters of detail or a specific or routine nature to be dealt with by secondary legislation, in particular such matters as –

    (i)   numbers and distributions of posts, or classes, ranks and grades?

    (ii)   recruitment and promotion procedures, including methods of examination or ensuring competition?

    (iii)   processes of performance appraisal?

    (iv)   working hours?

    (v)   conditions governing leave?

    (vi)   levels of remuneration, and conditions and levels of allowances?

    (vii)   disciplinary procedures?

(c) should authority be given to some central authority to develop and issue a code of conduct/ethics and a code of discipline?

Cost Factors

5.1. Is it clear how cost factors relevant to the civil service are to be dealt with in the context of the state budgetary system?

5.2. In particular, is it clear --

(a) how and by whom the costs of the civil service (e.g., remuneration, allowances, pensions, operational expenditure, etc.) are to be determined and controlled?

(b) how and by whom the numbers of civil servants, overall and in individual ministries/agencies are to be determined, monitored and controlled, consistently with the state budgetary process?

(c) whether additional procedures need to be provided to enable parliament to exercise control over personnel costs and staffing levels and to ensure efficiency in the public service?

5.3. If these matters are not adequately covered by existing law, should they be dealt with in this Act or in accompanying legislation (e.g., the budget law)?

Entry to the Civil Service System

6.1. Is the system of appointment to be a career system or a post system, or some combination of both? That is, does the Act make clear whether civil servants are appointed to --

(a) the civil service in a class and grade, thereafter moving forward through grades as their career progresses; or
(b) specific posts from which they may seek to move to another such post as they advance in age or experience?

6.2. Are the legislative provisions concerning selection (and remuneration, promotion and mobility) fully consistent with the system adopted?

Qualifications

6.3. Does the Act provide comprehensively with respect to the qualifications for entry to the civil service? In particular -

(a) does the Act contain a statement of the general qualifications and disqualifications that apply in all cases?
(b) is it clear how particular or specialist qualifications for particular appointments are to be determined and made public (e.g., by secondary legislation, job description)?
(c) does the Act state the circumstances in which entry may be open to persons who do not hold local nationality?

6.4. Does the Act provide for how and by whom more detailed regulations should be made in this context?

6.5. Is it necessary to include in the legislation detailed provision as to the formal educational achievements required, especially requirements that are tied rigidly to particular classes or grades or levels of posts?

6.6. Are any special forms of educational qualifications (e.g., specialist training in public administration at a national institution) to confer priority for entry or entry to particular class or categories of post, etc. (e.g., "fast stream")?

Mode of Entry

6.7. Does the Act require entry to be by open competition on merit amongst those qualified?

6.8. If a career based system is adopted, does the Act require some form of open examination for entry to the civil service as a whole?

6.9. If competition is not required, is it clear how selection will be made, and by whom, in ways that preclude patronage or nepotism, prejudice and partiality?

Legal Relationship

6.10. Does the Act make clear –

(a) that the legal relationship is between the civil servant and the state rather than the individual ministry/ agency?
(b) who has the authority to enter into that legal relationship on behalf of the state (e.g., the head of the ministry/agency)?

6.11. Is the structure for decision-making on appointments so designed as to prevent nepotism and partiality and to facilitate mobility between ministries/agencies?

6.12. Is the council of ministers, or some other central body, given responsibility for -

(a) appointment of the most senior level of state official?
(b) oversight of the overall appointment process?

6.13. Does the legislation prescribe how the appointment is to be formally recorded and when it is to begin?

6.14. Should the taking of an oath be a pre-requisite of appointment ? If so, what is the consequence of a failure to take the oath?

Probation

Note: To appoint a civil servant on tenure involves a long-term financial commitment on the part of the state. Many OECD countries therefore require appointees to complete a period of probation satisfactorily before the appointment is confirmed.

6.15. Is provision made for the initial appointment to the service or a post to be subject to satisfactory completion of a probationary period?

6.16. If so, is the:

(a) probationary period set long enough for a fair assessment to be made?
(b) performance to be assessed in a way that will guarantee a professional and fair judgment?
(c) appointment to be confirmed or terminated by a decision at a level that will prevent nepotism and partiality?
(d) civil servant who is not confirmed entitled to have the period extended or the termination reviewed?
(e) civil servant eligible for entitlements during the probationary period (if so, what are the entitlements)?

Conditions of Service

Personnel File

7.1. Is provision made for the institution and maintenance of a personnel file for each civil servant and for which authority is to have the responsibility in that respect?

7.2. Does the legislation require the confidentiality of the files but at the same time guarantee civil servants the right to inspect and to challenge the contents of their own personnel file?

7.3. Is provision made determining which body is to have power to issue detailed regulations in this respect?

Advancement and Promotion

7.4. Does the legislation provide for when and how civil servants may advance in their career and may be promoted, and by whom decisions in that regard are to be made?

7.5. Will the decision-making be at a particular level and in ways that it will -

(a) make advancement possible elsewhere in the state administration?
(b) prevent nepotism and partiality?

7.6. Does the Act provide for a system of performance appraisal for civil servants?

7.7. If so -

(a) how, by whom, and how frequently is the appraisal to be carried out?
(b) is appraisal to be linked to, and form the basis of, advancement and promotion?
(c) will the civil servant have the right to see the appraisal in writing and to challenge the assessment?

7.8. Are advancement and salary increases to be automatic as a result of achieving seniority or of completing prescribed periods of service or should they be related, in whole or part, to performance?

7.9. Are bonuses ("primes") to be payable for special service ? If so, in what circumstances and by whom are the relevant decisions to be made?

7.10. Are further qualifications and/or examinations to be required for advancement to a new grade or for appointment to a new post? Can such requirements be better dealt with by terms of service rather than by the legislation?

7.11. In what circumstances are promotions and appointments to new posts to be subject to open competition on merit, and is it made clear that the use of competition is to be determined and the competition itself conducted in ways that will prevent nepotism and partiality?

7.12. Are vacant posts in a ministry/agency to be open to all civil servants holding the relevant qualifications or merely to those in the same ministry/agency?

7.13. If vacancies are to be open to all, does the legislation require general advertisement throughout the civil service?

Transfers

7.14. To what extent and in what circumstances may a civil servant transfer to a different ministry/agency?

7.15. Given that transfers should normally be at the request or with the consent of the civil servant, are there exceptional circumstances in which a civil servant can be required to transfer?

7.16. Do civil servants who are to be made redundant have a priority right to be transferred to an equivalent position in another ministry/agency when a vacancy arises?

7.17. Does the decision-making structure provide for the possibility of using transfer as a means or career development or of avoiding redundancy?

Termination

7.18. Does the Act contain a statement of the circumstances in which the legal relationship may be terminated? In particular, does the legislation prescribe the conditions under which service may be terminated for -

(a) ill health?
(b) incompetence/unsuitability in the job or poor performance?
(c) redundancy or closure of the ministry/agency, in the case of those without tenure?
(d) misconduct?
(e) a civil servant's resignation/request?

7.19. Does the Act provide that the same authority that makes appointments is the body authorized to terminate, and does it provide for the procedures and for rights of appeal/review in respect of termination of service?

7.20. What rights (e.g., allowances, pensions, re-appointment) has a civil servant whose employment has been terminated in the various circumstances?

7.21. What special rights has a civil servant without tenure whose employment has been terminated for redundancy or in consequence of the closure of a ministry/agency (e.g., enhanced pension rights, limited continuance of pay)? Are the costs of those rights provided for in the state budget ?

7.22. Are there provisions in the legislation or elsewhere regulating the procedure, and the order of priority, by which civil servants are to be identified for termination of their employment when redundancy is necessary, in ways that prevent nepotism and partiality?

Duties of Civil Servants

Special Duties

8.1. Does the Act contain or provide for a full range of special duties upon civil servants, as state officials, that are aimed to ensure their neutrality, probity, loyalty to government and the state, efficiency and accountability?

8.2. In particular, does the Act provide for -

(a) a duty to comply with the lawful orders of hierarchical superiors, and the circumstances and procedure by which the civil servant may refuse to carry out an order that is improper?
(b) a duty to provide the public with requested information unless it is secret as defined by a law on secrecy, and the duty of confidentiality in relation to matters that fall within that legal definition of secrecy?
(c) the extent to which there is a duty not to undertake other paid work or business activities (and by whom permission may be obtained for such work when it is not incompatible with the civil servant's responsibilities)?
(d) the circumstance in which there may be a duty to reside in a particular location or to transfer, for a period, to another place or to other responsibilities?
(e) the duty not to solicit or take financial or other rewards or benefits from third parties for discharging civil service functions?
(f) the duty to appear before a medical commission for assessment of physical or mental capacity to perform the functions of office?
(g) a general duty to perform functions loyally, conscientiously and without delay, without bias and uninfluenced by political opinions or allegiances, and without misusing power, and generally to act respectably and to refrain from behavior that is incompatible with membership of the civil service?

Code of Conduct

8.3. Does the Act provide for the publication of a Code of Conduct that provides detailed guidelines to civil servants as to the ways in which the various duties specified in the Act are to be complied with in the circumstances in which they are most likely to arise?

Discipline of Civil Servants

9.1. Does the Act establish a system for disciplinary action against civil servants that is transparent and meets judicial quality standards?

9.2. In particular -

(a) are the grounds for disciplinary action adequately identified in the Act in terms that meet the standards of legality, and is their relationship with the statutory duties and the Code of Conduct clearly indicated?
(b) does the Act set out a complete statement of the penalties that may be imposed for proven misconduct, and the cases in which each can be ordered?
(c) does the Act identify the bodies which may exercise disciplinary functions and differentiate those cases that can be dealt with by a hierarchical superior from those that must be heard by a disciplinary tribunal?
(d) does the Act make provision with respect to the composition of disciplinary tribunals (which do not include those who initiate or prosecute the proceedings) of a sufficient size and in sufficient numbers to perform their expected task?
(e) is the composition of such tribunals such that it can be expected to reach independent decisions?
(f) are there adequate safeguards included in the Act for a fair hearing, including the right to receive legal assistance, to be represented by a person of the accused's choice, to know the charge and to hear the evidence, to be heard in defence and to appeal?
(g) is provision made for a general appeal body for all disciplinary tribunals to ensure common standards of decision-making?
(h) does the Act authorize the making of a standard set of rules of procedure or Code of Discipline with respect to the initiation, prosecution, hearing and decision of cases?

(i) does the legislation require the destruction, after a prescribed period, of adverse findings that have been entered into the personnel files of civil servants?

(j) does the legislation specify the circumstances in which civil servants may be suspended pending the outcome of disciplinary proceedings, and their rights during suspension and if found not guilty?

Rights of Civil Servants

Specific Rights

10.1. Does the Act contain the basic framework of specific rights to which civil servants are entitled?

10.2. In particular, should the Act authorize the following rights (subject to stated limitations as necessary) -

(a) the right of equal access of qualified persons to the civil service?

(b) the right to a salary (and whether this may be performance-related rather than tied to seniority or years of service)?

(c) the right to have salary levels settled by a process that involves collective bargaining/negotiation?

(d) the right to a written order of a hierarchical superior if the lawfulness or propriety of the order is in question?

(e) the right to join a trade union or a professional association, and the right to strike?

(f) the right to join and hold office in a political party and to participate in political activities that are not incompatible with the performance of the individual's functions?

(g) the right to a prescribed minimum period of annual leave and to take unpaid leave?

(h) the right to go to court or to some other independent authority to settle disputes relating to the employment relationship?

(i) the right to take prescribed forms of outside employment, unless incompatible with the performance of functions?

(j) the right not to be transferred without consent, unless necessitated by the exigencies of the service?

(k) the right to receive and undertake appropriate training at state expense, and to take study leave?

(l)   the right to special allowances (e.g., for work in remote areas, official travel, on transfer, during illness, for housing, overtime, and for especially onerous work)?

(m) the right to special employment conditions (e.g., maternity/paternity leave, medical treatment for self and the family, pensions and disability payments for self and the family)?

10.3. Does the Act provide that the detailed features of these rights (e.g., numbers, amounts, conditions of entitlement) may be determined from time to time by other means, such as secondary legislation, job descriptions, administrative directions?

Costs of Implementation

10.4. Have the costs of implementing the contemplated rights been calculated?

10.5. Are those costs capable of being met from the state budget? If not, should any provisions be excluded or modified or some procedure provided for suspending particular rights, until such time as they can be afforded?

Personnel Participation

11.1. Does the legislation make provision for the participation of civil service personnel or their representatives in management decision-making processes?

11.2. In particular -

(a) does the legislation make clear the extent and the ways in which trade unions or professional associations have the right to be involved in personnel matters?

(b) are the functions of unions or associations confined to acting in a collective capacity (e.g., salary negotiations, consideration of changed employment conditions or new legislation on entitlements)?

(c) or do they extend to representing the interests of individual civil servants (e.g., in employment disputes or in disciplinary proceedings)?

(d) are unions or associations entitled to perform collective representative functions for all civil servants in individual ministries/agencies or are they confined to an overall civil service role?

(e) or should collective representation in individual ministries/agencies be provided by consultative or grievance bodies elected by the civil servants there?
(f) are unions or associations entitled to representation on disciplinary tribunals?
(g) should there be provision for the establishment of a single national consultative body in addition to the unions and associations?

Training

12.1. Does the legislation make adequate provision for training, linking it to advancement and promotion?

12.2. If the Act provides for the right and the duty to receive training, what arrangements are provided to ensure and monitor that training is fully and systematically planned and provided throughout the service?

12.3. Does the legislation adequately indicate upon which bodies the responsibility for the provision of training is to fall, and the role of any national training institutions in that regard?

12.4. Is there a mechanism by which the costs of training are to be estimated and by which they will be included in the state budget?

Transitional and Saving Provisions

13.1. Does the Act contain or provide for the making of all transitional arrangements necessary to bring existing circumstances, as governed by the present law, into line with the requirements of the new legislation?

Timetables and Commencement

13.2. Has a timetable been developed (e.g., using flow and critical path charts) to determine how the new civil legislation will be phased in by stages?

13.3. Does the Act enable its provisions to be brought into force in accordance with those stages?

13.4. Is it clear that no provisions of the Act will become law until other provisions upon which they are dependent have become fully operational?

13.5. Do the proposed dates for commencement of particular parts allow a realistic time for the preparation for their implementation prior to commencement?

Conversion of Existing Civil Servants

13.6. Does the legislation include provisions which deal with the position of persons who are already engaged in state administration and therefore at present subject to existing law? In particular, does it provide with respect to:

(a) the means by which the status of those at present performing civil service functions ("existing civil servants") will be brought into line with the new civil service system (whether career or post) and their new grades or posts, and their salary entitlements, determined?

(b) the status and conditions of service of existing civil servants, and those to be recruited in the transition period, until this conversion process is completed?

(c) the position of existing civil servants who do not hold qualifications required by the Act or who are disqualified under the Act?

(d) what special allowance may be made for unqualified existing civil servants by reason of long service or to enable them to acquire needed qualifications?

(e) whether special redundancy or pension terms are to be made for existing civil servants who leave, or are required to leave, the civil service consequent upon the coming into force of the legislation?

(f) the procedures, authorities and time-table by which decisions on the future of existing civil servants are to be made?

General Transitional Matters

13.7. What will be the status of those formerly employed in the state administration (e.g., retired persons) and their families, vis-a-vis any special privileges enjoyed by them under existing law (e.g., medical or pension allowances)? In particular -

(a) are their rights under that law to be preserved?

(b) or are they to be equated with those who are in similar positions under the new legislation?

13.8. What is the status of disciplinary proceedings instituted, or disciplinary action being implemented, against existing civil servants under the existing law? In particular, are those proceedings to be discontinued, or to be completed under the existing law or brought within the scheme of the new legislation?

13.9. What is the status of on-going employment disputes involving existing or former civil servants? In particular, are these to be completed under the existing law?

13.10. What are the status and entitlements of persons (if any) who, under existing law, were treated as, or equated with, existing civil servants? In particular, are they to continue to be governed by the existing law, or are they to be put into a similar position under the new legislation?

13.11. To what extent is a period of past service under the existing law to be counted in calculating any qualifying period for the purposes of any benefit conferred under the new legislation?

13.12. Is provision needed to ensure the maintenance and transfer of personnel records established under the existing law, for use as records under the new legislation?

13.13. What period of grace should be allowed within which existing civil servants are to bring their affairs into line with requirements of the legislation, and any Code of Conduct, concerning financial and commercial interests or other incompatibilities?

13.14. Should any relevant secondary legislation made under the existing law, be continued in force, to the extent that it is consistent with the new Act, until new secondary legislation is made for the purposes of the new Act?

13.15. Should there be a requirement that references in other legislation to provisions of, or to authorities named in, any law that is being repealed are to be read as references to the relevant provisions or authorities in the new legislation?

Repeal Provisions

13.16. Does the Act contain a complete statement of the extent to which existing law relating to the civil service is repealed?

13.17. Does the Act fully identify provisions of that existing law which are to be saved (i.e., to continue in force) for any specific purpose or period?

Structure of the Act

Note: The following questions can usefully be borne in mind both when the provisions of the Act are in the process of being written and, later, when drafts of the text of the Act are being checked. Similar questions should be asked with respect to the secondary legislation made to supplement the Act.

14.1. Is the Act structured in a systematic and ordered way that will facilitate its debate in parliament and its ready comprehension by those who need to use it?

14.2. In particular, does the Act satisfy the following general principles, commonly adopted in OECD countries?

(a) If provided, the objectives of the Act should be stated at the beginning, since they set the context in which the provisions that follow must be read.
(b) Basic concepts or terms used in the Act should be explained or defined before they are put to use.
(c) The application or coverage of the Act (i.e., the statement of general cases dealt with and not dealt with) should come before the provisions that apply to those cases.
(d) Primary (or basic) provisions should come before those subsidiary provisions that develop or expand or depend upon them.
(e) In particular, general propositions should come before a statement of exceptions to them.
(f) Provisions of universal or general application should come before those that deal only with specific or particular cases.
(g) Provisions creating bodies should come before those that govern their activities and the performance of their functions.
(h) Provisions creating rights, duties, powers or privileges ("rules of substance") should come before those that state how things are to be done ("rules of administration or procedure").

(i) Provisions that will be frequently referred to should come before those which will not be in regular use.

(j) Permanent provisions should come before those that will be in force or have application for only a limited time (e.g., during a transitional period).

(k) Provisions affecting a series of related events or actions should be set out following the chronological order in which those events or actions will occur.

(l) Terminology should be used consistently throughout the Act and all secondary legislation; the same term should be used for the same case, and a different term used for a different case.

(m) Related provisions should be gathered together in the same part of the Act, and distinct groups of related provisions should be created as separate parts of the Act.

(n) Groups of provisions, and parts, should be ordered according to the same principles that govern individual provisions.

(o) Cross-reference should be made expressly in the Act to all other legislation of importance that supplements the Act (e.g., the Labor Code and the laws relating to pensions, health insurance or remuneration).

(p) Cross-reference should be made in provisions of the Act to other provisions of the Act with which they are linked, by reference to their correct numbering.

Notes

[1] Transcription of the document: Organization for Economic Cooperation and Development (OECD), "Civil Service Legislation Contents Checklist", *SIGMA Papers*, no. 5, Paris, 1996.

[2] "State officials" in Great Britain refers to officials in the centralized public administration.

Appendix B

"Next steps": separation of policy and operation

The Next Steps Program began in 1987 as a series of interviews with managers of various levels. The interviews gave the following results regarding the situation of the public administration:

1. An important issue of the functions of the government is the execution of policies. The separation of policy and execution would help each part to do its own work efficiently.
2. The government is not homogeneous and should not be administered as if it were.
3. The civil service is resistant to change. Therefore, a program of reform should be headed from above by assigning a high-level project manager.

To overcome these obstacles the Next Steps program was created. The program was announced in 1988 with four elements:

1. To identify the executive functions of the government and to organize them as isolated agencies.
2. The agencies should negotiate freedoms and flexibilities based on an analysis of the necessities of the business or area. And working on the premise of these freedoms and flexibilities, performance would improve.
3. To announce the creation of each agency with its objectives in Parliament.
4. To assign a project manager to make sure that the program works.

Although the agencies are under the command of the ministers, they are managed by chief executives, selected specifically for this job. They have delegated responsibility in finances and human resources in managing their respective agencies. The ministers are the ones who set the operational objectives of the agencies by means of a *framework document*.

The framework document is kind of a contract between the minister and the executive agency, which specifies the objectives expected of the agencies and the norms under which it operates.

There is a central Next Steps team that has a manager and depends on the Cabinet Office. At the beginning of the program, the function of this team was to identify possible agencies, to convince the authorities of the benefits of the program and finally to form these agencies. Now their function is rather to transmit better practices among the different executive agencies.

The process of selection of Next Steps executive agencies is part of a more general initiative that the government has followed in order to modernize the public administration, which involves:

1. Analyzing first if the activity in question is necessary.
2. If so, deciding if it is necessary for it to be under the government's responsibility.
3. If so, analyzing whether it is necessary for the government to carry it out (or for it to subcontract it).
4. If so, then analyzing how the efficiency of the department can be improved.

Once the candidate agency has been selected, its chief executive is chosen and the terms under which it will operate are established. Thus, the Next Steps team helps, but does not interfere in the process of selection or design of packages of incentives made to measure for the chief executive of the agency. The Treasury has a say in this process because of the financial risk. In order to attract capable candidates with vision, who could be agents for change, attractive compensation packages are prepared and they are paid according to their performance.

"Citizens' charter": program of performance measurement

This program was created in 1991 with the double purpose of measuring the agencies' performance and getting them closer to the customer, in this case the citizenry. The charters operate at the individual level of each agency and regularly publish their operative results, comparing them against the objectives that have been set for them. The performance evaluation for each agency contemplates the following points:

1. Operation standards.
2. Information and transparency.
3. Ease of option and consultation.
4. Courtesy and utility.
5. Value for their money.

Besides publishing the agencies' performance, the Citizens' Charter offers service to the client so that (s)he can submit any complaints and interests regarding the service offered by its different departments.

The justification for this program derives from the fact that previously, except for some political pressures, there was no incentive to give the client good service. In addition, at the moment of the administrative decentralization, in order to be able to assign resources to different items inside a department, it was necessary to know the priorities of the clients.

At the moment, in Great Britain there exist more than 8,000 Citizens' Charters covering diverse suppliers of local services such as policemen, firemen, hospitals, etc.

Examples

The patients' charter

Launched in 1991, it specifies the rights of the patients as to guaranteed waiting time, the right to receive written answers quickly, etc. The objectives of this program were mailed to every home in the United Kingdom.

The British rail charter (1992)

This program sets standards of punctuality for the British Rail System. The users can ask to have their money reimbursed if a train is delayed. The employees are to wear name tags, and their wages are related to their overall performance. *British Rail* must publish its punctuality report every month.

The underground user charter

Users can ask for a reimbursement of their ticket if they have to wait more than twenty minutes on the platform of the underground, or if the train is delayed more than twenty minutes in arriving at its destination.

The Citizens' Charter began as merely a form of evaluating the agencies' performance. It was limited to questioning the users about whether or not they were satisfied with the service. Users can now also suggest changes that could be implemented in order to improve the service.

Results of "Citizens' Charter"

This communication with the clients has helped agencies determine what "quality" means to the users, because the concept of quality that the users of the public services have does not usually coincide with that of the suppliers. Surveys made by the agency into the benefits of social security revealed that the users were not as interested in factors of comfort, such as having plants and carpets, as they were in questions of privacy at the moment they were explaining their case. In addition it was learned that people are more concerned about *knowing* exactly how long it would take to obtain an answer, than the length of the process itself.

Appendix C

Comparative analysis of critical points of the career civil service of OECD countries: United Kingdom, New Zealand and France

In order to carry out this analysis, the structure of the civil service was divided into eight critical points that represent the elements detected as most important for the case of Mexico.

Degree of autonomy in human resources management

Table C.1 Structures and Recruitment

United Kingdom	New Zealand	France
Departments decide on their salary scales and structures; in the *Senior Civil Service* they do not decide on the salary scale. Departments decide on their practices and criteria for selection and recruitment, provided certain general norms are observed such as open competition based on merit. When power was devolved in Great Britain there already existed institutions such as Citizens' Charter and Next Steps which facilitate performance evaluation, thus helping to have a meritocratic system with devolution of autonomy. In fact, the devolution of human resources management was developed agency by agency as they were prepared with systems of information and evaluation.	Chief executives of departments have total autonomy over salary scales and structures. Chief executives of departments have total autonomy over recruitment and selection, subject to certain basic principles.	Salary scales and structures are centralized by corps. Recruitment and selection practices are centralized by corps (such as the corps of accountants or lawyers). The totally open and delegate system of New Zealand functions by means of two systems: the formal, which is made up of norms and institutions, and the informal, which is turned into ethical, effective behavior through group pressure. This is due to the size of the country's population and its strongly ethical culture.

Comments

The need for decentralization of human resources both in the United Kingdom and in New Zealand was the result of the devolution of power and autonomy to the departments. The reason why this flexibility worked is because both countries had adequate incentives to make the model work; in the case of Britain, the principle of *accountability*, and in the case of New Zealand, the model of group pressure.

Table C.2 Negotiations with unions

United Kingdom	New Zealand	France
Negotiation with the unions depends on the agency or department. Decentralized recruitment and selection have facilitated informal, monthly meetings to discuss mutual points of interest. The evaluation systems were designed in conjunction with the unions. And the unions, for their part, adapted to the reform.	Negotiation between the chief executive and the union for the agency. The chief executive consults with the State Services Commission in order to have an idea of what the arrangements are like in other places.	Negotiation centralized by corps. The need to have a common negotiating front in the face of growing unionism was one of the main reasons for creating a civil service.

Entry and separation

Table C.3 Entry

United Kingdom	New Zealand	France
Two ways: free designation and by competition	It is all free designation, but based on merit	Entry to the service, not to the post, by competition.
Free designation is only used under exceptional conditions, and there is a committee that authorizes a great number of these cases.	If anyone in an agency does not agree with a designation of a chief executive, he can ask for a revision to be made of the choice and for the State Sector Commission to review it.	Only in cases of high rank can there be free designation. Personnel hired by contract, but without entering the service.
Entry to the service is possible at any level.	Entry to the service is possible at any level.	Entry to the service is only possible from the bottom.
The competition is open to attract a greater number of candidates	Open competition	Open competition is only for entering the service and certain corps.

Table C.4 Separation

United Kingdom	New Zealand	France
Anyone can be dismissed for justified causes such as decline in performance.	The chief executive can dismiss someone if he thinks it necessary. The State Services Commission, with the authorization of the cabinet, can dismiss a chief executive. The total discretion in the case of New Zealand does not lend itself to injustices due to the informal system of group pressure mentioned in point I.	When a person enters the service, he acquires a guaranteed job for life and it is nearly impossible to fire him. The career system with work guaranteed for life in France has hampered the competitiveness and efficiency of government employees.

Table C.5 Promotion

United Kingdom	New Zealand	France
The departments decide on their own practices, but this must be based on merit and performance evaluation.	The chief executive is responsible for these practices, but based on merit.	Promotion from class to class based on merit and by evaluation. Stepwise promotion within a class (or grade) is automatic year by year. The automatic promotion model in France generates an incentive for inefficiency

Table C.6 Performance evaluation

United Kingdom	New Zealand	France
Each department has its own system of evaluation (except for the higher posts of the Senior Civil Service). By March, 1999, it is expected that everyone will be using this system (Senior Civil Service). There also exists evaluation by the citizenry through the "Citizens' Charter". For example, in the Land Registry Office of the United Kingdom, the evaluation is made between the worker and his supervisor, comparing the goals set, with the achievements (later on, goals are set for the following year). The case of the Citizens' Charter in the United Kingdom means that the same market evaluated the performance of the agencies and of the chief executives. This gives the advantages of objectivity and low cost.	The State Services Commission is responsible for the evaluation of the chief executives and the agencies separately. The results of the evaluation of the chief executives is reported to the ministers responsible.	Only for those employees who are going to move from one grade or class to another. The evaluation is made by a committee of approximately 6 persons, half of whom work with the person being evaluated (including the boss) and the other half in the department of human resources of the department.

Incentives and remuneration systems

Table C.7 Salary scale

United Kingdom	New Zealand	France
As of April 1, 1999, ministers and officials in charge of departments and agencies can decide on their own salary scale. For higher positions it is centralized (see appendix on Senior Civil Service)	Heads of department have total autonomy over the salary scale of the department.	Salary scale centralized by corps

Comments

1. One advantage of having a central salary scale is that it facilitates the mobility of employees both between departments and within them, because there is a uniform structure of payments.
2. On the other hand, if the government is heterogeneous (as happens in most cases, including Mexico), it can be difficult to adjust the different pay structures to a central salary scale.

Table C.8 Bonuses

United Kingdom	New Zealand	France
Agencies and departments decide whether to give them.	The head of department decides on everything related to the granting of bonuses	A bonus of a maximum of three months' salary is given for performance.

Table C.9 Support organizations

United Kingdom	New Zealand	France
The Office of the Public Service, which is part of the Cabinet Office, depends on the Prime Minister and is responsible for the operational efficiency of the central government and the development of public service reforms. Finance department sets the budget for the secretariats.	The State Services Commission is responsible for assigning activities and responsibilities among the departments. Authorizes the assignation of high posts and evaluates the performance of the chief executives. Is responsible for promoting training and development.	The general direction of administration and public function depends on the Prime Minister and is in charge of the coordination of the secretariats and the civil service.

Table C.10 Introduction: how gradual it is

United Kingdom	New Zealand	France
The departments decide whether to open the existing positions to competition or whether everyone retains his position. In the case of HMSO (Her Majesty's Stationery Office) of the United Kingdom, positions were opened to competition and a lot of personnel competed and won better posts than before the restructuring. This meant that other personnel lost their jobs but the process was effective in creating an awareness of the need for change.	Employees keep their jobs with the decentralization of the human resources administration.	

Table C.11 Scope of the civil service

United Kingdom	New Zealand	France
From the base to the under-secretary	Includes base and chief executives of the departments	Includes base

Evaluation of governments

International Forum of Davos, Switzerland

Graph C.1 shown below was prepared using information obtained from the World Economics Forum in Davos, Switzerland. These results are based on interviews with citizens.

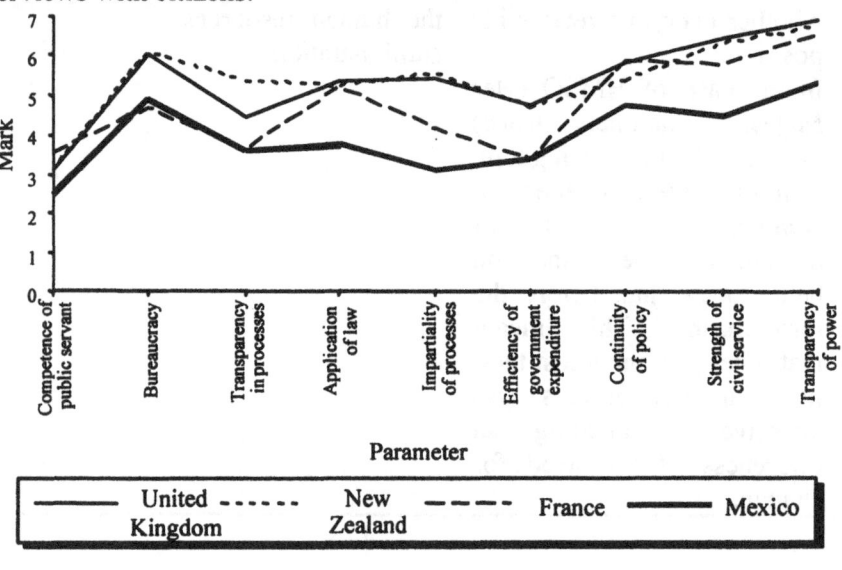

Average	
United Kingdom	5.35
New Zealand	5.39
France	4.76
Mexico	3.96

Graph C.1 Comparison of OECD countries

Appendix D

Comparative analysis of critical points in the career civil service in Latin American countries

In order to make this analysis, the structure of the civil service is divided into eight critical points that are useful for the Mexican context:

1. Degree of autonomy in human resources management
2. Entry and separation
3. Promotion
4. Performance evaluation
5. Incentives and remuneration systems
6. Support organisms
7. Introduction: how gradual it is
8. Scope of the civil service

Level of autonomy in managing human resources

Table D.1 Structures and recruitment

Chile	Argentina	Colombia	Bolivia
The Treasury Ministry assigns the financial resources that may be used for human resources remuneration. Each organization is free to use these funds and set salary scales they consider appropriate. The Chilean Act establishes basic selection and recruitment principles that the organizations must follow, but the organizations have sufficient autonomy to decide on the procedures that are most suitable.	Due to the similar structures of most of the organizations regulated by the Act, all processes are designed and controlled centrally.	Follows the French model of centralization. The Treasury Ministry assigns financial resources and the items into which he wishes to distribute them. The structures and processes of selection and recruitment are centrally controlled by the CNSC; however, the organizations may make modifications they consider appropriate, upon agreement with the CNSC.	The Bolivian Act grants autonomy to all agencies in regulating management processes. Each agency proposes its own salary scales and organizational structures based on the policy issued for this purpose by the governing body.

Comments

1. The civil service systems in Latin America are generally controlled centrally.
2. There are few decentralized control mechanisms and performance agreements between the organisms, the Executive and the citizenry.
3. Chile and Bolivia are the countries that grant greatest freedom to their organizations in defining the most convenient organizational structure, and the way in which it distributes its human resources funds. This freedom is the basis of an efficient public administration because after all the public sector competes against the private sector for better trained human resources. However, if unqualified employees cannot be separated out, one runs the risk of having twin or ghost organizations that can negatively affect the efficiency (due to duplication of functions) and considerably increase operation costs.

Table D.2 Negotiations with unions

Chile	Argentina	Colombia	Bolivia
There are no unions in the public administration, since they are prohibited by law. There exists a National Fiscal Employees Association (ANEF, for its initials in Spanish), which does not have the same force as a union. The career civil service includes all professionals belonging to the ANEF, but does not include secretaries, chauffeurs, and similar levels.	There is the Civil Personnel Alliance of the Nation, which has sufficient force to reject changes that may be damaging to its members.	The Colombian Act does include all members below the level of chief of division (equivalent to section director); however, it only considers those of the professional level and up, qualified for promotions, excluding the administrative (secretaries) and auxiliary staff (chauffeurs, messengers, etc.) The administrative, auxiliary and some professional levels belong to a union that does not have much force.	The Bolivian Act includes all employees in public agencies, including unionized personnel. However, in the event of a union existing that is characterized by its specific strength, each agency is free to regulate the Act as it feels appropriate in order to avoid conflicts.

Comments

1. Three of the four Latin American countries analyzed have different union systems: in Chile, unions for bureaucrats are nonexistent; in Colombia they enjoy little power; and in Argentina they are so powerful that they have neutralized the plans for modernizing the public administration.
2. Chile and Argentina include analysts and professionals in the Career Civil Service System (in Mexico these workers correspond to base analysts). Bolivia and Colombia also include auxiliary positions (chauffeurs, gardeners, etc.).
3. The case of Bolivia is different from the others. The agencies have enough autonomy and regulate their processes as they consider appropriate in order to carry out their administration and avoid conflicts with the unions.

Entry and separation

Table D.3 Entry

Chile	Argentina	Colombia	Bolivia
Two possible ways: through competition or free designation. Free designation is for a limited period (maximum of one year) and performance is constantly evaluated. Does not belong to the civil service. The competition is normally closed, intended only for members of the civil service. In the event there are not 2 or more candidates with the necessary qualifications, an open competition is announced.	Closed, only those registered in the Career Civil Service may participate. Only the lowest level of the career hierarchy participate in open competitions. The selection process is very strict and complicated, based on theoretical knowledge and solving real cases.	Two ways possible: by competition or by free designation. Free designation is used in specific cases and for a period of not more than 4 months. The employee designated in this way is to be constantly evaluated and will not belong to the civil service. The competition is normally closed, intended only for members of the civil service. In the event there are not 2 or more candidates with the necessary qualifications, an open competition is announced.	The agencies are able to select the type of competition that will be held: by direct invitation, closed competition, or open competition. Each agency is able to select the process and tests to be applied to select the ideal candidate, as well as the point value that each test will have in the final mark.

Comments

1. Chile, Argentina and Colombia give preference to the public servants already registered, which gives an important advantage with respect to continuity (institutional memory). However, the disadvantage lies in the fact that the best officials may be overlooked by not giving them the opportunity to compete against registered officials.
2. Bolivian law grants the agencies the freedom to choose the type of competition, the criteria for evaluating candidates and the weighting of each criterion. This scheme can be corrupted and fall into nepotism or string-pulling, in a similar way to what happens under a scheme of free appointment or designation.

Table D.4 Separation

Chile	Argentina	Colombia	Bolivia
Establishes clear conditions under which an employee may be dismissed from the civil service, mainly for poor performance. Resigning is "voluntary", but an employee's resignation may be requested. If the employee refuses to submit his resignation, his post is declared vacant.	The Act specifies that there will be dismissal after the first deficient mark in the performance evaluation. In addition, there are other discretionary reasons, such as "abusing a superior", which may warrant the dismissal of the civil servant.	Establishes that, at the first deficient evaluation of the employee, the post will be declared vacant. An employee cannot be dismissed if he is under investigation in the National Civil Service Commission.	The Act specifies the reasons for which an employee may be dismissed from the civil service. Poor performance, as witnessed by the performance evaluations, is also a reason for dismissal. The Act does not specify the rights of an employee when he is dismissed from the civil service.

Comments

1. In general, the criteria for separation are very strict as far as unsatisfactory performance evaluations are concerned, creating great pressure on the evaluator.
2. In Chile, an employee may be asked to resign, which causes a loss of responsibility for the organization and is a way of avoiding the procedures determined by law.

Table D.5 Promotion

Chile	Argentina	Colombia	Bolivia
Is done by closed competition and only those employees who satisfy the necessary requirements as well as good performance evaluations may participate. The employee who holds the first post in the promotion ladder below the vacant one has a right to be promoted if he fulfills the minimum requirements.	There are three guiding principles to consider: performance evaluation, training and seniority. Each of the posts has a specific profile defined which an applicant must cover.	Is done by closed competition where only those employees who fulfil the basic requirements and have good performance evaluations may participate.	Promotions are given through closed competition or by direct invitation. Only those employees who fulfil the requirements of the vacant post and have satisfactory performance evaluations over the last two years may participate.

Comments

All the countries, and more so in the case of Argentina, promote those employees who are already registered in the civil service. The possibilities of being hired as an external person are limited, which has the advantage of generating continuity (institutional memory), but the disadvantage that it may not acquire the best officials by not giving them an opportunity to compete against registered officials.

Table D.6 Performance evaluation

Chile	Argentina	Colombia	Bolivia
The Act establishes basic principles for the process. Each organism is free to create its own procedures according to the basic principles defined. Based on a system of merits and demerits throughout the year.	Defined centrally, held six months after entry and thereafter once a year.	The Act defines the items to be evaluated and the weight given to each in the final mark. The organisms only decide – based on the definition of functions – the range over which each item will be evaluated.	Measures principally three aspects: efficiency, effectiveness and economy of management. The Act only describes the basic principles of the overall process. The regulations are made by each agency according to its needs.

Comments

1. The performance evaluations have proven to be a failure in these three countries: in Chile, 98% of all career officials are graded as excellent; in Argentina 0.5% of the officials have been fired for poor performance; and in Colombia there is a similar phenomenon to the one occurring in Chile.
2. The process of performance evaluation is vital for the promotion, training and termination processes, which are critical points in the civil service system. A process of performance evaluation that is really effective guarantees the continuance and progression of the best civil servants and, consequently, a more efficient public administration.

Incentives and systems of remuneration

Table D.7 Salary scale

Chile	Argentina	Colombia	Bolivia
Each organization defines its salary scale providing it does not exceed the budgetary ceiling set by the Treasury Ministry.	Centralized	Centralized	The salary scale is defined by each department based on the country's salary policy. The Treasury Ministry sets a budgetary ceiling for the payroll.

Comments

Argentina and Colombia determine salary scales and salary levels centrally. Chile and Bolivia are free to adapt their salaries and thus to compete with the private sector, recruiting suitable personnel for each vacant position.

Table D.8 Bonuses

Chile	Argentina	Colombia	Bolivia
Based on performance evaluation; the Act does not specify the amount of the bonuses.	The Act does not go deeply into the topic of bonuses; they are defined centrally.	The Act does not specify the amount of the bonuses nor the way the performance evaluation affects the granting of bonuses.	Based on the performance evaluation. Every year bonuses are given to those assessed as "excellent". The maximum amount of the bonus is one month's basic salary.

Comments

1. None of the laws goes deeply into the topic. Except for Chile and Bolivia it is understood that they are controlled centrally. Most cases are defined according to performance evaluation.
2. Bolivia is the only country that limits the amount of the bonus to a month's salary and to budgetary availability.

Table D.9 Support organizations

Chile	Argentina	Colombia	Bolivia
The Act establishes that the Treasury Ministry, through a sub-direction, is to oversee compliance with the norms regarding the civil service. However, it fails to define the methods of control that are to be used.	The National Administrative Profession System (Sinapa, its abbreviation in Spanish), administered by the Secretariat of the Public Function, is in charge of the administration of personnel belonging to the Career Civil Service in questions of entry, promotion, training, evaluation, remuneration and separation. The Public Servants' Training and Instruction Program is responsible for training human resources who aspire to be government administrators and belong to the Career Civil Service.	Has a National Civil Service Commission, subdivided into section commissions. These commissions are in charge of establishing the norms for the civil service and overseeing compliance with them. In addition, there is a Committee in each organism that attends to the every-day, local situations.	The Treasury Ministry is in charge of the Personnel Administration System through three levels of organization: Normative and consulting level, the responsibility of the governing body of the Personnel Administration System. Executive level, represented by the maximum authority of each agency. Operative level, consisting of a unit in charge of administering the personnel of each agency.

Comments

1. Chile has few support mechanisms and delegates most of the responsibilities to the same organizations. However, the Ministry of the Treasury, through a Sub-direction, has the ability to modify the Law and interpret it in administrative matters.
2. Argentina has an integrated system that reaches very high levels (Secretariat). Several organizations are coordinated for the development of human resources and to solve the problems that derive from the introduction of laws in this area.
3. Colombia organizes the administration of the civil service through a National Commission and through Section Commissions of the Civil Service that carry out all activities including the creation of norms, overseeing their observance, the auditing of processes, the authorization of modifications to processes, and the resolution of controversies, among others. It has a simple organization, seemingly easy to introduce. In spite of this, it has lately been overloaded with work, which gives the impression of inefficiency and excessive red tape.
4. Bolivia makes up its Personnel Administration System at different levels of the central government; from the normative and advisory level, directly dependent on the Ministry of Treasury, to the operative level that is part of the civil service in each agency. It is a complicated model because each level has its specific powers, which can on occasions cause differences between one level and another; for example, the normative level issues general guidelines that the departments must follow, but it is the responsibility of the operative level to regulate those general guidelines.

Table D.10 Introduction: how gradual it is.

Chile	Argentina	Colombia	Bolivia
When the Act went into effect, all existing posts were respected, without considering a maximum term for converting them into civil service positions.	Its introduction has been taking place for years together with other efforts at public administration modernization. It does not establish a term for converting all of the positions into civil service positions.	The Act set a limit of six months for converting all posts into civil service positions by means of open competitions.	Gave all agencies a limit of four months to develop an inventory of personnel of the agency to prepare the specific regulations for matching. Later gave one year to adjust the profiles of the agency to the required profiles. This decided the ratification of an employee, his training, reallocation or removal from the institution.

Comments

1. Different schemes have one point in common: the non-removability of the public servants before introducing the Act. This point has become a critical one because the inefficiency of the previous officials makes the creation of a twin or ghost structure necessary, that carries out the same functions at a higher cost.
2. The ideal at this point is to carry out the changes gradually, with definition of profiles and adequate functions, opening the positions voluntarily to competition, up to a term of not over a certain number of years, by the end of which all the posts will become civil service positions.
3. The scheme that seems most gradual and best planned of the four countries is that of Bolivia, which establishes a clear procedure by means of which first the current situation is analyzed, in order to then propose the solution that is really necessary. Later on the two situations are compared to identify areas of opportunity and to begin the adaptation of organizational and staff structures. The adaptation has a period of execution of one year, after which all the positions will be of the civil service.

Table D.11 Scope of the civil service

Chile	Argentina	Colombia	Bolivia
From posts of analysts to posts of heads of department (similar to section director).	From lower to medium high professional posts within the organization.	From posts of analysts to posts of division heads (equivalent to section director).	Up to higher levels (undersecretaries) from the lowest unionized levels.

Comments

1. All countries define their highest sphere as designated, calling the positions of free designation outside the scope of the Career Civil Service. On occasions, this sphere penetrates as far as the third and fourth levels below the head of the organism, significantly diminishing the quantity of levels in the public official's career.
2. In all cases the Career Civil Service System includes the analysts and professionals (in Mexico they correspond to the base analysts).

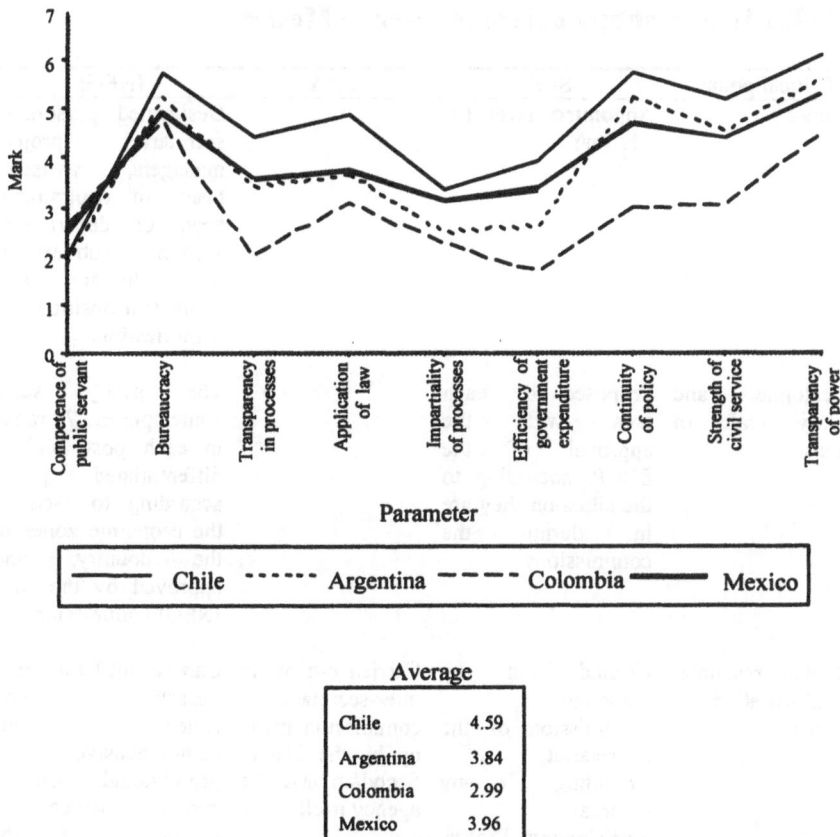

Average	
Chile	4.59
Argentina	3.84
Colombia	2.99
Mexico	3.96

Graph D.1 Comparison of the Latin American countries analyzed

Appendix E

Inter-institutional comparison and evaluation of departments with career civil service in Mexico

Table E.1 Inter-institutional comparison in Mexico

Critical points	SRE	CNA	INEGI
Scopes	Appointed level (to advisor)		Designated personnel: secretaries, project managers, assistant heads of department, head of department, section subdirector, area director and equivalent positions by authorization.
Catalogue and salary scale of posts	Proposed by each area with the approval of the SHCP, according to the situation they are in during the commissions.		The salary scale contemplates 7 ranks in each post, and is differentiated according to each of the economic zones in the country, and approved by the SIP-INEGI commission.
Human resources administration system	Carried out by Personnel Commission of the Secretariat, excluding any external participation. That is, the External Affairs Secretariat carries out this work autonomously.	Carried out by an inter-secretarial commission made up by the SHCP, Secodam and the agency itself.	Carried out by a cross-departmental body called the comprehensive professionalization system, which is responsible for the organization and functioning of the designated public servants.

234

Table E.1 Inter-institutional comparison in Mexico (cont'd)

Critical points	SRE	CNA	INEGI
Regulations for selection of personnel	Each department establishes the personnel recruitment and selection regulations, and is the one who applies the evaluation criteria, namely, it is a system generated from within and applicable outward.	The personnel management dependent on the sub-direction of administrative services carries out personnel selection generally according to the needs of each area or department.	The establishment of the norm is the job of the SIP-INEGI Commission, with a function that is completely autonomous of the normative departments of the federal public administration.
Performance evaluation	The performance evaluation is done by the Personnel commission of the Mexican foreign civil service. This consists of competition exams in order to rise stepwise on the promotion ladder for which a term of 7 years is allowed.	Each area sets the evaluation criteria for the personnel. The evaluation is done annually by the administrative units of personnel management. A criterion for dismissal of the employee from his post is having an unsatisfactory evaluation on two consecutive occasions.	The performance evaluation criteria are set by the SIP-INEGI commission, holding a periodic evaluation every three years; in the event this exam is not passed, the employee will undergo a training program, and if this is not passed, this will constitute grounds for terminating the labor relation without any responsibility on the part of the INEGI.

Table E.1 Inter-institutional comparison in Mexico (cont'd)

Critical points	SRE	CNA	INEGI
Incentives	If not, the personnel will be assigned to a lower level in the department. Within the Mexican foreign civil service a system exclusively designed for career personnel is not contemplated; what does exist is a function of the budgetary savings of the secretariat, by approval of the SHCP.	Incentives are granted for the employee's performance and training. The economic bonus depends on authorization by the SHCP.	Posts by free designation are: the president of the INEGI, coordinators, directors general, regional directors, as well as equivalent posts according to norms.
Free designation	Free designation is seen at levels of: ambassadors and general consuls, for which names and backgrounds of candidates are proposed by the secretary of External Affairs to the president of the Republic. In the event of these being members of the SCEM, they do not lose their prerogatives.	Director general, staff of consultants, general subdirectors and managers. (May be carried out by the secretary of the Semarnap, governors of the states or the head of the Federal Executive).	The posts held by free designation are: the president of the INEGI, coordinators, directors general, regional directors, as well as equivalent posts according to norms.
Removal of a public servant	In the SCEM not passing the competition exams that are expressly applied to determine the level of professional development of the worker, directly related to performance, is considered a cause for removal from his position.	The removal of a civil service employee by the free designation of a superior, is not possible on the sole basis of an unsatisfactory evaluation on two consecutive occasions.	The SIP guarantees the continuance in one's post as long as an optimum performance is shown, so that the worker cannot be dismissed on the free designation of a superior.

Table E.1 Inter-institutional comparison in Mexico (cont'd)

Critical points	SRE	CNA	INEGI
Competition for position	The competitions for positions are open. However, to enter the SCEM, it is necessary to complete an academic training course specified by law.	In the first phase, candidates are proposed to occupy a vacancy; in the event that this phase is declared void, an external competition will be opened for these posts.	The system is open, remaining subject to the discretion of the commission whether the competition is to be open or closed.

Bibliography

Aguilar Villanueva, Luis (1996) 'Current Challenges of the Mexican State and of Mexican Public Administration', *International Journal of Public Administration*, vol. 19, no. 9, Pennsylvania State University.

Ai Camp, Roderic (1996) *Politics in Mexico*, 2nd ed., Oxford University Press.

Alchian, Armen A. (1959) 'Private Property and Relative Cost of Tenure', Phillip D. Bradley (ed.), *The Public State in Union Power*, University of Virginia Press.

_____ (1961) *Some Economics of Property*, Rand Corporation.

_____ and Harold Demsetz (1972) 'Production, Information Costs, and Economic Organization', *American Economic Review*, vol. 62.

Alderman, Harold, Sudharshan Canagarajah and Stephen S. Younger, (1993) *Consequences of Permanent Lay-off from Civil Service: Results from a Survey of Retrenched Workers in Ghana*, Cornell Food and Nutrition Policy Program (Work Document no. 35), Ithaca, N.Y, February.

Alessi, Louise de (1980) 'The Economics of Property Rights: A Review of the Evidence', *Research in Law and Economics*, vol. 2.

_____ and Robert J. Staaf, (1988) 'Property Rights and Choice', *Law and Economics: An Introduction*, 2nd ed., Academic Press.

Arellano, David (1997) *Unequal Advances and Unclear Intentions: The Mexican State Reform and the Managerialist Strategy*, CIDE, Mexico City, mimeo.

_____ (1973) *Case Studies Methodology in Social Sciences: Elemental Bases* CIDE (Work Document no. 46), Mexico City.

Armstrong, William (1973) *El Informe Fulton: tres estudios sobre el servicio civil británico*, Escuela Nacional de Administración Pública, Madrid.

Bale, Malcolm and Dale, Tony (1997) *Public Sector Reform in New Zealand and Its Relevance to Developing Countries*, World Bank, Washington, mimeo.

Bardach, Eugene (1998) *Getting Agencies to Work Together: The Practice and Theory of Managerial Craftsmanship*, Brookings Institution Press, Washington.

_____ (1998) *Los ocho pasos para el análisis de políticas públicas. Un manual para la práctica*, Centro de Investigación y Docencia Económicas, Miguel Ángel Porrúa, Mexico City.

Barenstein, Jorge (1982) *El análisis de la burocracia estatal desde la perspectiva weberiana: los administradores en el sector público mexicano*, CIDE, Mexico City.

Barzelay, Michael (1992) *Breaking through Bureaucracy*, Berkeley, University of California.

Beck, Birgitta Thellman, Johansson Erik y David H. Fretwell (1995) *Privatization and Restructuring: Issues Related to Divestiture of Labor and Social Assets*, draft no. 3, World Bank, Washington, April, mimeo.

Becker, Gary (1993) 'A Theory of Competition among Pressure Groups for Political Influence', *Quarterly Journal of Economics*, vol. 98.

Berke H., J. Perry y T. Tbonen (1996) Civil *Service Systems in Comparative Perspective*, Indiana University Press.

Betancourt, Ernesto (1995) *Documento de trabajo para la formulación de una política macroinstitucional para la reforma del gobierno de Nicaragua*, United Nations Development Program (UNDP)/ Management Development Program (MDP), January, mimeo.

_____ (1995) *Documento para la discusión de una política macroinstitucional para la reforma de la administración pública de Nicaragua*, PNUD/ MDP, April, mimeo.

_____ (1995) *Informe final: propuesta para proyecto piloto, Servicio Gerencial y Técnico de Estado (SGTE)*, Republic of Nicaragua, May, mimeo.

_____ (1996) *Sugerencias para integrar la implantación de las reformas de la administración pública de Bolivia*, January, includes *Guía para la Suscripción de Convenios de Fortalecimiento Institucional* (m), MOSTA-SENDA Project, Consejo Nacional de Modernización del Estado (Conam), Ecuador, May, mimeo.

_____ *A New Approach to Develop Institutional Infrastructure*, paper presented at the National Conference of the American Society for Public Administration, July, 1996.

Bozeman Barry (1998) *La gestión pública, su situación actual* (introductory study by Enrique Cabrero Mendoza), Fondo de Cultura Económica/Colegio Nacional de Ciencias Políticas y Administración Pública/Universidad Autónoma de Tlaxcala (Nuevas Lecturas de Política y Gobierno series), Mexico City.

Bravo Ahuja, Víctor (coord.) (1989) *Tendencias contemporáneas de la administración pública. Ensayos sobre la modernidad nacional*, Diana, Mexico City.

Buchanan, James M. (1972) 'Politics, Property, and the Law: An Alternative Interpretation of Miller *et al.* V. Schoene', *Journal of Law and Economics*, vol. 15, no. 2, October.

Camp, Roderic Ai (1996) *Politics in Mexico*, 2nd ed., Oxford University Press.

Campbell, Colin (1995) 'Does Reinvention Need Reinvention? Lessons from Truncated Managerialism in Britain', *Governance: An International Journal of Policy Administration*, no. 4, October.

Campbell, Tim (1997) *Innovations and Risk Taking: The Engine of Reform in Local Government in Latin America and the Caribbean*, World Bank (Discussion Document of the World Bank, no. 357), Washington.

Campos, José Edgardo y Sanjay Pradhan (1996) *Budgetary Institutions and Expenditure Outcomes: Binding Governments to Fiscal Performance*, World

Bank (Work Document on Political Research, no. 1646), Washington, September.

_____ 'Evaluating Public Expenditure Management Systems: An Experimental Methodology with an Application to the Australia and New Zealand Reforms', *Journal of Policy Analysis and Management,* vol. 16.

Chaudhry, Shahid Amjad, Reid Gary J. and Waleed Haider Malik (eds.), (1994) *Civil Service Reform in Latin America and the Caribbean: Proceedings of a Conference,* World Bank, (Technical Document of the World Bank, no. 259).

Coase, Ronald H. (1961) 'The Problem of Social Cost', *Journal of Law and Economics,* vol. 1.

Cooter, Robert and Ulen Thomas (1984) *Law and Economics,* Harper Collins.

Diamond, Larry (1997) 'Repensar la sociedad civil', *Revista Metapolítica,* vol. 1, April-June.

Dror, Yehezkel (1996) *La capacidad de gobernar,* Fondo de Cultura Económica, Mexico City.

Embassy of France, 'La función pública en Francia', *Hechos y cifras,* no. 42, Regional information service.

Federación de Sindicatos de Trabajadores al Servicio del Estado (1996) *La reforma de la administración pública y la modernización sindical,* March.

_____ (1997) 'Servicio Civil de Carrera, sin pérdida de los derechos adquiridos', *Acontecer Sindical,* Mexico, March.

Fiszbein, Ariel (1992) *Labor Entrenchment and Redundancy Compensation in State Owned Enterprises: The Case of Sri Lanka,* World Bank, (Internal Discussion Document, Southern Region of Asia), Washington, December.

Fukuyarna, Francis (1995) *Trust,* Free Press Paperbacks, Division of Simon and Schuster, New York.

Furubotri, Erick G. y Rudolf Richter (eds.) (1991) *The New Institutional Economics: A Collection of Articles from the Journal of Institutional and Theoretical Economics,* Texas A & M University Press, College Station.

Ganley, J. A. And Cubbin J. S. (1992) *Public sector efficiency measurement,* Elsevier Science, Holland.

García Ruiz, José Luis (1997) *Retos y condicionantes para el establecimiento de un sistema de servicio civil en México,* CIDE, Mexico City, mimeo.

Geddes, Barbara, *Politician's Dilemma, Building State Capacity in Latin America,* University of California Press, 1994.

_____ (1997) 'Reform as a Collective Good: Political Entrepreneurs and Democratic Politics', chap. 2 of *Politician's Dilemma: Building State Capacity in Latin America,* University of California Press, Berkeley.

Government of the United States (1997) 'Improving Performance in a Balanced Budget World,' Section IV of *Budget, Fiscal Year 1998,* Washington.

Goel, S. L. (1984) *International Civil Service Principles, Practice and Prospects,* Sterling, India.

Gómez, Henry (1997) *Government Reform in Latin America: How Far Have We Come?,* paper presented to the International Association for Administration Schools and Institutes, Quebec, July.

Gore, Al (1993) *From Red Tape to Result: Creating a Government that Works Better and Costs Less: Report on the National Performance Review*, Random House.

_____ (1994) *Un gobierno más efectivo y menos costoso*, Edamex.

Graham, Carol (1996) *Raising the Stakes in the Social Services, Social Security and Privatization in Peru*, draft, April.

_____ (1997) *Building Support for Market Reforms in Bolivia: The Capitalization and Popular Participation Programs*, draft, May.

Grindle, Merilee S. (1977) 'Patrons and Clients in the Bureaucracy: Career Networks in Mexico', *Latin American Research Review*, vol. 12.

Guatemala (1997) *Anteproyecto Ley de Servicio Civil*, January.

Guerrero, Omar (1986) *La teoría de la administración pública*, Harla.

Haggard, Stephen (1996) *The Reform State in Latin America*, mimeo.

Hays, Steven W. and Kearney Richard C. (1995) *Public Personnel Administration*, Prentice Hall, USA.

Ibarra, Luis Guillermo (1997) Notes on a lecture given during the 'Foro de Consulta sobre el Servicio Civil de Carrera: Dignificación, Profesionalización y Crítica del Servidor Público', organized by the FSTSTE, February.

Ingraham, Patricia W (1995) *The Foundation of Merit Public Service in American Democracy*, Johns Hopkins University Press, Boston and London.

_____ and Kettl Donald E (1992) *Agenda for excellence*, Chatham House, EUA.

_____ and Rosenbloom David H. (eds.) (1992) *The promise and paradox of civil service reform*, University of Pittsburgh Press, EUA.

Instituto Apoyo, *Apoyo al Congreso*, several issues, Lima, 1991 - 1993.

_____ (1995) *El Sistema de Remuneraciones y Pensiones del Sector Público* Lima,.

Johnson, Ronald and Libecap, Gary (1994) *The Federal Civil Service System and the Problem of Bureaucracy*, The University of Chicago Press, USA.

Kaufman, R. (1996) *The politics of state reform: a review of theoretical approaches'*, mimeo.

Kettl Donald F. (1997) 'The Global Revolution in Public Management: Driving Themes, Missing Links', *Journal of Policy Analysis and Management*, vol. 16, p. 460.

Kim, Paul S. (1988) *Japan's Civil Service System*, Greenwood Press, USA.

Kliksberg, Bernardo (ed.) (1994) *El rediseño del Estado: una perspectiva internacional*, FCE-INAP, Mexico City.

Klinger, Donald E. and Nalbandian, Donald (1993) *Public Personnel Management: Contexts and Strategies*, Prentice Hall, USA.

Klitgaard, R. (1995) *Information and Incentives in Institutional Reform*, Center, Maryland.

Klitgaard, Robert (1996) *Healing Sick Institutions: The Case of La Paz, Bolivia*, prepared with Ronald MacLean-Abaroa for the World Bank, March, mimeo.

_____ (1997) *Cleaning Up and Invigorating the Civil Service,* report prepared for the Department of Operations Evaluation, World Bank, Washington, March.

Koh, Byung Chul (1989) *Japan's Administrative Elite,* University of California Press, USA.

Kreps, David M. (1990) *A Course in Microeconomic Theory,* Princeton University Press.

Laking, Rob (1996) *Public Management Lessons for Developing Countries and the World Bank: Summary of Background Papers,'* World Bank, Washington, mimeo.

Langston, Joy. (1995) 'Sobrevivir y prosperar, una búsqueda de las causas de las facciones políticas intrarrégimen en México', *Política y Gobierno, vol. 11,* no. 2, CIDE, Mexico City.

Méndez, José Luis (1994) 'La reforma del Estado en México: alcances y límites', *Gestión y Política Pública, vol. 3,* no. 1.

Mény, Yves (1990) *Government and Politics in Western Europe. Britain, France, Italy, West Germany,* Oxford University Press, USA.

Mercuro, Nicholas and Ryan, Timothy P. (1984) *Law, Economics and Public Policy,* JAI Press.

Merino Huerta, Mauricio (1996) 'De la lealtad individual a la responsabilidad pública', *Revista de Administración Pública,* no. 91, INAP, Mexico City.

_____ 'Servicio Civil', *Diccionario de Política y Administración Pública,* Colegio de Licenciados en Ciencias Políticas y Administración Pública, Mexico City.

Metcalfe, Les (1993) 'Public Management: From Imitation to Innovation', *Australian Journal of Public Administration,* no. 3, September.

Mills, Bradford y David E. Sahn, *Reducing the Size of the Public Sector Work Force: Institutional Constraints and Human Consequences in Guinea,* Cornell University, Ithaca, NY, May, 1993, mimeo.

Ministry of Finance. (n.d.), *Guidelines for Drafting Performance Agreements with State Enterprises in Thailand,* Government of Thailand.

Ministry of Treasury (1997) *Reglamento para el Personal Eventual de Programas y Proyectos del Sector Público,* La Paz, Bolivia, June.

Moctezuma, Esteban (1997) *Iniciativa de Ley para la Profesionalización y Evaluación del Desempeño de los Servidores Públicos de la Administración Pública Federal Centralizada,* Senate of the Republic, Mexico City.

Moore, Mark H. (1995) *Creating Public Value, Strategic Management in Government,* Harvard University Press, Cambridge, Mass.

Mueller, Dennis C. (1989) *Public Choice II,* Cambridge University Press.

_____ (1997) 'Constitutional Public Choice', in Dennis C. Mueller (ed.), *Perspectives on Public Choice: A Handbook,* Cambridge University Press.

Niskanen, William A (1994), 'The peculiar economics of bureaucracy', *American Economic Review,* Papers and Proceedings, no. 58, 1968.

_____ *Bureaucracy and Public Economics,* Edward Elgar.

Nye, Joseph S., Zelikow Philip D. and King , David C. (1997) *Why People don't Trust Government,* Harvard University Press.

Olson Mancur (1965) *The Logic of Collective Action: Public Goods and the Theory of Groups,* Harvard University Press.

Organization for Economic Cooperation and Development (1988) *Why Economic Policies Change Course*, Paris.

Osborne, David and Gaebler, Ted (1992) *Reinventing Government*, Addison-Wesley.

_____ (1982) *The Rise and Decline of Nations*, Yale University Press.

Oszlak, Oscar (ed.) (1984) *Teoría de la burocracia estatal: enfoques críticos*, Paidós, Argentina.

Pardo, María del Carmen (1995) 'El servicio civil de carrera en México: un imperativo de la modernización', *Gestión y Política Pública*, vol. *IV*, no. 2, CIDE, Mexico City, second semester.

Pommerelme, Werrier W (1978) 'Institutional Approaches to Public Expenditures: Empirical Evidence from Swiss Municipalities', *Journal of Public Economics*, vol. 9.

Rauch, James E. and Evans, Peter B. (1997) 'Bureaucracy and Growth: A Cross-National Analysis of the. Effects of 'Weberian' State Structures on Economic Growth', draft, Department of Political Research, World Bank, Washington, May, 1997; includes John Talbot, *A Description of the 'Weberian State' Comparative Data Set*, draft, April.

_____ (1997) *Bureaucratic Structure and Bureaucratic Performance in Less Developed Countries*, draft, Center for Institutional Reforms and the Informal Sector, May.

Reid, Gary J. (1992) *Civil Service Reform in Latin America: Lessons from Experience*, World Bank, (LATPS Occasional document, no. 6), Washington, May.

_____ (1995) *Jamaica Public Sector Modernization Project Executive Agency Strategy Materials*, memorandum, October.

_____ (1997) *Note on Imposing Sensible Management Controls*, note, February 24.

_____ (1997) *Sequencing Issues in Institutional Modernization Processes*, note, February 24.

_____ (1997) *Normas básicas: Sistema de Administración de Personal* (SAP) *Comments*, letter, March.

_____ (1997) *Public Sector Training and Public Sector Modernization Programs*, note, March.

_____ (1997) *Making Evaluations Useful*, note, April 9.

_____ (1997) *Policy Implementation: Meeting the Organizational Challenge*, paper presented in the Caríbbean Quest congress: New Directions for the Reform Process, Port of Spain, Trinidad and Tobago, June 25-26, (document delivered during the mission of August 21-25).

_____ and Mitchell, Olivia S. (1995) *Social Security Administration in Latin America and the Caribbean*, Reporte no. 14066, World Bank, March.

_____ and Scott, Graham. (1994) *Public Sector Human Resource Management: Experience in Latin America and the Caribbean and Strategies for Reform*, Report no. 12839, Technical Department for Latin America and the Caribbean,

Regional Studies Program, March, (document delivered during the mission of August 21-25).

Robbins, Donald J., González Rozada, Martín and Menéndez, Alicia (1997) *Public Sector Retrenchment and Efficient Severance Payment Schemes: A Case Study of Argentina*, draft, Harvard University and Boston University, October, 1996.

Roemer, Andrés, *Derecho y economía: políticas públicas del agua*, Miguel Ángel Porrúa.

_____ (1998) *Introducción al análisis económico del derecho*, 1st repr., Instituto Tecnológico Autónomo de México/Sociedad Mexicana de Geografía y Estadística/FCE.

Sánchez, José Juan (1999) 'Profesionalización del servicio público: antecedentes y perspectivas en México', *Enfoques de Políticas Públicas y Gobernabilidad*.

Santerre, Rexford E. (1986) 'Representative versus Direct Democracy: A Tiebout Test of Relative Performance', *Public Choice, vol. 48.*

_____ (1989) 'Representative versus Direct Democracy: Are there any Expenditure Differences?', *Public Choice, vol. 60.*

Schick, Allen (1996) *The Spirit of Reform: Managing the New Zealand State Sector in a Time of Change*, report prepared for the Commission of State Services and the Treasury Department, Wellington, New Zealand, August.

Schmidt, Allan A. (1988) 'Law and Economics: An Institutional Perspective' *Law and Economics: An Introduction*, 2a. ed., Academic Press.

Schwartz, Herman M. (1997) 'Reinvention and Retrenchment: Lessons from the Application of the New Zealand Model to Alberta, Canada', *Journal of Policy Analysis and Management*, vol. 16.

Scott, Graham, Ball, Ian and Dale, Tony (1997) 'New Zealand's Management Reform', *Journal of Policy Analysis and Management*, vol. 16.

Senge, Peter (1990) *The Fifth Discipline: The Art and Practice of the Learning Organization*, New York, Doubleday.

Shepherd, Geoffrey y Sofia Valencia (1996) *Modernizing the Public Administration in Latin America: Common Problems, No Easy Solutions*, article presented at the congress on State Reform in Latin America and the Caribbean, Spain, October 14-17.

Simon, Herbert A. (1991) 'Organizations and Markets', *Journal of Economic Perspectives, vol. 5*, no. 2, spring.

Stigler, George J. (1961) 'The Economics of Information', *Journal of Political Economy, vol. 69*, no. 3, June.

Sunat (1993) *Reforma del Sistema y la Administración Tributaria*, Lima, June.

Svejnar, Janand Terrell, and Katherine (1990) *Labor Redundancy in the Transport Sector: The Case of Chile*, World Bank, Washington, July, mimeo.

Tendler, Judith (1997) 'Good Government in the Tropics', chapter 1 ('Introduction') and 6 ('Conclusion: Civil Servants and Civil Society: Governments Central and Local'), The Johns Hopkins University Press, Baltimore, MD.

Toinet, Marie-France (1994) *El sistema político de los Estados Unidos*, FCE, Mexico City.

Trivedi, Prajapati (1994) Improving Government Performance (What Gets Measured, Gets Done)', *Economic and Political Weekly*, Bombay.

Valdés Romo, Héctor (1997) 'El servicio civil de carrera: dignificación, profesionalización y ética del servidor público', *Acontecer sindical*, year 3, no. 29, March.

Van Humboldt, Guillermo (1943) *Escritos políticos*, FCE.

Wilson James Q. (1989) *Bureaucracy, What Government Agencies Do and Why They Do it*, Basic Books.

Williamson, Oliver E. (1996) *'The Mechanisms of Governance'*, Oxford University Press, New York.

Wolfe, A. (1980) *Los límites de la legitimidad. Contradicciones políticas del capitalismo contemporáneo*, Siglo XXI, Mexico City.

World Bank, *Technical Annex: Ecuador Modernization of the State Technical Assistance Project*, World Bank, November, 1994 (document delivered during the mission from August 21 - 25).

_____ (1996) *Perspectives on the Caribbean Public Sector*, draft (supporting document for Report no. 15185-CRG), Washington, January.

_____ (1996) *Caribbean Countries: Public Sector Modernization in the Caribbean*, Report no. 15185-CRG, Washington, April.

_____ (1997) *World Development Report 1997: The State in a Changing World*, Oxford University Press, Washington.

Yin, Robert, *Case study research: Design and methods*, Sage, Newsbury Park, USA.

Documents and journals

Álvarez Medina, Gabriel (1991) *Marco jurídico, social y político de la burocracia en México*, thesis, Faculty of Law, UNAM, Mexico City.

Britain's System of Government, Foreign and Commonwealth Office London, March 1995.

Civil Service Code 1995, Civil Service Code of the United Kingdom.

Civil Service Commission, *Civil Service Commissioners' recruitment code*, 2nd. ed., United Kingdom, April, 1996.

Civil Service Commission, *Selection on merit – Fair and open competition – Equal opportunity*, Annual Report 1996-1997, United Kingdom.

Constitución Política de los Estados Unidos Mexicanos, Ministry of the Interior, 1995.

Este País (1999) 'Qué tanta confianza tiene usted en mí' no. 55, Mexico City, February.

Federación de Sindicatos de Trabajadores al Servicio del Estado (1996) La *Reforma de la Administración Pública y la Modernización Sindical*, Mexico City, March.

Federación de Sindicatos de Trabajadores al Servicio del Estado, *Servicio civil de carrera, sin pérdida de los derechos adquíridos*, Mexico City, March, 1997.

Gasca Santos, Jorge Gabriel (1997) *Servicio civil de carrera en México: las posibilidades de una meritocracia*, CIDE, August.

INAP – Colegio Nacional de Ciencias Políticas y Administración Pública (1996) *Foro Nacional: La profesionalización del servicio público* (Serie Praxis, no. 91), Mexico City.

Instituto Internacional de Ciencias Administrativas (1991) *Revista Internacional de Ciencias Administrativas*, Madrid, vol. 57, no. 3, September.

International Journal of Public Administration, vol. 19, no. 9. Pennsylvania State University, 1996.

Irwin, Tim, *An analysis of New Zealand's new system of public-sector management.*

Ley Orgánica de la Administración Pública Federal, Porrúa, Mexico City, 1994.

López Presa, José Octavio (1996) *La profesionalización del servicio público*, paper, Mexico City.

Mauro, Paulo (1993) *Corruption, country risk and growth*, Harvard University, November.

OCDE-PUMA (1996) *Integrating People Management into Public Service Reform*, Paris.

OCDE-PUMA (1996) *Ministerial Symposium on the Future of Public Services*, Paris, March.

OECD (1995) *Governance in Transition. Public Management Reforms in* OECD *Countries*, Paris.

Programa de Modernización de la Administración Pública 1995-2000, the Federal Executive, Mexico City, 1996.

Propuestas para el establecimiento de un sistema de profesionalización de Servicio Civil de Carrera en las áreas de control y evaluación de la gestión pública, Transcript of the 9th National States and Federation Comptrollers' Meeting, Government Control, Secogef-Government of Mexico state, year IV, no. 8.

PUMA/OECD (1996) *Ethics in the Public Service. Current issues and practice*, (Occasional papers no. 14), Paris.

Reglamento de la Ley del Servicio Exterior de México, SRE, 1994.

Reid, Gary J. (1997) *Implementación de una política. Alcanzando los retos organizacionales*, World Bank.

Schick, Allen (1996) *The spirit of the reform: Managing the New Zealand State Sector in a time of change*, New Zealand, August.

Scott, G., P. Bushnell and N. Sallee, 'Reform of the Core Public Sector: The New Zealand Experience', *Governance, vol. 3, no. 2*.

Senior Civil Commission (1996) *Guidance on civil service commissioners' recruitment to senior posts*, 2nd ed., United Kingdom, July.

State Sector Act 1988, Civil Service Code of New Zealand.

State Services Commission (1996) *New Zealand's State Sector Reform: A decade of Change*, Wellington, New Zealand.

State Services Commission (1997) *Responsibility and accountability: Standards expected of public service chief executives*, New Zealand, June.

The Civil Service: Continuity and Change, document presented in Parliament by the Prime Minister, London, July.

U.S. Government, *Chiefs of State and Cabinet Members of Foreign Governments*, USA, 1988-1993.

World Economic Forum (1997) *The Global Competitiveness Report 1997*, Davos, Suiza.

About the Authors

"A NEW PUBLIC MANAGEMENT... is an extraordinary and important book on a topic of burning actuality in Latin America's agenda of development: New Public Management and Civil Service Reform".
ENRIQUE V. IGLESIAS, President of the Inter-American Development Bank.

"A constructive, useful, creative work that offers the reader an excellent frame of reference for identifying problems and contributing solutions in the field of Management and Public Policy. It is a trailblazing, pioneer work in Latin America on how to accomplish reform of the institutional and administrative State, and consolidate an efficient, result-oriented career civil service".
MICHAEL BARZELAY, professor of Public Administration, London School of Economics and Political Science; author of Breaking through bureaucracy: a new perspective of public administration, Berkeley, University of California, 1992.

"Esteban Moctezuma Barragán and Andrés Roemer develop a profound analysis of the administrative problems that governments face in the light of the new millennium. The result is an exceptional investigation, one of the few that incorporate an analytic and comparative focus about the efforts of administrative modernization worldwide. The book will allow public policy-makers, academics interested in the subject and society as a whole, to learn about this fascinating topic".
KATE JENKINS, Head of the Administrative Modernization Unit of the British Government during Margaret Thatcher's administration and consultant for several Latin American governments on this subject.

Esteban Moctezuma Barragán was born in Mexico City on October 21, 1954. He has a B. S. in Economics from the National Autonomous University of Mexico (UNAM). He obtained his Master's degree in Political Economy at Cambridge, Great Britain. Among the positions that he has held are: Secretary of the Interior from 1994 to 1995 and consultant to the President of the Republic on topics of the New Federalism in 1995. In the academic environment, he has taught at the Colegio de México. He was Senator of the Republic in the 57th Legislature, during which time he promoted the Career Civil Service Act, as well as Secretary for Social Development, 1999-2000.

Andrés Roemer was born in México City on July 12, 1963. He has a B. A. in Law given by the National Autonomus University of México (UNAM) and a B. S. in Economics given by the Technological Autonomus Institute of México (ITAM) (Both Suma Cum Laude). He has a Masters degree in Public Administration given by the Kennedy School Government at Harvard University, where he was awarded with the Don K. Price Award (given only to one student of the masters program every two years) and he obtained his Phd. in Public Policy with special academic distinction from Berkeley University. Andrés Roemer is also the author of: Introduction to Law and Economics, FCE, México, 3rd edition, 2000; Law and Economics: A Survey of the Literature; Economics of Crime, Noriega Editores, México Unido Contra la Delincuencia, Club de Industriales, México 2001; The Policies and Politics of Water, Miguel Angel Porrúa, México, 2nd edition, 2000; and Sexuality, Law and Public Policy, M. Porrúa, 1998. At the present time Andrés Roemer is President of the Latin American and Caribbean Law and Economics Association.